Rethinking Gender

Rethinking Gender

Edited by

Roli Misra

RAWAT PUBLICATIONS

Jaipur • New Delhi • Bangalore • Hyderabad • Guwahati • Kolkata

ISBN 978-81-316-0610-0

Published by
Prem Rawat for **Rawat Publications**
Satyam Apts, Sector 3, Jawahar Nagar, Jaipur 302 004 (India)
Phone: 0141 2651748 / 7006 Fax: 0141 2651748
E-mail : info@rawatbooks.com
Website: www.rawatbooks.com

Delhi Office
4858/24, Ansari Road, Daryaganj, New Delhi 110 002
Phone: 011 2326 3290

Also at *Bangalore, Hyderabad, Guwahati* and *Kolkata*

Typeset by Rawat Computers, Jaipur
Printed at Chaman Enterprises, New Delhi

Dedicated to

Ma and **Papa**

for teaching me to never give up personally as well as professionally.

Contents

Preface

The development of civilization across the world overlooked the contribution of women since the dawn of history. She has nurtured mankind not only as a mother but also stood in need of the hour to support, encourage, console as well as motivate man's endeavour for development. Yet astounding applauses for women often resulted in feeble claps. How sad, it is? The present collection on various issues related to woman enkindles sympathy for her invaluable contribution and her own silent voices and to really appreciate her dedicating spirit which we hardly care about. I am also hopeful that the present book will not only be an addition to the literature of gender equality but would also definitely spur the thinking to establish a more egalitarian society and also motivate the planners to come into the play and make commendable contribution in the making of a new social order which would be really humane in thought and spirit.

I have no words to express my gratitude to all the eminent academicians who have contributed their scholarly papers so as to give this book a shape. I would like to place on record my sincere thanks to the former head of the department, Shri S.J. Srivastava for his prodigious knowledge and putting his valuable inputs during the process of editing. I would also like to thank my family and friends whose belief in me has always been a motivating spirit and also for supporting me all through the journey of translating my efforts into this reality. This book salutes all the wonderful women for their struggles and victories.

Contributors

Manju Agrawal, Director, Amity Institute of Behavioural and Allied Sciences, Amity University, Lucknow.

Mir M. Amin, Assistant Professor, Department of Commerce, Islamia College of Science and Commerce, Srinagar.

Gomati Bodra, Assistant Professor, Department of Sociology, Jamia Millia Islamia, New Delhi.

Vibha Chaturvedi, Department of Philosophy and Director, Women's Studies and Development Centre, University of Delhi.

I.D. Gupta, Former Professor, Department of Economics, University of Lucknow, Lucknow.

Mukulika Hitkari, Associate Professor, Department of Economics, D.G. College, Kanpur.

Meeta Malhotra, Faculty, Amity Institute of Behavioural and Allied Sciences, Amity University, Lucknow.

R.P. Mamgain, Professor of Economics, Giri Institute of Development Studies, Lucknow and Managing Editor, *The Indian Journal of Labour Economics.*

Shyam Kartik Mishra, Associate Professor, Department of P.G. Studies and Research in Economics, L.B.S. College, Moghalsarai, Chandauli and General Secretary, UPUEA.

Roli Misra, Assistant Professor, Department of Economics, D.B.S. College, Kanpur.

Mohd. Muzammil, Vice Chancellor, Dr. B.R. Ambedkar University, Agra and M.J.P. Rohilkhand University, Bareilly and former Visiting Fellow, University of Oxford, UK.

Vibhuti Patel, Head, Department of Economics, SNDT University, Mumbai.

Tulika Saxena, PhD Scholar, College of Arts and Social Sciences, Australian National University, Canberra, Australia.

T.V. Sekher, Associate Professor, International Institute of Population Sciences, Mumbai.

Farooque Ajaz Shah, Assistant Professor, Department of Commerce, Islamia College of Science and Commerce, Srinagar.

A.K. Singh, Assistant Director, Regional Centre of Environment and Urban Studies (RCUES), University of Lucknow, Lucknow.

Anupama Srivastava, Faculty, Amity Institute of Behavioural and Allied Sciences, Amity University, Lucknow.

Parvin Sultana, Research Scholar, Centre for Political Studies, Jawahar Lal Nehru University, New Delhi.

Niharika Tripathi, Research Scholar, International Institute of Population Sciences, Mumbai.

P.S. Tripathi, Associate Professor, Department of Economics, D.B.S. College, Kanpur.

Introduction

Gender, in sociological and feminist thought, denotes the cultural constitution comprising notions, perceptions and premises concerning feminity or masculinity and the ways in which these serve ideologically to maintain gendered identities. Gender is a matter of culture. The downgrading of gender to sex may be understood as a key move in the ideological justification of patriarchy. The primary identity of a person in a human society is that of gender, which according to psychologists, gets fixed in early infancy. Feminist expositions have assembled considerable evidence to drive home the point that gender is culturally constructed (Krishnaraj, 1999).

Over the past many years we witnessed tremendous change in the worldwide outlook of the people largely influenced by the social dynamics of the West and also the languishing steps of the East. Efforts by great social reformers directed to imparting women education have helped in bringing them out of the *purdah* system and have resulted in a progressive and happy society in terms of regard for the half world. Gender inequality springs from many sources, and it is so often difficult to determine which form of inequality is declining by the effects of globalization, and which change being undermined. Empowering women is an indispensable tool for advancing development and reducing poverty, yet discrimination against women and girls, together with gender-based violence, economic discrimination, reproductive health inequalities and traditional dogmas, remains so wide and persistent.

There is no dearth of literature on gender issues. However, the thrust is uniformly the same – the unequal status of women in one form or the other, under different pretexts, and their consequences. Given this status gender biases are exhibited both implicitly and explicitly with the exceptions of few protests by progressive men and women.

We all understand that women in the design of this creation have been a complementary factor in the development of individual and society and there is no superiority or privilege assigned to any particular gender. Industrial development in the recent past has extended vast employment opportunities and made women economically independent. They have new aspirations, vitalized enthusiasm and raising hopes for their better accommodation in society. However, in the present set-up, both the people and the government seem like a silent spectator in the general dogma of progress leaving behind much acclaimed values of the Indian Vedic society and unique regard for women worshipped in the form of *Shakti.* What perturbs to an enthusiastic person is the slow pace of change to alter the outlook of people in the light of cultural values emerging with the advancement of science and technology and dominance of elites. Contrary to these changes is the capitalistic order which has brought media in the frontline in influencing the approach of people both to crime and punishment.

National development policies have, by and large, neglected gender dimension in development theory and practice. The invisibility of woman as an economic entity is at the root of her low status. Many macro and micro researches have documented that in development, women's economic status has stagnated, especially in developing countries (Dixon-Mueller, 1988). Efforts to increase the economic contribution of women should be viewed not only as a means to make fuller use of all human resources for economic development, but also as a way of improving income distribution. Women should be recognized not merely as targets of welfare policies in the social sector, but as critical group of development (Joseph, 2007). This recognition was reflected at the time of formulation of the Sixth Five-Year Plan, with a chapter titled, 'Women and Development'. 'This shift in recognition represents reassertion of the principle of women's equality of rights to participate effectively in the process of development, ensuring thereby movements in the direction of the constitutional goals' (GoI, 1985).

Work towards eliminating gender inequality in the framework provided by the Beijing Platform for Action has created awareness, monitoring and alleviation of the externalities that the new global system creates for women. Progress towards eliminating gender inequality in the future depends on investment and policy framework where the global approach strengthens women's security and welfare, and fighting the issues, mostly in the economic realm, where women are made worse off by the new global system. Gender equality, which is first and foremost a human right, is withering away in the name of development and change, resulting in expansion of religion, fundamentalism and feminization of poverty. Empowering women is an indispensable tool for advancing development and reducing poverty, yet discrimination against women and girls, including gender-based violence, economic discrimination, reproductive health inequalities, discriminatory traditional practices, etc., remains the most pervasive and persistent form of inequality. Development seems to have bypassed women who constitute about half of the population of a nation. A nation cannot afford development without mainstreaming women who are significantly contributing to its economy, society and polity. Major changes are taking place in the composition of the workforce in terms of gender, age and educational qualifications across the world. An increasing number of women are entering the workforce, especially in the developing countries, where relatively few women have been absorbed so far. A larger presence of women at workplace will have an influence on the working conditions and terms of employment.

While many countries have made progress towards gender equality, yet there are regional disparities. Moving towards gender equality is not a technocratic goal but it is a political process which requires new way of thinking giving way to new philosophy that regards all people, irrespective of their sex, as essential agents of change. The human development paradigm, which puts people at the centre of its concern, must be fully engendered. The rhetoric of gender equity and women's empowerment has become common place in government policy, non-governmental advocacy, media and academic research. The national government of India has initiated important steps to improve the status of women. National perspective plan for women (1988–2000), national plan of action for girl child (1991–2000) and national draft policy for women (2001) are some of the key policy initiatives. Besides, the government has also initiated woman-centred programmes for their development and empowerment.

However, gender discrimination has been identified as one of the most pervading forms of institutional deprivation. The mad dominance of greed over all human goodness has undermined the position of women in the patriarchal set-up. It is important that women must be regarded as agents of beneficiaries of change. Investing in women's capabilities and empowering them to exercise their choices is not only valuable in itself but is also the surest way to contribute to economic growth and development. The engendered development model, though aiming to widen choices for both women and men, should not predetermine how different cultures and different societies exercise these choices. What is important is that equal opportunities to make choice exist equally for both women and men. Legal, economic, political or cultural barriers that prevent the exercise of equal rights should be identified and removed through comprehensive policy reforms and strong affirmative action.

A collection of essays in this book portrays the position of women in the so-called civilized society. Women from East to West have been subjected to unabated violence ranging from treatment like a commodity, down to a born slave. In view of the rapid advancement of knowledge and new emerging human rights and global outlook, we need a series of social and legal changes and the provisions given to fair sex who rear and nurture the sea of humanity performing different roles and simultaneously writing new chapters.

I.D. Gupta in his paper 'Women Empowerment in the Globalized World Today' has examined the gender issue for its poverty part as also the other side of women empowerment. He deftly examines the fact as how swiftly exploitation culture has crept into the entire framework of market economy and globalization, which just undermines human dignity and the complementarity between the man and machine. The position of women discussed in historical perspective as well as in the globalized era is perhaps the merit of this paper.

Mohd. Muzammil in his paper entitled 'Muslim Women in India: Educational, Health and Economic Status' has attempted to analyse the educational, health and economic status of Muslim women within the pluralistic nature of Indian society. It examines the various aspects of their educational status and also the most legitimate barriers to their educational backwardness. Conclusions point to the need for adoption of a policy for their educational awakening by dismantling the stranglehold of the traditionalism and ritualism with a view to pave the way for their modernization by enabling them to play a meaningful part in formal work and decision-making.

Another paper on very contemporary issue is by Vibha Chaturvedi on 'Sexual Harassment at Workplace' which examines the problems of sexual harassment, discussing the historic judgment in Vishakha vs State of Rajasthan. The paper also raises the problems of identification of kinds of sexual harassment giving examples from Delhi University.

The paper 'Female Foeticide and Sex Selection' by Vibhuti Patel talks about new reproductive technologies (NRTs) in India and how consumerist culture-oriented economic development, commercialization of medical profession and sexist biases in our society, as a whole, have created a sad scenario of 'missing girls'. In this context, Patel has raised a crucial question: Can we allow Asian girls to become an endangered species?

A.K. Singh talks about the problems faced by women in urban areas and how they have been sidelined in the process of development in his paper 'Gender Mainstreaming in Urban Administration'. Infrastructure development is not gender-neutral. Lack of basic services affects both men and women; however, women in cities, especially in low income communities and slums, are more severely affected by inadequate and poor services. In absence of access to toilets, women are forced to defecate in open which is unsafe and undignified while it is also a serious health and environmental threat. Though gender budgeting in urban sector is limited, however, gender mainstreaming, engendering urban development and gender budgeting, is imperative in urban sector in order to address the needs of urban women and their empowerment.

A brief endeavour has been made in the paper entitled 'Conceptualization and Manifestation of Women Empowerment' by S.K. Mishra, to survey the efforts made to conceptualize the term 'women empowerment' and also to identify the indicators that manifest this term and facilitate empirical researches in this field. In this paper, despite disagreement on issues of origin, definition, indicators and measurement related to term 'empowerment', there is global consensus, irrespective of discipline, that access to power is unevenly distributed within and between the classes of human society.

The next paper on 'Women Employment: A Comparative Analysis of Scheduled Castes and Other Social Groups in Uttar Pradesh' by Rajendra P. Mamgain attempts to examine the pattern of women's participation in work in a most populous state of Uttar Pradesh in a comparative all-India framework. The paper briefly touches upon the economic and demographic features, trends and patterns of women's workforce participation and educational levels of women workers in Uttar Pradesh.

P.S. Tripathi and Mukulika Hitkari in their paper entitled 'Social Demography: Gender Perspectives and Prospectives' have attempted to relate women health care with the socio-economic status, living conditions, high risk behaviours and differential discriminatory sex status, etc. The substantive content in this paper deals with varied demographic indicators crucial for female health care in metropolitan cities. Moreover, the underlying perspective is not to highlight the calculations pertaining to fertility rates, life expectancy, crude birth and death rates, morbidity, mortality rates (maternal and infant) as also nutritional levels, but to inductively analyse their contributory demographic status in the global scenario of developing economies like India, coupled with the relevant challenges as pertinent to urban women's health in the above mentioned domain.

The paper on 'Mental Health of Women' by Manju Agrawal, Meeta Malhotra and Anupama Srivastava focuses on the status of mental health of women, possible factors and policy implications associated with their mental health. Gender differences in mental illness are also discussed. The authors examined the relationship between reproductive health and mental illness among women. The effects of psycho-social and economic factors like multiple roles, marginalized social position, gender violence, globalization, etc., on mental health are also explored and discussed. The paper advocates a gender-sensitive approach in developing policies and plans while addressing the mental health concerns of women. It also emphasizes study and action plan on gender-specific risk factors of mental illness.

The paper 'Daughter Dispreference: Experiences from Rural Community in Uttar Pradesh' by Roli Misra focuses on a very important social issue of female foeticide. Misra's paper articulates genesis, processes and consequences of declining sex ratio in the state of Uttar Pradesh on an empirical basis. Issues like violence against women, bride purchasing, polyandry as re-emerging phenomenon, mismatched marriages, and problems of social exclusion have emerged in the surveyed areas. Further, the paper highlights the mindset of the people in the rural areas and prevailing socio-cultural stereotypes, which encourage such barbarous practice of eliminating girls even before their birth.

Gomati Bodra's paper 'Image and Reality: Portrayal of Tribal Women in Media' discusses the question of media representation of tribal women in relation to the popular discourses. The subordination of tribal women operates at various levels especially which lies in the various male-centric perceptions and definition of most discourses which are decidedly mainstream. It gets further complicated in case of communities that are completely alienated from all structures of power. The mindset which goes into the construction of the image of tribal women in media is well explained in this paper.

Mir M. Amin and Farooque Ajaz Shah, in their paper on 'Changing Face of Women Entrepreneurship in the Globalized Indian Economy', demonstrate that women entrepreneurship is still in its nascent stage in India due to a number of factors that need to be taken care of by breeding the culture of producing women entrepreneurs and facilitating them to conduct their business activities effectively and easily. This may be only possible when India has a clear-cut policy for the women enterprises because in the present era of liberalization and globalization, women entrepreneurship has tremendous potential of empowering women and transforming society.

In the next paper entitled 'Sex Education in India: Expectations and Experiences of Young Women' by Niharika Tripathi and T.V. Sekher, an attempt has been made to understand the expectations and experiences of young women aged 15-24 years in India regarding family life education (FLE). The study illustrates that an overwhelming majority of women are in favour of introducing FLE at school level. Majority also felt that FLE should be introduced in schools from standard 8th onwards. The findings emerging from these nation-wide surveys strongly support the acceptance and need for sex education among youth in India.

Tulika Saxena in her paper on 'Indian Women and Domestic Violence: Victories and Struggles in the Movement for Law and Justice' has discussed the issue of domestic violence in India and has tried to review the status of the landmark PWDVA 2005 and the problems faced in its effective implementation.

The last paper by Parvin Sultana on 'Baring Bodies: Resistance through Resignification' deals with a very unusual subject. Because bodies can be humiliated, they can also be resignified to humiliate the humiliator, hence, bodies can also be the site of resistance through resignification, that is, subverting the meaning that is imposed on a humiliated body and investing newer meanings in the same body which renders it more powerful. The author also talks about the naked parade of women that took place at Kangla fort in Manipur to oppose the rape and murder of Thangjam Manorama in July 2004 and tries to situate the incident in the larger discourse of how body has been used time and again as the site of humiliation, exploitation and resistance.

In general, the collection of different papers in this volume provides a multidisciplinary perspective to understand the varied facets of gender issues so as to enhance and share knowledge about the various aspects of gender development. Trends clearly indicate that the future development will bank upon the skilled development of women in terms of their education, health, empowerment and promotion mechanism that strengthen the positive aspects and consequences of globalization with respect to gender equality by providing them increasing opportunities to work in solidarity at regional, national and international levels to demand their rights. The basic point here is what a woman is and what she has been struggling for? Obviously, this is her identity blurred in the mainstream of development overlooked for many years and a positive change that is still awaited. Does the present framework support her in her struggles? Sexual prejudices work as obstacles for the women to register their role as well as their participation in policy framework. The set of articles in this book shall be a pointer towards the existing policies formulated for the upgradation of women in the society so as to make development a gender-neutral process.

References

Dixon-Mueller, Ruth and Richard Anker, Assessing Women's Economic Contribution to Development, ILO, Geneva, 1998.

Government of India, *Women in India-Country Paper*, Ministry of Social and Women's Welfare, New Delhi, 1985.

Joseph, Molly 2007. *Women Participation and Development Strategies*, Kanishka Publishers, New Delhi.

Kathryn, Ward B. 1988. Women in the Global Economy in Gutek Barbara, A. et. al., *Women and Work: An Annual Review*, Vol. 3, Sage, U.S.A.

Krishnaraj, Maithreyi.1999. A Gender Critique of Economic Theories of Population. in Maithreyi Krishnaraj, Ratna M. Sudarshan and Abusaleh Shariff (eds.), *Gender, Population and Development.* New Delhi: Oxford India Paperbacks.

1

Women Empowerment in the Globalized World Today

I.D. Gupta

Gender issue has acquired significance for quite sometime in development economics. Globalization has added a new dimension to it. In the backward economies of the world the deplorable condition of the second gender in cultural, social and economic spheres had been a cause of concern for social reformers and economic activists for a long time. However, the issue has acquired new momentum with the strengthening of democracy and the democratic institutions in the developing world where demands for equality of status and economic liberty is being raised quite vigorously. Amartya Sen, the Nobel laureate considers 'development as freedom'. It is a multidimensional concept of freedom which revolves around freedom from slavery in society as well as demands for political and economic participation and cultural status. Based on the works of Nozick and John Rawls the concepts emphasizes on Rawlsian justice and empowerment through entitlements as developed by Robert Nozick. The provisioning of primary goods is basic to development as per Rawls.

In the backward societies which are also economically and intellectually backward, women are considered as commodities to be traded like slaves. In social and family ladder they are the followers of the wishes of the first gender. In this distorted picture of a sick society the girl child is eliminated at its first notice or is pushed into prostitution after attaining puberty in many of the instances. However, in the better stock of population too they are bound with several kinds of un-freedoms including economic dependency over her master husband. Even in culturally and intellectually advanced parts of society in India, like in West Bengal and other parts, the status of women had not been more than that of a maid servant doing household chores and facing drudgeries of life obeying the orders of the householder. Therefore, economic independence and basic education caught the attention of missionary institutions and social reformers as the first pre-requisite of development and freedom of women in society.

In a large part of the Middle Eastern countries even today law prescribes for having more than one woman at a time in life. Bearing and rearing of children had been the primary function of women in society. In the case of Mughal emperor Shahejahan who loved his wife so much that he built Tajmahal in her memorial which is a world renowned treasure of architectural beauty and excellence, his wife Mumtaj Mahal had to bear 14 children for the king in her 17 years of married life.

In the modern society of twenty-first century the instances of female foeticide and domestic violence in the countries of Asia, Africa and the Middle East have taken such a dangerous proportion that it has become a major issue of human rights. Instances of large-scale human rights violations are recorded from those countries that are on the path of sustained economic development like China and India. It is said that the regimented societies are more prone to human rights violations than the countries having democratic political system. Countries like India are facing demographic imbalance in their population structure due to constantly decreasing female ratio to men population. The dependent status of women in house, in society, in economic, political, and cultural spheres is a common perception.

It is to be noted that when we talk of women's status in a society, the society cannot be taken as one unit. Society is a composite of different strata. Usually, a society is divided into lower, middle, and high class. These sub-divisions have further sub-divisions of lower lower, middle lower and upper lower; lower middle, middle middle, and higher middle and sub higher and higher classes. These divisions have different ramifications for economic and socio-cultural empowerment. The most vulnerable are those who are in the lower and lower middle strata of society. The women in high income group have their different slangs. They sometimes trespass the commonly prescribed rules and expectations for the women in society. Breaking of common moral codes of conduct and barriers imposed by society are more often with the higher strata of society. Promiscuity and things like that are taken as status symbol, in some cases, for the men and women in society. Hence, in social expectations and behaviour it is the middle class which is considered as the torch bearer and the backbone of the society. Therefore, it is said that in the society where the percentage of middle class population is high the society is healthy and strong and where the middle class percentage is slender or absent, the society is sick. The health of the society in the case is depending upon the number of followers of the basic values that society craves for. It is for the upliftment of its people and smooth functioning of society.

Karl Marx visualized that capitalism has wiped out the middle class and created a system where only labour class and bourgeois class existed. The importance of money multiplied manifold in the industrial culture and in the post-Industrial Revolution era. This was the rise of social behaviour and materialism in society. Status was attached, wrongly, with the acquisition and possession of promissory notes of the government or other forms of wealth where money had a limited purpose in life. It is not all. It does not command each and everything in life. Owing to this misdirection, now the development economics is searching for the purpose of and meaning of development as it has driven the industrial society at the brink of devastation and misery. Money has created frustrations. Larger and larger numbers of people are slipping in depression arising out of complexities in life created by industrial society. The environmentalists' warnings for limiting such a pattern of industrial development has a meaning in view of climatic changes and global warming which has made the life of people on this planet earth unsustainable.

In Hindu society the three basic causes of disputes are: *Zar, Zoru* and *Zameen*, i.e., money (wealth), women and the land. They had been the causal factors behind every acrimonious happening and disputed in life from the time immemorial. Marx too presented materialistic interpretation of history. It states that every happening in history had had materialistic underpinnings.

In its right perspective the concept of wealth is not attached to the money only. The perception of being wealthy is not the perception of a moneyed man. It (wealth) has several connotations. One is wealthy in the real sense when he commands a good health; when one is in possession of intelligent and obedient offspring; when one commands a high moral standard. Therefore, it is said, when wealth is lost, nothing is lost. When health is lost, something is lost. And when character is lost, everything is lost. Wealth also takes the form of glory and fame. It is sometimes considered opulence. In Vedic hymns the prayers are for opulence (being lord of Rayee). The purpose of writing this is to understand the proper meaning of development for which the economists and others are craving for. Understanding the purpose of life gives meaning to life and provides direction to the functioning. Happiness lies in simplicity and not in complexity which the industrial society and development has provided to the mankind in the last two centuries. The misdirection is the basic cause of warnings from the nature in the form of environmental disturbances and changing climates.

After deliberating upon the real meaning of development and progress, we turn towards the gender issue. That society is considered healthy and orderly where there is no discrimination between men and women because they have been created in this world by the Supreme Lord as complimentary to one another. They are, in scientific language, forms of positive and negative 'energies' which completes the circuit.

In Vedic literature it is narrated that the Supreme Creator created man and woman out of one unit of nature and bestowed his *Tejas* in them in the form of soul (consciousness). *Atman* brought with it *pran, manah*, memory and intelligence. These are the faculties of *Atman*. *Pran* made five main and five sub-divisions and took charge of different parts of the body. When this intelligent module was created he asked them to enjoy life and his heavenly creations. In his system men and women have no different identities. They all are the same.

He created this world by his *Tapah* and he is all the time performing a *Virat* (magnificent) *Yajna* so that this universe could remain in order so that his sons and daughters may live in happiness. He created sky and stars, this planet earth, air and water, sun and moon and other planets. He created fire. He created different types of fruits and flowers, birds and butterflies, oceans and rivers, mountains and seasons. He created an order in which the sun and the moon and different planets are revolving on their axis at a certain speed and voyaging through a defined route in the planetary system. By his command everyday sun rises and sets without fail from time immemorial. By his command sky pours water in the form of rains in different areas which make the land fertile and rivers are filled up, seasons come and go breaking the monotony of man's life. By his command cool breeze flows to make His children happy.

He himself contains the properties of man and woman and therefore, he is taken as *Ardhnarishwar.*

Christianity too visualizes the formation of man and woman in the like manner with the only difference that the man and woman, the Adam and Eve, were sent to the Garden of Eden with the instructions not to touch the apple, the fruit of the garden. It was the forbidden apple. And since the two tasted the forbidden fruit they were denounced to have committed sin. Consequently, all the men and women born out of Adam and Eve are sinful by their creation. Vedic origin of species is not sinful and therefore, the best part of God's creation, men and women need not bear the feeling of sin in their creation. They have come here to enjoy the bliss of life.

In scientific language of the day everything requires basic material (*Prakriti*) and energy or power for its creation. When that energy performs the function of creation of human beings and other species, it is named *Prajapati* or *Brahma*; the energy that sustains the living and non-living beings is Vishnu, the sustainer; and the energy that destroys the created things is named as Rudra. This metaphorical statement when interpreted in its right perspective, presents a significant insight into the creation, creativity and the grand design of the energy forms. It is a Trinity concept of power. The understanding that men and women are born equal in this grand creation of the Almighty gives life a meaning and a purpose. Those who are blind to understand the design and system of the Omnipotent and Omnipresent are the baser ones of creation.

Women in Historical Perspective

Women enjoyed high status in ancient Indian society. In the Vedic period and that of the Upanishads women like Gargi, Maitrayee and Katyayani had attained high intellectual status as that of the Maharshis and Seere like Yajnavalkya.

The quote of the time is:

> 'Yatra Naryastu Pujyante, Ramante Tatra Devatah'
>
> [The family and society where women are adorned there lay the eternal bliss and happiness of this world.]

In ancient India women have had equal status in society. In *Brihadaranyak* Upanishad there is a famous debate between Gargi and Maharshi Yajnavalkya over the origin of universe and the enquiry about Brahman. Gargi had thrown very difficult questions over the Maharshi like, what it is that surrounds the earth, the *antariksha* and the *dwulok*; the answer was that it is all surrounded by the space. Then the question was what it is that surrounds the space; the answer was that the space or the sky is surrounded by *akshar*, that which is eternal. Maharshi had to reprimand Gargi when she asked about the cause of Brahman as it was an *ati-prashna* (excessive argumentation), the reason being that everything has a cause (*kaaran*) behind it; and as the *Nyaya* philosophy states nothing could happen without a cause; there could be no cause of the cause and hence Gargi was reprimanded by Yajnavalkya.

In *Tretayuga,* queen Kaykeyi had gone to the battle field with King Dasharath and helped him win the battle by supporting him when the axles of his chariot was broken. Two boons were bestowed on her for this praiseworthy work by the king.

Sita was famous for her celibacy and purity of character and still today she is an ideal for the women of the world.

In *Dwaparyuga,* around five millennium back, Queen Gandhari willingly opted to remain blindfold for life as her husband King Dhritarashtra was a blind man.

Not so long ago even in the present period Rani Laxmibai and so many others fought for the nation and are the epitomes of bravery and sacrifice.

In the pre-independence period in India many of the social reformers like Raja Ram Mohan Roy and Swami Dayanand fought for the upliftment of women by giving them right to education and reading the Vedas, and banishing *sati pratha* of burning wife on the funeral pyre of the husband. Right to remarry by the woman whose husband was no more, banning child marriage, educating girls and giving them right to perform *yajna* and all other Vedic rituals (*karma kand*) form part of the basic agenda of Arya Samaj which was founded in 1875 by Swami Dayanand in Bombay and which today has millions and millions of followers in India and in many countries of the world. Many of the basic agenda like removal of untouchability, education to girls, raising the age of marriage of girls, right to remarriage and many of the things which empower women economically, socially and culturally were accepted by the national government in the post-independence period. Many of the Muslim leaders like Sir Syed Ahmad Khan and many of the Christian missionaries have done commendable work in providing quality education to the women and making them eligible to compete the highest national services like civil services and educational services. Women are in large numbers in universities, civil and administrative services, army, police services, Corporate world, and so many other fields contributing to the progress of nation systematically. This was the vision of Free India of Mahatma Gandhi, Pandit Jawaharlal Nehru, Sardar Patel, Maulana Azad, Rafi Ahmad Kidwai and so on so forth, the visionary leaders of Indian freedom struggle.

Gender Issue of the Day

The concept of development and progress has taken different connotation and forms in modern times. The time in which we are living is roughly the post-Second World War period in which attempts were made by the saner elements of civilized society to bring an order in this world so that the mistakes are not repeated which caused devastation to the nations in the form of two world wars within a century in which more than 50 million people were killed and injured in the Second World War alone. Several institutions were formed at the world level to reconstruct and develop the wounded economies. The world, however, was divided on the political and economic system which could enable this reconstruction and lead the path of nations towards progress. While Nazism and Fascism were held derogatory to progress and mainly responsible for human suppression and sufferings, democracy is being held in high order which could alleviate sufferings of humanity and ensure fundamental human rights to citizens, men and women. However, in the economic sphere the clash between capitalism and communism could not be resolved until 1985 when the Union of Soviet Socialist Republic, the USSR, gave way to Glasnost and Perestroika and economic liberty and disintegrated. It was a revolt of the people against regimentation and violation of human rights. The regimes of Hitler and Mussolini were the regimes when humanity suffered at a massive scale and human rights violations were unprecedented. The era of globalization came thereafter. Globalization is seen as a package of the three: market supremacy, privatization and liberalization of international trade and capital flows. These are basically capitalist prescription to progress.

The intellectual society occupying the international institutions like the United Nations and its various sub-divisions, the International Monetary Fund (IMF), the World Bank, the World Trade Organization (WTO) and others, mainly from the high income industrialized countries of the West, have a myopic vision of development since its inception. They decided to move vigorously on the path of industrialization so that lots of manufacturing goods could be produced for human consumption. For the poorer nations at the time (in 1950s) it was translated into the dictum 'industrialization is a synonym of economic development'. They ran after this path and invited different kinds of imbalances in their economic system, in the trade front, on the balance of payments front, on the agricultural front, on the distributive justice front and so on. Poverty not only continued despite industrial development rather it escalated owing to lower priority given to agriculture and infrastructure. Villages where the masses of India were living starved of investments and productivity suffered. Growth rate of food production remained slow or stagnant. With the fast growing population in the independent era the shortage of food grain production led to a crisis situation in the country many a time despite the Green Revolution of the 1960s and 1970s. In the era of globalization even today where the dependency of population on agriculture is 67 per cent, the production contribution of agricultural sector to the national income is at the level of only 17 per cent. And, the sector's annual growth rate is moving around 2 per cent or even less than that, escalating further the economic divide of the country.

The next prescription of the intellectual society commanding the world institutions became Physical Quality of Life (PQLI) and Human Face of Development. Yet another prescription came in 1990s for human development associating economic parameters of income growth with social factors of education and healthcare taking into consideration the Gender Development Index (GDI) and Gender Empowerment Measure (GEM). The data creating institutions and their analyzers ran after preparing Human Development Indices for different regions of the world. The development agenda then moved on the pathways of women and child development and yet another socio-politico angle was added of human rights of the people and its violations. The role of state in development or more clearly the quality of governance and its association with a capitalist market economy system is on a scrutiny in the new system after globalization. The whole scenario, or the whole conception of holistic development, is misdirected giving rise to issues of social and economic justice once again to the forefront.

As per the data available despite the progress that has been made world over six out of 10 poorest people are still women and girls, who must, as the primary family caretaker and producer of food, shoulder the burden of tilling land, grinding grain, carrying water, and cooking. In Kenya, as per the reports of the United Nations Development Programme (UNDP), women can burn up to 85 per cent of their daily calorie intake by just fetching water. Yet some 75 per cent of world's women cannot get bank loans because they have unpaid or insecure jobs and are not entitled to property ownership. This is one reason why though women comprise 50 per cent of total population but own only 1 per cent of world's wealth.

Equality between men and women is more than a matter of social justice – it is a fundamental human right. Gender equality also makes economic sense. When women have equal access to education and go on to participate fully in business and in economic decision-making, they are a key driving force against poverty. Women with equal rights are better educated, healthier, and have greater access to land, jobs and financial resources. Their increased earning power in turn raises household incomes. By enhancing women's control over decision-making in the household, gender equality also translated into better prospects and general well-being of children, reducing poverty of future generations. Gender equality is a condition for inclusive, democratic, violence-free and sustainable development.

The Other Side of Empowerment

Power corrupts and the absolute power corrupts absolutely, is the saying. While at the time we talk of women empowerment we may not afford to be swayed away in an unqualified manner in the direction without taking care of the other side of the empowerment. For a balanced view to be formed one may have to study both sides of human nature, the good and bad in it, and then prescribe a path of progress. Progress which does not hurt others' rights, liberties and entitlements. Justice to all should be the dictum.

To understand human nature one will have to go to the basic attributes of man and the good and evil spirit in him. It is said that the 'spirit' (*atman*) is pure but as it comes into association with body, three *gunas*, surround it. They are the *sattva*, the *rajas* and the *tamoh guna.* They are in different proportion in each individual. Their different proportions in each individual make him different to each other. That is the reason why the two men even being identical do not possess the same *swabhav* or the nature and they react differently to a given situation. It is the combination of the *gunas* that defines the nature of the man and the direction of his action and his functioning. While *sattva* is divine, *rajas* is baser and the *tamas* is the baser most. Evils mostly arise out of the higher proportion of *tamas* and *rajas*. *Tamas* is also considered 'darkness'. *Ahankar* (ego) is one of the basic attribute or qualification of the two.

Kautilya in his epoch-making book, *Arthshastra*, depicts that it is very difficult to understand the true nature of a man while he is not in action. He compared man with the horse who while pegged to his stand grazing green grass appears so gentle and nice. But when attached to a chariot he starts revealing his true nature. In the like manner man's nature could only be revealed when he is put to test and given power and deployed to certain functioning. The examples are men like Hitler who at their own whims (inflated ego) caused large-scale suffering to humanity and put the world to devastation. He massacred millions of Jews in concentration camps and was mainly responsible for the Second World War.

Dating back to five millennium years, in Dwaparyuga, Dhritrashtra by his inflated infatuation towards son was not ready to listen to the reasoning of justice and Duryodhan by his evil nature and jealousy compelled the country to a war in which 18 divisions of army were destroyed and the earth became devoid of brave men and the intellectual as they all perished in the war. It is said *Kaliyug* (Black Period) began since then.

The strange phenomenon is that the man is good and bad at the same time depending upon his differing reactions to a particular situation. His reaction to a particular situation cannot be predicted. Therefore, as Stephen Hawkins, the noted physicist wizard, says the future cannot be predicted as, it cannot be predicted what would be the reaction of a person to a particular situation in future? Man behaves differently to the same situation at different points of time. And it cannot be visualized forehand. Therefore, science of foretelling becomes unscientific in the event of depiction of man's nature and his behaviour pattern. Future can only be estimated it cannot be conclusively foretold.

Women in India have largely been empowered through democracy in the country constitutionally and legally and they are at par with men in a system of 'one man one vote'. So much so that in independent India they are shouldering the burden of nation-building and taking it to glorious heights. Our country had a woman prime minister and a president too. But here too India is divided as the larger masses of population are still far behind. They are educationally and economically backward. Their condition is miserable. They are subject to domestic violence and, prostitution and other types of social horror. The purpose of the present deliberation is to focus them in the limelight. The issue is associated with the larger issue of poverty in the country. However, gender issue requires more attention vis-à-vis the general issues of poverty. Poverty and injustices lie more with the women particularly the rural women who are the most vulnerable lot facing different types of unfreedoms and voicelessness. It is a matter of human rights and social and cultural identity and status and self-esteem.

When we delineate the things and go into deeper analysis, the nuances of rural and urban women are different. The urban minority predominates the scene as they have status and more voice but the situation is different with the rural women particularly those belonging to certain social groups like scheduled caste, schedule tribe and other backward classes. They are the poorest of the poor and where the light of freedom has not yet reached. They are the wretched ones of the society looking at the goodwill and mercy of the upper strata of society and government institutions.

In the urban society where women are mainly educationally and socio-culturally advanced the problem is different. It has been found that higher education many a times inflates the ego of the person and he/she becomes obstinate and arrogant which drastically reduces his/her adaptability and adjustment capability in the family institution. Clash of interest arises mainly due to differing temperament and inflated ego and false sense of superiority, and the family and children are the casualty. That is the reason why in the new era of light and learning in India families are breaking down at a faster rate. Hundreds and thousands of cases of divorce and marriage dissolution are registered in the family courts of metropolitan cities and towns every month. The number and pendency of the cases are frustrating. The education and economic empowerment is causing family and social disorder to a worrisome proportion.

Yet another dark side of educational empowerment is where both the spouse are working for some corporate institution away from the joint family home. There they taste the culture of capitalist market system whose basic motive is profit maximization. It is a competitive world where the survival is through efficiency and hard work. In pursuance of the fulfillment of the target in the corporate world there is hardly any time for the person to be with the family and the child and to enjoy the leisure. Again family institution is at stake. Enough money is there but the manager of the house is absent from the house. What is the fate of the child who is devoid of mother's care, only the time will tell to them when in pursuit of money what they have lost is the real essence of life? Capitalism is exploitative. The only difference with the earlier Industrial Revolution phase is that at that time working hours were excessively attached with low wages, now the same exploitation is there with higher wages.

Therefore, while the gender issue highlights the poverty side of the problem it also entails exploitative nature of the corporate world where a large number of educationally empowered women are joining force which have for them another type of socio-cultural shock where family institution is breaking down and the very essence of life is missing in pursuit of the material wealth. This is the enigmatic side of globalization and women's empowerment.

Concluding Remarks

We discussed the gender issue for its poverty part as also we discussed the other side of women empowerment and discussed the exploitation in the market economy system brought about by globalization. Exploitation and injustices are inherent in the capitalist system. But the system has come and there is no going back. We have to be cautious and shall have to learn to manage how best we could utilize the system for the betterment of the suffering lot in abject poverty. How best we could safeguard our social institution like family and family bondage is up to intelligent society to decide.

The purpose of education and empowerment should be to enhance the higher qualities of the person so that she/he could live a life of self-esteem and dignity and could contribute towards alleviating the sufferings of not only the human beings, but also the sufferings of other living and non-living beings of nature.

References

Brihadaranyak Upanishad.

Kautilya, *Arthashastra.*

Mahabharat.

Nozick, Robert. 1974. *Anarchy, State and Utopia*, Blackwell Publishing Limited, United Kingdom.

Rawls, John. 1971. *A Theory of Justice*, Harvard University Press, United States of America.

Sen, Amartya. 2000. *Development as Freedom*, Oxford University Press, New Delhi.

2

Muslim Women in India

Educational, Health and Economic Status

Mohd. Muzammil

Since the publication of the Sachar Committee Report in 2006 the socio-economic condition of Muslim minorities has received greater attention by researchers in social sciences. The focus on education, women empowerment, elimination of gender discrimination, and ensuring gender budgeting in all social sector spending has led to giving relatively larger attention to the study of educational and economic status of Muslim women.

Further, this is not only a national issue in India – now it is a matter of global concern. The United Nations Development Programme (UNDP) is focusing on Gender Development Index (GDI) and Gender Empowerment Measurement (GEM). The Dakar Declaration under the title of Millennium Development Goals (MDGs) also includes promotion of gender equality and improving maternal health as its goals to be achieved by 2015. The onus is more on uplifting the females of deprived minorities, and this assumes greater significance if their number is fairly substantial. There is no denying fact that minorities in the world in general are often less educated and less developed. When the Human Development Report was launched in 1990 and it touched upon the issue of gender in the context of human development ingredients, there was not much literature available to reckon with (Muzammil, 1990). Gradually, the focus shifted to women development and gender empowerment at the global level. National, regional and group specific studies came to occupy the concerns of researchers.

India is no exception. In fact, it is one of the least literate societies in the developing world from the view point of women's literacy. The economic development of the country has not been literally translated into human development. In fact women have been 'a late starter in education' across the globe. Campaigns for education of Muslim women came still later and in many societies it is yet to take off. Ester Boserup made a name when she published her book *Women's Role in Economic Development* in 1971 and focused on women's education and drew the attention to the stark conditions of gender disparity in education (particularly) in developing countries. Within this broader picture of educational and social disadvantage, the literacy levels of Muslim men and women are found to be further skewed towards the bottom. The position of women is more serious and worrisome in the Muslim minority community than in other minority groups.

Demographic Size and Caste Ratio

The size of Muslim population in India is very substantial. It is more than the total population of the Arab countries. Muslims are the largest minority in India and the number of Muslim women (about 60 millions) in India (in 2001) was larger than the total population of United Kingdom or France (Table 1).

Table 1

Minorities in India: Proportion in Total Population

Category	*Ratio in population in India 2001 (%)*	*Adult sex ratio (women per 1,000 men)*	*Child sex ratio (girls per 1,000 boys)*
Hindus	81.4	931	925
Muslims	12.4	936	950
Jains	00.4	940	870
Sikhs	01.9	893	786
Christians	02.3	1,009	964
Buddhists	00.8	953	942
Others	00.7	992	976

Note: Child sex ratio is for 0–6 years of girls per 1,000 boys.

Source: Government of India: Eleventh Five-Year Plan 2007–12, Vol. II, Box 6.3.

The Muslim women are unevenly distributed in the country concentrating mostly in Bihar, Uttar Pradesh and West Bengal apart from Jammu and Kashmir where Muslim population is predominant. The gender disparity is typically larger in states where Muslim (women) population is high. The provision of reservation has adversely affected the employment position of Muslim community and Muslim women.

The reason is simple. While 22.2 per cent of the Hindu population is under Scheduled Caste (SC) category, then only 0.8 per cent Muslims come under this head. Similarly, while 9 per cent of the Hindus are classified as Scheduled Tribes (ST) only 0.5 per cent Muslims belong to this group. Even in the Other Backward Caste (OBC) category, where the ratio of substantial even in Muslim community is still lower (39.2%) as compared to the ratio of OBC in the Hindu community (42.8%). There have been demands for reservation to the Muslim community but there also have been arguments on the reverse. Table 2 gives the distribution of different categories of religion/caste wise population. It shows the dominance of general category among the Muslims to the order of about 60 per cent as compared to 26 per cent for Hindus.

Table 2

Distribution of Population by Caste Categories

Religion/caste	*SC*	*ST*	*OBC*	*Gen*	*All*
Hindu	22.2	9.1	42.8	26.0	100
Muslim	0.8	0.5	39.2	59.5	100
Christian	9.0	32.8	24.8	33.3	100
Sikh	30.7	0.9	22.4	46.1	100
Jain	0.0	2.6	3.0	94.3	100
Buddhist	89.5	7.4	0.4	2.7	100
Zoroastrian	0.0	15.9	13.7	7.4	100
Others	2.6	82.5	6.2	8.7	100
Total	19.7	8.5	41.1	30.8	100

Source: Based on the Report of 61st Round of the NSSO, Compiled from the Sachar Committee Report.

Educational Status

As per the Sachar Committee Report, Muslims are the poorest minority in India and the womenfolk of this community are educationally most deprived. Economically they are very poorly empowered and least autonomous. Educational deprivation leads to lesser social awakening and results into economic dispossession. In the field of bare literacy the Committee has found that the literacy rate among Muslims is very much below the national average. The gap between Muslims and the general average is greater in urban areas and more so among the womenfolk. Some 25 per cent of children of Muslim parents in the age group of 6–14 years have either never attended school or have dropped out. The worst sufferers in this category are girls (see for details, Sachar Committee, 2006).

In general, female literacy is lower than male literacy. This is true almost globally. Women's deprivation in education is therefore obvious. Thus, female literacy rate in India for Muslims is 50 per cent and for Hindus 53 per cent. Thus, figures for female literacy are almost identical for both Hindu and Muslim women in rural India. There is a marginal difference between figures for Hindu and Muslim women's primary education for rural India, which subsequently widens across middle, secondary and graduate levels of education. A similar trend is also observed in the data for women's education in urban India. Furthermore, about 60 per cent of Muslim women are illiterate in urban India, as compared to 40 per cent of Hindu women and 23 per cent of Christian women who come under this category (Table 3).

Table 3

Minorities in India: Total Literacy and Female Literacy

Category	*Total literacy (%)*	*Female literacy (%)*
Hindus	65.1	53.2
Muslims	59.1	50.1
Jains	94.1	90.6
Sikhs	69.4	63.1
Christians	80.3	76.2
Buddhists	72.7	61.7
Others	47.0	33.2

Source: Government of India: Eleventh Five-Year Plan 2007–12, Vol. II, p. 187.

Economic backwardness is often the result of educational deprivation. The low literacy level of Muslims and Muslim women is well documented in various research studies. The condition of Muslims in education is not much different from that of the scheduled caste and scheduled tribe communities (Table 4). In the mid 1960s literacy levels of both these groups were low, and far lower than that of 'Others'. The literacy rate among Muslims in 2001 was 59.1 per cent. This is far below the national average (65.1%). If the SC/ST, (with an even lower literacy level of 52.2%) and Muslims are excluded, the remaining category of 'Others' would show a high literacy level of 70.8 per cent. In urban areas, the gap between the literacy levels of Muslims (70.1%) and the national average is 11 percentage points and in relation to the 'Others' category, this gap is of 15 percentage points.

Although the rates of literacy are lower in rural areas (52.7% for Muslims), the gap between the two categories is also narrower. Along with the low educational status of Muslim women, it is important to note, however, that the SC/ST are still the least literate group in both urban and rural India. Although the literacy levels of 64 per cent and 68 per cent amongst male SC/ST and Muslims respectively are not low, they are far below the level for 'Others' which is 81 per cent. In contrast, Muslim women with a literacy level of 50 per cent have been able to keep up with women of other communities and are much ahead of the SC/ST women in rural India.

A general analysis at the state level presents a relatively better picture for Muslims. In as many as 10 out of the 21 selected states literacy rates among Muslims are higher than the state average. These include, in particular, Jharkhand, Karnataka, Maharashtra, Andhra Pradesh, and Gujarat. The Sachar Committee notes that 'such estimates can be deceptive and hide the low levels of attainment among specific groups. In quite a few of these states higher aggregate literacy rates are associated with low urban literacy levels.'

There are several reasons responsible for the sympathetic state of affairs of Muslim women. In the most populated states like Bihar and Uttar Pradesh, the condition of education of Muslim women is very deplorable and this is one of the reasons of their economic subordination and over all poor living conditions.

Table 4

Literates as Percentage of Population by Age Groups

Age groups (in years)	*Hindu*			*Muslim*	*Other minorities*
	General	*OBC*	*SC/ST*		
6–13	90.2	80.8	74.7	74.6	86.5
14–15	95.7	87.5	80.0	79.5	91.9
16–17	95.0	85.2	78.6	75.5	91.3
18–22	91.4	76.9	65.0	70.5	85.8
23 and above	74.0	50.6	36.5	46.1	67.0
Total	80.5	63.4	52.7	59.9	67.0

Source: Based on NSSO 61st round data (2004–05).

The condition of education of Muslims is poor across the board. There is some semblance of parity between urban Hindu and Muslim women with reference to primary education which widens considerably for corresponding figures for middle school – 25 per cent for urban Hindu women and 15 per cent for Muslim women – the difference being much greater when compared to Christian women (35%). Only about 5 per cent of urban Muslim women have secondary education, compared to 11 per cent of Hindu women and 22 per cent of Christian women. The number of urban Muslim female graduates is negligible (0.8%, against

4.2% of Hindu women and 5.5% of Christian women) according to the NSS data.

The relative gap between the figures for educational enrolment for Muslim women in comparison to Hindu or Christian women can also be highlighted. Unlike the percentage difference between Muslim, Hindu and Christian women in primary education, Muslim women in both rural and urban India lag behind their counterparts in school enrolment from the very beginning. This initial disadvantage is further exacerbated across subsequent educational enrolment categories. The figure of about 30 per cent for rural Muslim females attending school in the 5–9 age group (compared to 45% Hindu women) or 1.4 per cent for Muslim rural female enrolment for the 20+ age group (7.4% for Hindu women) is still more favourable than the corresponding figures for urban India.

Mean years of schooling for Muslims is also lower than the mean years of schooling for general and other categories. Similarly, the enrolment ratio is also lower for Muslims than for other categories. The gender disparity is more visible in case of enrolment ratio. This ratio is far better in case of boys than in girls.

Thus, the enrolment figure for urban Muslim females (52%) compares poorly to the corresponding figure of 71 per cent for Hindu females, which further widens across subsequent age categories to end with 4.7 per cent of Muslim females attending educational institutions, compared to 10.2 per cent of Hindu women or 18.2 per cent of Christian women.

Clearly, Muslim women in urban India are much worse off than their rural counterparts, not only in terms of their overall educational status as citizens of India, but also in terms of their relatively poor educational status when compared to Hindu or Christian women. This trend is all the more alarming when this situation is compared to the advances in Muslim female education achieved at the turn of the century.

As many as 25 per cent of Muslim children in the 6–14 years age group have either never attended school or have dropped out. In the drop out students girls far outnumber the boys and also among those who have never been to school, the number of girls is much larger than the number of boys. The obvious reason for this is the discrimination against the girl child in many ways and also the lack of suitable opportunities for the education of the female child in Muslim dominated areas.

In present days, only literacy does not matter. A minimum level of schooling is supposed to be desirable, For example an education up to matriculation may be treated as minimum school education which is worth the name. While in general for persons in the age group of 17 years and above, 26 per cent persons have achieved this level, i.e., completed matriculation. But this proportion is only 17 per cent among Muslims.

Thus, as was the case for literacy, even at the matriculation level, expansion of educational opportunities since independence has not led to a convergence of attainment levels between Muslims and 'others'. Rather, the initial disparities between Muslims and 'others' have widened in all four groups disaggregated on the basis of place of residence and gender. The increase in disparity is most apparent in urban areas for females and among rural males.

The gap between urban males has not changed significantly, rather it has remained persistently high at about 30 percentage points. The gaps are vast and increasing over time, contrary to the expectation that as the overall educational system improves disparities will be reduced. However, some degree of catching up can be seen for SCs/STs, especially in the case of urban males and females, and also for rural males.

State-wise analysis of data suggests that these patterns exist even in educationally advanced states like Kerala. In spite of the achievements at lower levels of education, the inequality between Muslims and 'others' for both urban males and females in the state has increased significantly.

In West Bengal, the percentage of urban males (completing matriculation in the 'others' group) has remained roughly constant at 50 per cent. Thus, it (low rate) has made it easy for the Muslims to catch-up. While relative deprivation has been lower in rural areas and among females, in West Bengal, the position of Muslim women on the whole has worsened over time by more than 10 percentage points in both rural and urban areas.

Andhra Pradesh is the exception in the sense that Muslims, with higher levels of attainment initially in urban areas, have not fallen significantly behind other communities. However, their rate of progress has been slow, so much that 'others' caught up with them in the last two decades. In rural areas, although Muslims have fallen behind other groups, the gap is still not significant. This is a very encouraging sign both for males and for females in the Muslim community in this state.

In general, however, the educational disadvantage of women in Muslim community is worrisome indeed. The government has not been able to secure primary and secondary education for most of its citizens and its policies have deprived people of their right to education until very recently. The waqf property of the Muslim community has also not been utilized for the educational and economic betterment of the Muslim community and women have almost no say in the management of the waqf property. Participation of honest, intelligent and active people in the management of community property has been lacking and thus community property or its income could not help in educating the Muslim children (Muzammil, 1998). Our study has revealed that while

Muslim wakf property could not be used for the educational betterment of Muslim children, the Gurudwaras of the Sikh communities was better utilized for education of the children of this community (see for details, Muzammil, 2001).

It could also be assumed that Muslim girls' schooling is not always encouraged. The female literacy rate is an appalling 28.1 per cent. An improvement in the overall literacy rates for Muslims would not just lead to a corresponding increase in Muslim enrolment in higher education (universities and professional courses) but would also ensure more social opportunity for Muslim women (and men).

This initial disadvantage, i.e. Muslim women's poor literacy rates, completely precludes the possibility of their entering institutions of higher education. Due to this reason the Aligarh Muslim University and the Jamia Millia Islamia – minority institutions with the specific aim of furthering education among Muslims (male and female) in India, are unable to have a majority of Muslim women students in their professional programmes.

There have been regional initiatives like the formation of the Minorities Vikas Manch (Forum) in Jaipur, Rajasthan, to raise Muslim women's literacy levels in the state and to create awareness among the state's Muslims about state welfare schemes. A series of 'Public Hearings of Muslim Women', instituted by the National Commission for Women, highlighted the economic problems facing Muslim women. The overriding concern of these women was the lack of educational facilities for their children.

That is why, on several occasions, Muslim organizations have demanded the attention of the government, political parties and the media to the situation of education of Muslim women in India. They have also questioned the authority of Muslim political and religious leaders and urged a re-examination of the issues confronting the female members of the Muslim community. A new narrative based on critical self-awareness and identity has also been forged ahead. The Muslim Intelligentsia Forum has also held several meetings in various towns and cities in India for creating social awakening among Muslim women.

Health Status

Health implies more than the absence of sickness in the human individual. Health is an illusive concept as it indicates a state of harmonious functioning of body and mind in relation to the physical and social environment. Good health enables the individual woman to enjoy life to the fullest possible extent and to reach the maximum level of her productive capacity. Viewing thus, it is heartrending to note that the general health status of Muslim women is not as bad as that of their counterparts in other communities. But ironically the better health status of Muslim women did not result in ensuring better health of their children. Many health indicators of Muslim women are found to be superior to their counterparts in other communities. But better health indicators could not give them an edge in economic empowerment. Poor health condition of Muslim children is a drain on the family budget of Muslim families (Muzammil, 2003).

Defined as the complete possession of physical, mental, social and spiritual well-being, health status of Muslim women has rarely received due attention (ibid.). For convenience, usually female life expectancy at birth (average age) is taken as the proxy for women's health just as female literacy is taken as the proxy for the educational status of women. But there are many other components of greater significance in daily life.

Lack of adequate food and nutrition combined with rudimentary health facilities leads to low life expectancy and high mortality. Conversely, sumptuous and wholesome food consumption along with the intake of nutrients often ensures better health. Viewed from this angle Muslim women are found to be better placed than their counterparts in the majority community. However, there are many areas of concern as well. The National Family and Health Survey-2 (NFHS–2) examined in detail the consumption of the following items of food: milk and curd, pulses/beans, green and leafy vegetables, other vegetables, fruits, eggs, chicken, meat, and fish consumption. Among these items of food, Muslim women are found to be better placed in as many as five compared to their counterparts in the majority community. In the consumption of milk and pulses, however, Muslim women are relatively worse off. These facts are borne out by figures given in Table 5.

Table 5

Percentage of Ever Married Women Consuming Specific Food at Least Once a Week

Type of food	*Hindu women*	*Muslim women*
Milk or curd	55.7	46.8
Pulses or beans	88.5	83.7
Green, leafy vegetables	85.1	85.8
Other vegetables	93.0	93.8
Fruits	31.9	32.9
Eggs	24.9	44.1
Chicken, meat or fish	27.5	55.7

Source: Muzammil, 2003.

Natural height of women is not only socially significant and critical in settling marriages it is also important from health consideration. Natural height of women varies in different (community) groups of population. The cut off point for height below which a woman can be identified as nutritionally at risk is usually in the range of 145 to 150 centimetres. The mean height for women in India is 151 cms. Similarly the body mass index (BMI) is also used as an indicator for female health. BMI is defined as the ratio of weight in kilograms to the square of height in metres (kg/m^2). Related data for Muslim women are given in Table 6.

Table 6

Height and Body Mass Index (BMI) of Muslim Women

Specification	*Hindu women*	*Muslim women*
Mean height (in centimetres)	151.1	151.5
Percentage of women below 145 cms	13.5	12.3
Mean Body Mass Index (BMI)	20.1	20.5
Percentage of women below BMI 18.5 kg/m2	36.9	34.1

Source: Same as in Table 5.

The physical indicators given in Table 6 depict, in a sense, the effect of nutritional status of women which indicates the physical fitness and the physical fitness in turn ensures mental well-being.

The nutritional deficiency results into anaemia which is very common among women in India. It is characterized by a low count of haemoglobin (iron + protein) in the blood. Haemoglobin is necessary in the blood for transporting oxygen from lungs to other tissues and organs of the body. The youthfulness of women depends on the chemistry of her blood. They usually suffer from iron deficiency in blood. The position of Muslim women in this regard is found to be relatively better.

Table 7

Percentage of Ever Married Women suffering from Iron Deficiency (Anaemia by Degree of Anaemia)

Description category of anaemia	*Hindu women*	*Muslim women*
Women with any anaemia	52.4	49.6
Women with mild anaemia	35.5	34.2
Women with moderate anaemia	15.0	14.2
Women with severe anaemia	2.0	1.3

Source: Same as in Table 5.

Related data among the Muslim women is given in Table 7 which reveals that Muslim women are found to be less anaemic in all the three categories of anaemia – mild, moderate and severe, as compared to their counterparts in majority community.

It needs to be mentioned that iron deficiency is the most widespread form of malnutrition among women. Anaemia is viewed as a serious health problem among women.

Children's health is closely related with the health of mother. Muslim children are found to be suffering from cough and diarrhea. Interestingly, Muslim women are relatively more aware of the popular remedy, i.e., Oral Dehydration Salt (ORS) than their counterparts in the majority community. Relatively larger percentage of Muslim women takes the suffering child to a health facility provider.

Economic Status

Women as such are the poorest of the poor in the world. A study of the World Bank has shown that they have only 2 per cent of property ownership in their name (Muzammil, 2002). Since the Muslim community is a poor community in India, the general status of Muslim women is bound to be poor. They do not share in the economic benefits of the society on equal footing. That is why, 'women in Muslim community are not able to lead a fuller richer and more varied life, and often they are also deprived of a long healthy and creative life' (ibid.). Although Muslim women have been given by *Islamic Shariah* equal rights in economic matters like men, in practice, they are often denied those rights and are unable to participate and receive pecuniary benefits.

Educational empowerment comes from economic status. Relatively lesser percentage of Muslim women is self-employed. Muslim women's figures (percentages) are the lowest among all the three major religious categories. The ratio for Muslim women's employment as regular workers in urban areas is 15.7 per cent as compared to 27.7 per cent for Hindu women and 51.5 per cent for Christian women. This highlights their marginal presence in salaried jobs.

Figures for rural areas however, dismal as they are, also indicate a more or less similar employment status both for Hindu (3.6%) and Muslim (3%) women. The high self-employment rates and the corresponding low participation of Muslim women as salaried workers indicate their marginal presence as workers in the formal economy. This does not imply the absence of Muslim women as workers, rather it indicates their 'invisibility' as informal workers.

In the absence of existing research and analysis in the area of Muslim women's employment, it is difficult to pinpoint specific causes behind this, their poor employment status, although their educational status must presumably exert a significant influence on the form and levels of Muslim women's employment in both urban and rural areas. In the strictly religious households in Muslim society it is still not common to have women working outside for the family. Unless it becomes indispensable they are not allowed to move out to work for wages.

At a glance, Muslims have a poor socio-economic status, with a marginal presence in public life. More than 50 per cent of India's 112 million Muslims live below the poverty line, with a monthly income of ₹ 150 or less. Hindus who constitute 82.2 per cent of the population form 85.3 per cent of the elite; Christians comprising 2.6 per cent of the population are 3.5 per cent of the elite; Jains constituting 0.5 per cent of the population are 2.8 per cent of the elite; while Muslims who are about 12 per cent of the population constitute only 4.5 per cent of the elite (Shariff and Azam, 2004).

Furthermore, a group of Muslim women, lawyers and Muslim Personal Law Board members in Mumbai have worked out a model stipulating a set of minimal conditions to safeguard women's rights in education in association with the Muslim Personal Law Board. At a seminar on Muslim women in Mumbai held in collaboration with the National Commission for Women, a resolution calling for a dialogue with the Muslim Personal Law Board, and favouring reforms in Muslim personal law, has also been passed recently (vide, Muzammil, 2009).

Muslim women's education law in post-independent India is yet to undergo any reform, except for specific schemes. The politically influential section of the Muslim community has been resisting any big change so that the Islamic character of education is also maintained. But they also want a change in educational status. This is an important development. It symbolizes Muslim women and (men's) determination to challenge existing status and discuss ideas on women's rights which, in turn, are inextricably linked to current debates on Muslim women's professional education for jobs and the role of government in their educational and economic uplift.

Islam as such is a fashioner of development. It did not inhibit the educational or economic development of the community or its womenfolk. In many societies however, the man-made *Islamic Shariah* came in the way of the socio-economic uplift of the community (vide for details, Muzammil, 2002). Work participation rate of Muslim women is certainly lower among the minority communities but not the lowest (Table 8).

Table 8

Work Participation Rate of Muslim Women and Other Communities

Category	*Female work participation rate (%)*
Hindus	27.5
Muslims	14.1
Jains	09.2
Sikhs	20.2
Christians	28.7
Buddhists	31.7
Others	44.2

Source: Government of India: Eleventh Five-Year Plan 2007–12, Vol. II, p. 18.

The female work participation rate among Muslim women is half of that in Hindu community. Although it is lowest among the women in Jain community as is amply evident from the above table. The Sachar Committee has reported that overall about 44 per cent of women in the prime age group of 15–64 years in India participate in work, whereas 85 per cent of men in the same age group do so. But the overall work participation rate of Muslim women is only 25 per cent. In rural areas, the Committee notes that the female work participation rate is 70 per cent but that of Muslim women is only 29 per cent. Even upper caste Hindu women participation rate is as high as 43 per cent in rural areas. In urban areas, the work participation rate of Muslim women is only 18 per cent. This shows that they mostly have to stay at home and take care of siblings and the number of children population is higher in Muslim community. Some 23 per cent of the Muslim population is below nine years of age. This forces the women to stay at home and thus their work participation rate is low.

Another reason why Muslim female work participation rate is low is that they are less entrepreneurial and also because the loans disbursement to Muslims has been relatively much less as compared to other group of minorities. The Sachar Committee noted with concern that the average amount of bank loan disbursed to the Muslims is 2/3th of the amount disbursed to other minorities. In some cases it is only half. The Committee observes that the Reserve Bank of India's efforts to extend banking and credit facilities under the Prime Minister's 15-point programme of 1983 has mainly benefitted other minorities marginalizing Muslims, and more so Muslim women.

Conclusion

The general condition of Muslim women in India is causing concern although all is not dark and depressing. The plus points as mentioned above need to be capitalized to push them ahead in other areas of development. The position in case of demographic indicators is not depressing. The female educational scenario is bleak indeed. Economic status is really poor and work participation rate has serious gaps both in rural and urban areas. Muslim women remain grossly under represented in public services. They often suffer from 'double discrimination being Muslim and poor' (Das, 1992).

There is a need for an integrated approach of educational, social and economic development of Muslims and Muslim women. In a model that I suggested much earlier, it was advocated that micro models of uplift would work better than macro policy measures (vide, Muzammil, 1992). Further, the educational needs of the lower and middle class Muslim families are different from those of the rich class of the same community. The role of the government and the Muslim leadership is more important for the latter. Ensuring universal elementary education along the Muslim children will go a long way in helping India achieve the first of the MDGs (i.e., achieving universal primary education) by 2015. Promotion of secondary and higher education along with vocational and managerial specialization would also be helpful in educational uplift and reducing gender disparity within the Muslim community.

A suitably designed strategic mechanism needs to be found out for educational advancement and larger entry of Muslim girls (as well as boys) in the IIMs (Indian Institutes of Management) and IITs (Indian Institutes of Technology) and top universities and colleges of the country. It may lead to a real breakthrough in the vicious circle of illiteracy and poverty that plagues the Muslim community in India. Muslim intellectuals need to be proactive and come out to provide the real leadership to this community as the existing political captaincy of the community has been very weak which miserably failed to prevail upon the government for adopting developmental policies for this group. They would also be capable of seeing that religious instruction does not come in the way of educational awakening and socio-economic modernization of the Muslim community in general and Muslim women in particular.

Briefly stated and using the phrase invented by the UNDP, the national level macro and local level micro policy making for economic and social development of the Muslim community in India will be *endangered,* if it is not *engendered.*

References

Das, Arvind. 1992. *India Invented: A Nation in the Making*, Manohar Publications, New Delhi.

Muzammil, M. 1990. 'Education and Economic Development of Muslims: Problems and Prospects', *Azad Academy Journal*, August.

——. 1992. 'A Suggested Model of Socio Economic Uplift of Minorities', *Azad Academy Journal*, January.

——. 1998. 'Organisational Control of Waqfs', in S.N. Singh (ed.), *Waqf Administration: Status and Issues*, Spellbound Publications, Rohtak.

——. 2001. *Multi-Sector Plan for the Development of Minorities: District Pilibhit* (Report), Uttar Pradesh Development Systems Corporation (UPDESCO), Lucknow.

——. 2002. *Islamic Approach to Human Development*, New Royal Book Company, Lucknow.

——. 2003. 'A Study of the Health Status of Muslim Women in India', in S.N. Singh (ed.), *Muslims in India*, Anmol Publications, New Delhi.

——. 2011. 'Economic and Educational Status of Minorities: A Study of Muslim and Sikh Communities in Uttar Pradesh', in M.M. Verma (ed.), *Employment of Weaker Sections in India: Perspectives and Approaches*, Serial Publications, New Delhi.

Sachar Committee. 2006. *Social, Economic and Educational Status of the Muslim Community of India: A Report* (under the Chairmanship of Justice Rajinder Sachar), Government of India, New Delhi, November.

Shariff, Abusaleh and Mehtabul Azam. 2004. *Economic Empowerment of Muslims in India*, Institute of Objective Studies, New Delhi.

Siddiqui, M. Akhtar. 2004. *Empowerment of Muslims through Education*, Institute of Objective Studies, New Delhi.

3

Sexual Harassment at Workplace

Vibha Chaturvedi

The term 'sexual harassment' is of a comparatively recent origin. It was first used in United States of America in 1970s. Rowe is believed to have used the term in 1973 in a report on various gender issues prepared for the then President and Chancellor of Massachusetts Institute of Technology (MIT).[1] Susan Brownmiller observes that the term was coined by Cornell University activists in 1975. It was brought to public attention there by women's groups like working Women's Institute and Alliance against Sexual Coercion. However, the term remained largely unknown till early 1990s and really came into public notice after Anita Hill's testimony against Clarence Thomas in 1991.[2] Earlier in India words like 'eve teasing', 'molestation' and 'outraging the modesty of a woman' were generally used to refer to the kind of incidents now termed as sexual harassment. The use of the term 'sexual harassment' expresses the emphasis on gender equality and human rights. It is not an issue merely of problematic and inappropriate interpersonal behaviour between men and women but a serious violation of the dignity and human rights of women which should not be treated lightly.

Generally this term is used to refer to harassment of a sexual nature directed at women by men. But it has a wider sense, which is gender neutral. Therefore, it includes harassment where both the aggressor and the victim are of the same sex. It is important to realize that the victim can also be a male and both men and women can be aggressors. Cases where male students or workers were forced to extend sexual favours as a quid pro quo by their male teachers or superiors have been reported. However, women are the victims and men the perpetrators in most cases of sexual harassment that have been reported. In my discussion I will confine myself to harassment of women at the hands of men.

Sexual harassment of women has existed in society for centuries. It takes various forms ranging from staring, a certain kind of sizing up look, vulgar, sexually coloured comments directed at women to actual physical attack of a sexual nature. Majority of women have to face this kind of harassment during their life, especially when they are young. Perpetrators can be strangers but quite often, family members and neighbours also fall in this category. It is not an exaggeration to say that most women live under fear of molestation and rape and are subjected to sexual harassment at some point or other. Their mobility, their spontaneity, access to social goods, in short almost all aspects of their lives is seriously affected by this phenomenon. Unfortunately, quite often it is not taken as seriously as it should be.

Sexual harassment is a manifestation of objectification of women as they are perceived as mere objects for the gratification of men who feel that making sexual advances towards a woman is perfectly alright. In many incidents people view sexual harassment of women at public places as something women are supposed to learn to live with. Consequently there is an emphasis on teaching women strategies to deal with it quietly, rather than eliminating it. As far as sexual harassment of girls within the confines of the home and family is concerned, there is a strong tendency to make them quiet for the fear of social stigma or in the name of family honour.

Patriarchal thinking and objectification of women puts women in a situation of powerlessness and subjugation in all spheres of life. Men fail to see women as persons with agency and autonomy. The fact that they are also rational, moral agents and will like to set their own goals in life is not recognized, nor is it acknowledged that women are citizens and have a right to participate in decisions regarding the public world. Centuries of patriarchal practices have created a situation where most men continue to regard women as their property. Any assertion of will by women is regarded as undesirable, is discouraged and even suppressed. Since most women have also internalized patriarchal values, they also very often actively support in perpetuating and reinforcing such attitudes and practices.

Sexual harassment involves power dynamics. When men and women are placed in a situation of unequal power, then men may be encouraged to inflict inappropriate behaviour of a sexual nature on women who are under their control. In the patriarchal set up, women are in a subordinate position to men and remain unequal to men in respect of access to social goods, wealth and property and participation in decision-making processes both within the family and outside in the public sphere. Sexual harassment of women expresses an assertion by men of power and authority over women. Generally a woman faces such harassment at the hands of a man who enjoys greater power than her due to age or position. However, subjugation of women leads to a mistaken belief that men in general exercise power over women. As a result sometimes a woman may face harassment at the hands of a person who is subordinate to her or lower than her in social status. For example, a teacher may be sexually harassed by a student, or a girl may be harassed by a male household employee.

Sexual harassment of women at workplace is a part of this larger problem. 'Sexual harassment at workplace' refers to '... unwelcome sexual advances, requests for sexual favours and other verbal or physical conduct of a sexual nature that tends to create a hostile or offensive work environment'.[3] United Nations General Recommendation to the Convention on the Elimination of all forms of Discrimination against Women defines sexual harassment as 'unwelcome sexually determined behaviour' such as physical contact and advances, sexually coloured remarks, showing pornography and sexual demands by words or actions.[4] It is to be noted that the emphasis here is on unwelcome behaviour of a sexual nature. The behaviour may be physical or verbal. The important points are lack of consent of the woman and the detrimental impact of the behaviour on the woman towards whom it is directed.

As mentioned earlier, sexual harassment is now seen as a form of gender discrimination and violation of the principle of equality of all citizens. Moreover, it is now regarded as a violation of human rights. In India, it is a violation of the fundamental rights of a citizen as outlined in the Constitution. It is an infringement of life and liberty of a person. The Constitution of India guarantees equality of its citizens and prohibits any discrimination on the basis of gender. It also enjoins upon all citizens to renounce practices, which are derogatory to the dignity of women. Sexual harassment of women thus violates Article 15 of the Constitution, which prohibits any kind of discrimination on the basis of religion, race, caste, sex or place of birth and Article 19(1) (g) of the Constitution, i.e., the right of every person 'to practice any profession, or to carry on any occupation, trade or business'.

All working women, irrespective of their age, socio-economic status, religion, caste or race are vulnerable as far as the threat of sexual harassment is concerned. However, some sections of women are much more vulnerable than others. A report published by International

Labour Organization (ILO) observes that young women, separated, widowed or divorced women, women in unorganized or informal sectors of the economy and migrant workers constitute a more vulnerable section and are more frequent targets of sexual harassment.[5]

Rural women and women from economically weaker sections in India have worked outside the homes for centuries. They work most of the time in agricultural activities, construction work and other small enterprises. Most women work in unorganized sector and their working conditions are quite often unfriendly and exploitative, making them very vulnerable to exploitation of a sexual nature. Since most women have traditionally worked within the confines of their homes and the work is unpaid, very often workplaces in the public sphere are still perceived as spaces meant mainly for men. Their practices are tuned to men's needs and desires. When men interact with each other, they may talk in ways and do things, which women may find discomforting or offensive. Since independence, women's visibility and participation in economic activities in India has increased significantly. With increased access to education and rising aspirations, more and more women are now coming forward to work in paid jobs. However, the culture of the workplaces often fails to take note of this change and its implications and sensitivity to the needs of women and to behaviour appropriate in a mixed crowd continues to remain low.

Most women victims do not raise their voice against sexual harassment. They try to ignore it and keep hoping that the problem will disappear. Anyone who complains of sexual harassment generally faces social stigma. There is a widespread tendency to conclude that the complainant herself is somehow responsible for her plight and she has herself invited sexual advances as a result of inappropriate dress or behaviour. Therefore, it requires enormous courage and confidence for a woman to come forward and make a complaint. Even after making a complaint, the process to seek redressal tends to be extremely traumatic for the victim.

The issue of sexual harassment of women came into focus in India in 1997 as a result of a landmark judgment of the Supreme Court of India (Vishakha and others versus the State of Rajasthan and others).[6] The apex court declared that an instance of sexual harassment is a violation of fundamental rights under Articles 14, 15, 19(1) (g) and 21 of the Constitution. Gender equality demands protection from sexual harassment and right to work with dignity, which is a universally recognized basic human right. Moreover, the right to life demands that each person should be able to lead a dignified life. Sexual harassment violates Article 21, since it violates the right to dignity. The apex court has also stated clearly that the right to practice any profession, etc., is dependent upon the availability of a safe workplace. The Supreme Court issued guidelines for instituting a policy and mechanism for prevention of sexual harassment and providing redressal to victims in all organizations and institutions. The guidelines put the responsibility of providing a safe workplace on the employers and enjoined upon every institution to amend its existing ordinances and provisions to include a mechanism for prevention and redressal of sexual harassment. The Supreme Court reiterated its stand in another judgment in 1999 (Apparel Export Promotion Council vs Chopra) that sexual harassment is a violation of the fundamental right to gender equality and the right to life and liberty.

As a result of this judgment, generally referred to as the Vishakha judgment, organizations were forced to take note of the problem of sexual harassment at workplace. The salient points of these guidelines are as follows:

(i) Sexual harassment is defined as unwelcome sexually determined behaviour (whether directly or by implication), which includes physical contact and advances, a demand or request for sexual favours, sexually coloured remarks, showing pornography and any other unwelcome physical or verbal or non-verbal conduct of sexual nature.

(ii) The 'workplace' is defined to include educational institutions, places for providing services and other places where a sizable number of women work. It thus allows students, teachers, employees and consumers to avail of the mechanism for prevention and prosecution of sexual harassment.

(iii) It will be the duty of the employer or other responsible persons in workplace or other institutions to prevent or deter the commission of acts of sexual harassment and to provide the procedures for the resolution, settlement or prosecution of acts of sexual harassment by taking all steps required.

(iv) All employers, whether in private or public sector, should take appropriate steps to prevent sexual harassment as defined above.

(v) The guidelines emphasize that while dealing with complaints of sexual harassment, steps should be taken to ensure that the complainant or witnesses are not victimized or discriminated against.

It has been mentioned earlier that in complaints of sexual harassment what is important is the impact that a certain verbal or non-verbal behaviour has on the other party. The deciding factor here is not the intention of the person indulging in the behaviour but how it is perceived by the person towards whom it is directed and how it impacts her. One may point out that the impact will depend upon the nature of the relationship between the concerned persons and their comfort level with the concerned kinds of behaviour. A woman may be quite comfortable with certain kind of talk or gestures from a person who is her close friend but not from another person. Similarly, socio-cultural backgrounds and other factors also matter here. These introduce a certain element of subjectivity in decisions regarding whether certain piece of behaviour constitutes harassment or not for the woman in question. This will have an impact on whether a person makes a complaint or not. However, when we talk about norms of behaviour in workplaces, matters cannot be left solely to personal decisions of male and female workers. So general guidelines about appropriate and inappropriate behaviour are needed. It is evident that a person will complain against impermissible sexual behaviour of another person only when she feels discomfort at it and it impacts her adversely.

Impact and Implementation of the Supreme Court Judgment

Following the judgment, many institutions like government organizations, public sector organizations, private companies and universities and educational institutions have instituted a mechanism to address complaints of sexual harassment. Authentic data about the number of institutions that have implemented this judgement is not available. However, there is a general perception that a large number of organizations have still not implemented this. Moreover, in many cases, the mechanisms that are instituted are not in conformity with the Supreme Court guidelines. For example, quite often complaints committees consist entirely of nominated persons and persons in authority, or these do not have adequate representation of women. In 2006, the Supreme Court expressed concern over the non-implementation of Vishakha judgment and directed Chief Secretaries of States and Labour Commissioners to take steps to implement its directives.[7] As it is, the unorganized sector hardly ever takes measures to provide a safe and secure working environment to its female workers. At least the organized sector must try to do so. Such internal measures are likely to be more effective than police intervention. However, at present, the implementation of the Supreme Court directive still remains far from satisfactory. A policy is as good as it is implemented. My experience tells me that even after a mechanism is instituted its implementation has many complex and problematic dimensions.

There is a provision in Indian Penal Code (IPC) against outraging the modesty of a woman. Many complaints against sexual harassment are filed with police under this provision. However, we find that in most cases, the complaint is not investigated properly and adequate steps are not taken by Police to bring the culprit to book expeditiously. Rupan

Deol Bajaj case, Priyadarshini Mattoo case or Ruchika case are some of the high profile cases reported widely. All these cases are examples of the general apathy of the system to provide redress to the victim, especially when the harasser is a powerful and influential person. Even when the institution where a woman works, has a mechanism against sexual harassment, the complainants also often file a complaint with the police. In Delhi University, at least three cases are known where the complainants filed a complaint with the institutional complaints committees, as well as, with police. The committees inquired into them and gave their reports; however the police did not take much interest in investigating the cases properly. In one case, the police official entrusted with the inquiry came to me in my capacity as the Member-Secretary of the Apex Committee and requested me to provide the report of the Complaints Committee to the police, so that something could be written by way of progress of their inquiry. Cases of sexual harassment do not figure high on the list of the priorities of the police and hence a general apathy towards investigation of such complaints is the norm rather than an exception. It is, therefore, extremely important that organizations have a mechanism for dealing with the problem of sexual harassment and implement it effectively.

The Delhi University Experience

Let me share my experience of implementing the policy against sexual harassment at Delhi University. It gives insights into the complexity and difficulty of implementing measures against sexual harassment. I am sure the experience of others at different institutions must be similar in many respects.

Delhi University has instituted an ordinance to combat sexual harassment at workplace, which has incorporated several measures that are worth noting.[8] It envisages a pyramid like structure with the Apex Complaints Committee (ACC) at the top. To generate confidence in the victim the complaints committees are broad-based, including elected and nominated members. Every college is supposed to have a Complaints Committee (CCC) and at the University level, clusters of departments in different faculties have a Complaints Committee each (UUCC). For administrative offices, there is a separate complaints committee at each campus. The ordinance emphasizes that inquiries should be conducted expeditiously and in a gender sensitive manner. The Complaints Committees have elected representatives from each category of University community, students, teachers and employees of various categories. Besides the elected members, the committees also have co-opted members drawn from NGOs (non-government organizations) and activists. The Apex Committee consists of elected members from various categories drawn from the elected members of other complaints committees. In addition, it has nominated members, nominated by the Vice Chancellor from a panel of names given by the elected members of the Apex Committee. The chairperson is a person who does not belong to the university community. The Apex committee is the appellate and regulatory body. The Complaints Committees are envisaged to function independently of the administrative machinery. The authorities have the responsibility to implement the recommendations of the Complaints Committees in accordance with the University rules. The objective is to ensure that the Complaints Committees can function independently and are not subject to pressure from authorities.

I do not wish to claim that Delhi University's ordinance is the ideal formulation, but some of the special features of this mechanism can provide useful input to other institutions in framing their policies. The Supreme Court guidelines have made it clear that institutions should keep their specific needs in mind while following the general guidelines given by it. Each institution, therefore, is free to frame a policy according to its specific needs in keeping with the general guidelines.

Even after a policy is framed, its implementation in that organization is far from easy. The prevailing atmosphere is not supportive of implementation of such measures. Women are gradually becoming more vocal and assertive and this would work in favour of such progressive measures. In my experience of implementing the Ordinance in last four years, several problematic dimensions relating to both policy guidelines and implementation have been observed. It is a feeling that others entrusted with the implementation of the policy face similar challenges. Few points are made in the light of my experience.

One of the major difficulties is that most people do not take this issue with the seriousness it deserves. There is either an attitude of denial; 'such things do not happen here' or deep scepticism; 'we do not need another pro-woman measure'. There is a tendency to trivialize or treat lightly anything that concerns women alone. We found that getting the institutions in Delhi University to constitute the complaints committees alone required repeated and persistent efforts by Women's Studies and Development Centre (WSDC) even though the Ordinance had been there for four years or so.

Our experience shows that once the redressal mechanism is provided and publicized, more and more people come forward to file complaints. In the absence of such a mechanism, women have no option but to suffer in silence or resort to informal measures to resolve the problem. However, even after a mechanism has been instituted, the members of that institution can take advantage of it only when they are aware of it. For example, when a gender sensitization lecture was organized in a faculty in Delhi University, students of one department realized that what they were facing at the hands of a senior teacher comes under the ambit of sexual harassment. They later filed a complaint and action was taken by the university on this complaint. It is, therefore, very important that adequate publicity is given to the policy so that different sections of the institution know whom to approach and how to lodge a complaint.

The Supreme Court has directed that the Complaints Committee will be deemed to be an inquiry authority.[9] Its inquiry is not a summary inquiry or a fact-finding inquiry. Therefore, it becomes very important that general norms of departmental inquiries are followed. More importantly, it is essential that principles of natural justice are followed, since punitive measures can be imposed by the institution on the basis of the inquiry. However, an enquiry into a complaint of sexual harassment is quite different from an inquiry into an administrative or financial lapse or misdemeanour. It is also far more complex in certain respects. Certain general procedures of departmental inquiries become problematic in the context of inquiries into complaints of sexual harassment.

By its very nature the offence is such that there are no eyewitnesses. Nor does a victim rush to make a complaint the very first time somebody shows inappropriate behaviour towards her. As mentioned earlier, most women are reluctant to make such harassment public. Quite often a complaint is lodged only after the inappropriate behaviour is repeated on a number of occasions. This makes it extremely difficult for the victim to provide details like dates and time of the concerned incidents or produce documentary and other evidence of the incidents. One need to appreciate that in cases of sexual harassment, most of the time only circumstantial evidence is available and the inquiry committee needs to take a holistic view of the available evidence and come to a reasonable conclusion.

The other difficulty relates to the reluctance of the witnesses to come forward. We found that when the complaint is against a person in a position of power and authority, the students, junior teachers and office employees are very reluctant to give evidence against the accused for fear of victimization. Students are afraid of victimization in award of marks, recommendations for projects, admission in research programmes and placements, etc. Researchers are apprehensive about obstacles being created for completion of their research work, performance appraisal and finally in selections for academic positions. The employees are afraid of administrative harassment and adverse reports.

The fact that in most cases the administrative authority sides with the accused rather than the victim. It only complicates matters further. The complainant and her witnesses often have to face intimidation and threats from the accused and his supporters on the one hand and pressure from colleagues on the other to somehow settle the matter informally and not pursue the complaint. In most of the cases that we know of in Delhi University, witnesses insisted that their identities should not be disclosed. People also have apprehensions about the process of inquiry and making depositions before the inquiry committee. It does require time and energy on the part of witnesses to come forward in defence of the victim. Moreover, when a cross examination is done, even if it is through written questionnaires, witnesses may feel a lot of harassment because of the nature of questions and their number. In one case, the accused submitted more than 150 questions for the complainant and on average 60–100 questions for each witness. Many of these questions were totally irrelevant, intrusive and of a very personal nature. Witnesses may, therefore, themselves feel harassed during the course of inquiry.

A major issue concerns the process of cross-examination of the complainant and the witnesses. Due to the sensitive nature of the issue, it is important that confidentiality is maintained during the inquiry. Moreover, a direct encounter with the aggressor is bound to be very distressing and traumatic for the victim. Therefore, it is sometimes argued that cross-examination of the victim and witnesses should not be permitted. The inquiry committee should examine the veracity of the complainant's and witnesses' depositions by cross-questioning them at length. However, cross-examination seems necessary to make the decision of the inquiry committee legally tenable. In the course of a Special Leave Petition (SLP) filed by Delhi University the Supreme Court appreciated the argument that given the sensitive nature of the issue, direct face-to-face cross-examination is not appropriate and directed that an indirect cross-examination through written questionnaires should be conducted.

The issue of cross-examination is really complex. The point which needs to be emphasized is that an inquiry into a complaint of sexual harassment has to adopt a procedure in keeping with the sensitive nature of the issue, but also in accordance with the well-established principles of natural justice. Such inquiries also have to be conducted in a time-bound manner and expeditiously. If the inquiry drags on for years due to procedural complexities, the very purpose of the inquiry gets defeated. Therefore, our inquiry procedures and legal procedures need to take note of the new challenges and be made more gender sensitive. Offenses like sexual harassment, sexual abuse, rape, etc., are very different from other criminal offences. To be able to do justice to their sensitive nature, legal procedures need to be made suitable to dealing with these. However, the concerns and recommendations of feminist jurisprudence have, as yet, not been given due attention. These are early days of implementation of women-friendly policies and we hope that with time, greater gender sensitivity will be visible in the implementation of these policies.

We find that, in many cases, the complainant or the accused or both start a campaign to mobilize support and put pressure on the system. This may be in the form of a signature campaign, putting up posters, newspaper write-ups, protest marches, dharnas and other such activities. Such campaigns, even if well intentioned, create difficulties for the conduct of a fair and objective inquiry. People tend to prejudge the issue and view the findings with suspicion, if these are contrary to their opinion. But the requirement of natural justice demands that a conclusion should be reached only after a fair inquiry. All pressure tactics should be avoided. We have also noticed great reluctance on the part of appointing authorities to implement the recommendations of the inquiry committee in many cases.

There are widespread misconceptions about the issue of sexual harassment at workplace. It is often argued that such complaints are, in most of the cases, false or motivated by ulterior motives. So concerns are expressed about the misuse of the provisions. It is amazing how the threat of 'misuse' is widely discussed whenever a progressive measure in favour of women is implemented, be it against dowry or domestic violence or other such matters. Any law is open to the possibility of misuse and cases of misuse of laws are reported. But in cases of legislation in favour of women, this is employed either to raise a demand to dilute the law or scrape it altogether. As far as sexual harassment is concerned, authentic data on its prevalence is not available. But nobody doubts that it is very widespread. It is evident that very few victims come forward to make a complaint. Reason is that the complainant in most cases does not gain any advantage by making a complaint. On the other hand, the whole process of inquiry and its aftermath adds to the trauma the victim has already undergone. In most cases, the accused is given punishment in the form of a warning or stopping of increment, etc., and continues to be at the workplace. The interaction with the accused is bound to be stressful and traumatic for the complainant, especially if the accused is in a position of authority and the complainant cannot avoid such interaction. When the institution takes punitive measures against the accused, the accused in most cases challenges it in the court and a long drawn out legal battle ensues. In many cases, the complainants choose to move out of the institution to be able to put the unpleasant experience behind. It is, therefore, unlikely that a woman will make a false complaint against a male superior or colleague.

Men and women now work in close proximity in educational institutions and offices. Women have joined the workplace comparatively later and the institutional culture is quite often not well adapted to this development. Men quite often fail to understand that certain kinds of behaviour, which have been acceptable till now, are inappropriate in places where women are also present. For example, many male workers are in the habit of using gender-specific abuses liberally in their conversations. Most women find this very offensive and unpleasant. Similarly, men often have difficulty in accepting a woman as an equal colleague or a superior. As a result, they may resort to condescending and aggressive behaviour or make derogatory remarks against the concerned women or indulge in character assassination of these women. So long as family and social spaces do not imbibe gender sensitivity, such problems will remain for working women.

Sexual harassment is often closely related to other kinds of harassment, e.g., administrative harassment. Every case of harassment of a woman by a man does not constitute sexual harassment. It is also a misconception that only physical molestation constitutes sexual harassment. While a distinction can be drawn between sexual and administrative and other kinds of harassment of women, sometimes it is difficult to draw this line because other kinds of harassment is a result of resistance to sexual advances made by the aggressor. It becomes very important in such cases to appreciate that academic/administrative harassment is an integral part of sexual harassment.

Men and women now work together. Students also mix quite freely with members of the opposite sex. This has given rise to complex situations in educational institutions and other workplaces. Let me illustrate a few examples pertaining to students that came to my notice. When a female student wishes to opt out of a fairly long relationship with a male friend, the male friend may refuse to accept the situation and may resort to various kinds of harassment to teach the girl a lesson. In one case a boy and a girl were friends from childhood and continued their friendship through the college. Somehow, during the post-graduation the girl decided to distance herself from the boy. The boy then resorted to following her wherever she went, pestering her with phone calls and messages, maligning her before her class-fellows and other such activities. In another case, a girl refused to talk to her friend whom she had known for quite some time because he was pressurizing her for a physical relationship. The boy retaliated by approaching her under the false pretense of apologizing, drugged her with a cold drink and took her pictures in a state of partial undress. He displayed these on the internet and sent them to many of his friends. In another case when a female research scholar visited her male class fellow in his hostel he physically attacked her.

Thus, in many cases, if the girl breaks off her friendship with a male student or resists his sexual advances, she may be subjected to various kinds of harassment and character assassination. Conversely, if the relationship reaches a certain level of intimacy, quite often it may be misused by circulation of objectionable pictures, MMS (multimedia messages) of the girls in question. In some cases, such harassment has led to suicide by the victim. The point to be emphasized is that while girls and boys have become liberal enough to mix freely and enter into relationships, the demands of privacy and respecting the decision of the other party are not always respected. Networking sites, where young people reveal personal details, are also sometimes misused. This is a new area. There is an urgent need to spread awareness about the regulations governing such sites and the consequences of breaking these regulations. Unfortunately, awareness of cybercrimes is still very low and redress is also slow and inadequate.

We found that students are especially vulnerable to sexual harassment when they work in laboratories for long hours or go on study tours in mixed groups. Students are generally hesitant to lodge a formal complaint because they are afraid that they will be victimized in the evaluation of their work and in examinations. Research scholars are another vulnerable section. The progress of their research work and their scholarships are heavily dependent on the support of the supervisors. The supervisors, thus, exercise enormous control over their research scholars. Therefore, even if a scholar faces sexual harassment from the supervisor, she is generally very hesitant to make a complaint. In most cases, where scholars face very severe sexual harassment, they seek to leave the research programme rather than make a complaint. A student, who alienates her supervisor, faces much difficulty in finding another supervisor and pursuing her research work. Given the nature of academic requirements, it is inevitable that students and research scholars have to work under their teachers and supervisors. Here, the power dynamics is very evident. However, a few measures like making evaluation more broad based and transparent and formulating clear guidelines about the interaction between teachers and students can help in preventing students' harassment. I would like to give a few illustrations to support this contention.

In several cases of complaints of sexual harassment, we found that girl students are called by their supervisors to discuss matters at their residences or in their cabins in the institution late in the evening. Some supervisors ring up the scholars late in the night, show undue interest in their personal matters and invite the scholars for outings and, in general, shower attention in many ways and demand their company. When confronted, the supervisor generally responds by saying that such actions were prompted by a concern for the academic growth and welfare of the student in question. The scholars often find such behaviour intrusive and feel harassed. Foreign students who come on exchange programmes are also vulnerable to sexual harassment. Because of the difference in cultural and social norms, many of these students are comparatively liberal about going out with male colleagues and teachers and this is interpreted as their being available. In their case, it is even more difficult to get redress, since the students are here for a short period and cannot pursue the complaint once they leave the institution.

Till now, complaints and redress mechanism has been discussed. An important aspect of the fight against sexual harassment concerns prevention and awareness generation. Institutions need to take the issue of gender sensitization seriously. Awareness about gender sensitive and appropriate behaviour towards women is, by and large, very low in most places. The administrative hierarchy, in most cases, does not regard this as a priority area. There is a general tendency of denial and apathy. Gender sensitization is not going to be easy given the long established patriarchal and discriminatory attitudes towards women in society. But efforts have to be made in this direction. It is necessary to incorporate gender sensitivity into every aspect of institutions, be it infrastructure or curriculum or pedagogy or administrative decision-making. As things stand now, this is going to be a long battle.

Recently, the Government of India has tabled a bill against sexual harassment in the parliament. This aims at providing legal safeguards against sexual harassment. My preliminary assessment of the bill is that it is quite comprehensive in its scope and covers organizations of all kinds. It has put domestic workers also within its ambit. However, in my view the inquiry procedures could be made more gender sensitive. Let us hope it is adopted at an early date. Only time will tell how effective it proves in fighting sexual harassment at workplace. It is clear that the path to make workplace gender sensitive and safe for women is difficult. It requires comprehensive measures, long and sustained efforts for effective implementation of such measures. Above all it requires a society which respects women and their aspirations.

Notes

1. Wikipedia, the free Encyclopaedia, *en.wikipedia.org/wiki/sexual harassment* (accessed on 29 May 2012). The Encyclopaedia gives useful information about many issues like the meaning and definition of the term, impact of sexual harassment on the victims and the policies adopted in different countries on this issue.
2. Susan Brownmiller, *In Our Time: Memoirs of a Revolution*, 1999, p. 281. Wikipedia, the free Encylopaedia, accessed on 29 May 2012.
3. Legal dictionary: thefreedictionary.com/sexual+harassment, *http://www.google.co.in* (accessed on 29 May 2012).
4. Wikipedia, the free Encyclopaedia.
5. Deirdre McCann, *Sexual Harassment at Work: National and International Responses*, published by International Labour Organization, 2005. Reference is available on the website of ILO.
6. Vishakha Judgement, Vishakha and Others v. State of Rajasthan and Others, AIR, 1997, Supreme Court 3011, Justice J.S. Verma, Mrs Sujata V. Manohar and B.N. Kirpal.
7. Medha Kotwal Petition, *The Hindu*, 23 January 2006, as quoted in Soma Sengupta and Anindya Hazra, *Prevention of Sexual Harassment at Workplace: A Handbook*, Sanhita, Kolkata, 2007, p. 6.
8. Ordinance XV-D: Prohibition of and Punishment for Sexual Harassment, Policy on Sexual Harassment, University of Delhi, 2004, available on the University website.
9. Soma Sengupta and Anindya Hazra, op. cit., p. 6.

4

Female Foeticide and Sex Selection

Vibhuti Patel

The issue of female foeticide has gained focus of demographers, social scientist, policy makers, non-governmental organizations (NGOs) in last few decades. Asian countries are undergoing a demographic transition of low death and birth rates in their populations. The nation-states in South Asia are vigorously promoting small family norms. It is in this context India has adopted two-child norm and China has ruthlessly imposed 'one child per family' rule. Historically, most Asian countries have had strong son preference and have been witnessing declining child sex ratios. This article tries to examine gendered socio-cultural and demographic implications of new reproductive technologies (NRTs), with special focus on sex-determination and sex-pre-selection technologies. Sex ratios in Europe and North America and to some extent in Latin America and Caribbean are favourable to women as these countries neither kill/neglect girls nor do they use NRTs for production of sons. In the East Asia and Asia the sex ratios are adverse for women. India also has a comparative low sex ratio (Table 1).

There is an official admission to the fact that 'it is increasingly becoming a common practice across the country to determine the sex of the unborn child or foetus and eliminate it if the foetus is found to be a female. This practice is referred to as pre-birth elimination of females (PBEF). PBEF involves two stages: determination of the sex of the foetus and induced termination if the foetus is not of the desired sex. It is believed that one of the significant contributors to the adverse child sex ratio in India is the practice of female foetuses.'

Table 1
Women per 100 Men: Global Scenario

Europe and North America	105
Latin America	95
Caribbean	95
Sub-Saharan Africa	93
East Asia	83
Asia	91
China	92
India	93
Global	93

Source: The World's Women: Trends and Statistics, United Nations, 2010.

Historical Legacy of Declining Sex Ratio in India

In the beginning of the twentieth century, the overall sex ratio in the colonial India was 972 women per 1,000 men, it declined by –8, –11, –5, and –5 points in 1911, 1921, 1931, and 1941 respectively. During 1951 Census it improved by +1 point. During 1961, 1971, 1981, and 1991 it declined by –5, –11, –4, –7 points respectively and improved by +6 points and +7 points in census of 2001 and 2011 provisional (P) results (Table 2).

Table 2
Trends in Sex Ratio in India, 1901 to 2011

Year	*Overall Sex Ratio*	*Decadal Variation*
1901	972	—
1911	964	–8
1921	955	–11
1931	950	–5
1941	945	–5
1951	946	+1
1961	941	–5
1971	930	–11
1981	934	–4
1991	927	–7
2001	933	+6
2011(P)	940	+7

Source: Census Reports.

Legacy of continuing declining sex ratio in India in the history of Census of India has taken new turn with widespread use of NRTs in urban India. NRTs are based on principle of selection of the desirable and rejection of the unwanted. In India, the desirable is the baby boy and the unwanted is the baby girl. This is a result of the widespread use of sex determination and sex pre-selection tests throughout the country (including Kerala), along with high rates of female infanticide in the BIMARU (Bihar, Madhya Pradesh, Rajasthan and Uttar Pradesh) states, rural Tamil Nadu and Gujarat. Millions of girls have been missing in the post-independence period.

Professor Amartya Sen, in his world famous article 'Missing Women' has statistically proved that during the last century, 100 million women have been missing in South Asia due to 'discrimination leading to death' experienced by them from womb to tomb in their life cycles. In

India also the census results for the child sex ratio (0–6 years) have been alarming (Table 3) both for the rural areas as well as urban areas.

Table 3

Trends in Child Sex Ratio in India, 1981 to 2011

Years	*Total*	*Rural*	*Urban*
1981	962	963	931
1991	945	948	935
2001	927	934	903
2011(P)	914	919	902

Source: Census Reports.

To stop the abuse of advanced scientific techniques for selective elimination of female foetuses through sex determination, the Government of India passed the Pre-Natal Diagnostic Techniques (PNDT) Act in 1994. But, the techno-docs based in the metropolis, urban and semi-urban centres and the parents desirous of begetting only sons have subverted the Act. Sex determination and sex pre-selection, scientific techniques are to be utilized only when certain genetic conditions are anticipated but in India these are being used to eliminate female babies. People of all class, religious and caste backgrounds use sex determination and sex pre-selection facilities. The media, scientists, medical profession, government officials, women's groups and academics have campaigned either for or against their use for selective elimination of female foetuses/embryo. Male supremacy, population control and moneymaking are the concerns of those who support the tests and the survival of women is the concern of those who oppose the tests. The Forum against Sex Determination and Sex Pre-Selection had made concerned efforts to fight against the abuse of these scientific techniques during the 1980s.

Science in Service of Femicide

Advances in medical science have resulted in sex determination and sex pre-selection techniques such as sonography, fetoscopy, needling, chorion villi biopsy (CVB) and the most popular, amniocentesis and ultrasound have become household names not only in the urban India but also in the rural India. Indian metropolis are the major centres for sex determination and sex pre-selection tests with sophisticated laboratories; the techniques of amniocentesis and ultrasound are used even in the clinics of small towns and cities of Gujarat, Maharashtra, Karnataka, Uttar Pradesh, Bihar, Madhya Pradesh, Punjab, West Bengal, Tamil Nadu, and Rajasthan. A justification for this has been aptly put by a team of doctors of Harkisandas Narottamdas Hospital (a pioneer in this trade) in these words, '... in developing countries like India, as the parents are encouraged to limit their family to two offspring, they will have a right to quality in these two as far as can be assured, Amniocentesis provides help in this direction' (Patanki et al., 1979). Here the word 'quality' raises a number of issues that are examined in this article.

At present, ultrasound machines are most widely used for sex determination purposes. 'Doctors motivated in part by multinational marketing muscle and considerable financial gains are increasingly investing in ultrasound scanners' (George and Dahiya, 1998). But for past quarter century, amniocentesis, a scientific technique that was supposed to be used mainly to detect certain genetic conditions, has been very popular in India for detection of sex of a foetus. For that purpose, 15–20 ml of amniotic fluid is taken from the womb by pricking the foetal membrane with the help of a special kind of needle. After separating a foetus cell from the amniotic fluid, a chromosomal analysis is conducted on it. This test helps in detecting several genetic disorders, such as Down's syndrome, neurotube conditions in the foetus, retarded muscular growth, 'Rh' incompatibility, haemophilia, and other physical and mental conditions. The test is appropriate for women over 40 years because there are higher chances of children with these conditions being produced by them. A sex determination test is required to identify sex-specific conditions such as haemophilla and retarded muscular growth, which mainly affect male babies.

Other tests, in particular CVB, and pre-planning of the unborn baby's sex have also been used for sex determination and sex pre-selection tests. Diet control method, centrifugation of sperm, drugs (tablets known as SELECT), vaginal jelly, 'sacred' beads called Rudraksh and advertised Gender Select kit are also used for begetting boys (Kulkarni, 1986). Compared to CVB and pre-selection through centrifugation of sperm, amniocentesis is more hazardous to women's health. In addition, while this test can give 95–97 per cent accurate results, in 1 per cent of the cases the test may lead to spontaneous abortions or premature delivery, dislocation of hips, respiratory complications or needle puncture marks on the baby (Abraham and Shukla, 1983).

Through the Eyes of Medical Science

Amniocentesis became popular in the last 25 years though earlier they were conducted in government hospitals on an experimental basis. Now, this test is conducted mainly for sex determination and thereafter for extermination of female foetus through induced abortion carried out in private clinics, private hospitals or government hospitals. This perverse use of modern technology is encouraged and boosted by money minded private practitioners who are out to make Indian women 'male-child-producing machines'.

During 1980s, in other countries, the sex determination tests were very expensive and under strict government control, while in India the sex determination test could be done for ₹ 70 to ₹ 500. Hence, not only upper class but even working class people could avail themselves of this facility. A survey of several slums in Mumbai showed that many women had undergone the test and after learning that the foetus was female, had an abortion in the eighteenth or nineteenth week of pregnancy. Their argument was that it was better to spend ₹ 200 or even ₹ 800 now than to give birth to a female baby and spend thousands of rupees for her marriage when she grew up. The popularity of this test attracted young employees of Larsen and Turbo, a multinational engineering industry. As a result, medical bills showing the amount spent on the test were submitted by the employees for their reimbursement by the company. The welfare department was astonished to find that these employees were treating sex determination tests so casually. They organized a two-day seminar in which doctors, social workers, and representatives of women's organizations as well as the Family Planning Association were invited. One doctor who carried on a flourishing business in sex determination stated in a seminar that from Cape-Comorin to Kashmir people phoned him at all hours of the day to find out about the test. Even his six-year-old son had learnt how to ask relevant questions on the phone such as, 'Is the pregnancy 16 weeks old', etc. (Abraham, 1985).

Three sociologists conducted micro-research in Bijnor district of Uttar Pradesh. Intensive field work in two villages over a period of a year, and an interview survey of 301 recently delivered women drawn from randomly selected villages in two community developed blocks adjacent to Bijnor town convinced them of the fact that 'clinical services offering amniocentesis to inform women of the sex of their foetuses have appeared in North India in the past 10 years. They fit into cultural patterns in which girls are devalued' (Jeffery et al., 1984). According to the 1981 Census, the sex ratio of Uttar Pradesh and Bijnor district respectively, were 886 and 863 girls per 1,000 boys. The researchers also discovered that female infanticide practiced in Bijnor district until 1900, had been limited to Rajputs and Jats who considered the birth of a daughter as a loss of prestige. By contrast, the abuse of amniocentesis for the purpose of female foeticide is now prevalent in all communities.

A sociological research project in Punjab in 1982 selected, in its sample, 50 per cent men and 50 per cent women as respondents for their questionnaire on the opinions of men and women regarding sex determination tests. Among male respondents were businessmen and white-collar employees of the income group of ₹ 1,000 to ₹ 3,500 per month, while female respondents were mainly housewives. All of them knew about the test and found it useful (Singh and Jain, 1983). Punjab was the first to start the commercial use of this test as early as in 1979. A committee to examine the issues of sex determination tests and female foeticide, formed at the initiative of the government of Maharashtra in 1986, appointed Dr Sanjeev Kulkarni, a gynaecologist of the Foundation of Research in Community Health to investigate the prevalence of this test in Mumbai. Forty-two gynaecologists were interviewed by Dr Sanjeev Kulkarni. His findings disclosed that about 84 per cent of the gynaecologists interviewed were performing amniocentesis for sex determination tests. These 42 doctors were found to perform on-an-average 270 amniocentesis tests per month. Some of them had been performing the tests for 10–12 years. But the majority of them started doing so only in the last five years. Women from all classes, but predominantly middle class and lower class of women, opted for the test. About 29 per cent of the doctors said that up to 10 per cent of the women who came for the test already had one or more sons. A majority of doctors feel that by providing this service they were doing humanitarian work. Some doctors feet that the test was an effective measure of population control. With the draft of the Eighth Five-Year Plan, the Government of India aimed to achieve a Net Reproduction Rate of one (i.e., the replacement of the mother by only one daughter). For this objective sex determination and sex pre-selection were seen as handy; the logic being a lesser number of women means less reproduction (Kulkarni, 1986).

Academicians Plunged in the Debate

In such circumstances, 'Is it not desirable that a woman dies rather than be ill-treated?' asked many social scientists. In Dharam Kumar's words, 'Is it really better to be born and to be left to die than be killed as a foetus? Does the birth of lakhs or even millions of unwanted girls improve the status of women?' There was a continuous decline in the ratio of females to males across different census (Table 2). The situation is even worse because sex determination is practiced by all-rich and poor, upper and the lower castes, the highly educated and illiterate – whereas female infanticide was and is limited to certain warrior castes (Jeffery et al., 1984).

Many economists and doctors have supported sex determination and sex pre-selection by citing the law of supply and demand. If the supply of women is reduced, it is argued, their demand as well as status will be enhanced (Sheth, 1984). Scarcity of women will increase their value (Bardhan, 1982). According to this logic, women will cease to be an easily replaceable commodity. But here the economists forget the socio-cultural milieu in which women have to live. The society that treats women as mere sex and reproduction object will not treat women in more humane way if they are merely scarce in supply. On the contrary, there will be increased incidences of rapes, abduction and forced polyandry.

Another argument is that in cases where women have one or more daughters they should be allowed to undergo amniocentesis so that they can plan a 'balanced family' by having sons. Instead of continuing to produce female children in the hope of giving birth to a male child, it is better for the family's and the country's welfare that they abort the female foetus and produce a small and balanced family with daughters and sons. This concept of the 'balanced family', however, also has a sexiest bias. Would the couples with one or more sons request amniocentesis to get rid of male foetuses and have a daughter in order to balance their family? The author would like to clarify the position of feminist groups in India. They are against sex determination and sex pre-selection leading to male or female foeticide. What price should women pay for a 'balanced family'? How many abortions can a woman bear without jeopardizing her health?

Status of Women in Making Choice

Repeatedly it has been stated that women themselves enthusiastically welcome the test of their free will. 'It is a question of women's own choice.' But are these choices made in a social vacuum? These women are socially conditioned to accept that unless they produce one or more male children they have no social worth (Rapp, 1984). They can be harassed, taunted, even deserted by their husbands if they fail to do so. Thus, their 'choices' depend on fear of society. It is true that feminists throughout the world have always demanded the right of women to control their own fertility, to choose whether or not to have children and to enjoy facilities for free, legal and safe abortions. But to understand this issue in the Third World context, we must see it against the background of imperialism and racism, which aims at control of the 'coloured population'. Thus, 'It is all too easy for a population control advocate to heartily endorse women's rights, at the same time diverting the attention from the real causes of the population problem. Lack of food, economic security, clean drinking water and safe clinical facilities have led to a situation where a woman has to have 6.2 children to have at least one surviving male child. These are the roots of the population problem, not merely desire to have a male child' (Chhachhi and Sathyamla, 1983).

Economics and Politics of Femicide

There are some who ask, 'If family planning is desirable, why not sex-planning?' The issue is not so simple. We must situate this problem in the context of commercialism in medicine and healthcare systems, racist bias of the population control policy and the manifestation of patriarchal power (Wichterrich, 1988). Sex choice can be another way of oppressing women. Under the guise of choice we may indeed exacerbate women's oppression. The feminists assert – survival of women is at stake.

Outreach and popularity of sex pre-selection tests may be even greater than those of sex determination tests, since the former does not involve ethical issues related to abortion. Even anti-abortionists would use this method. Dr Ronald Ericsson, who has a chain of clinics conducting sex pre-selection tests in 46 countries in Europe, America, Asia and Latin America, announced in his hand out that out of 263 couples who approached him for begetting off-springs, 248 selected boys and 15 selected girls (Patel, 2003). This shows that the preference for males is not limited to the Third World Countries like India but is virtually universal. In Erricsson's method, no abortion or apparent violence is involved. Even so, it could lead to violent social disaster over the long term. Although scientists and medical professionals deny all responsibilities for the social consequences of sex selection as well as the sex determination tests, the reality shatters the myth of the value neutrality of science and technology. Hence we need to link science and technology with socio-economic and cultural reality (Holmes and Hoskins, 1984). The class, racist and sexiest biases of the ruling elites has crossed all boundaries of human dignity and decency by making savage use of science. Even in China, after 55 years of 'revolution', 'socialist reconstruction' and the latest, rapid capitalist development sex determination and sex pre-selection tests for femicide have gained ground after the Chinese government's adoption of the 'one-child family' policy (Junhong, 2001). Many Chinese couples in rural areas do not agree to the one child policy but due to state repression they, while sulking, accept it provided the child is male. This shows how adaptive the system of patriarchy and male supremacy is. It can establish and strengthen its roots in all kinds of social structures – pre-capitalist, capitalist and even post-capitalist – if not challenged consistently.

Attitude towards Women's Health

Centre for Enquiry into Health and Allied Themes (CEHAT) study (Bandewar, 2003) showed that 64 per cent of providers of NRTs revealed that they were against sex-selective abortions, 10 per cent of them stated that they too were against it but they had to do it, while 24 per cent of them approved of sex selective abortions of female foetuses. Among them, gender-based responses were quite interesting. Twenty-eight per cent of total male and 17 per cent of total female providers supported sex selective abortions, 68 per cent of total female and 61 per cent of total male providers were against it.

Social discrimination against women results into systematic neglect of women's health, from womb to tomb. Female infanticide and female foeticide are widely practised in BIMARU and DEMARU – Daughter Eliminating Male Aspiring Rage by Ultrasound (Punjab, Haryana, Himachal Pradesh, and Gujarat) states (Bose, 2001). This masculinization of sex ratio is as a result of selective abortion of female foetuses after the use of ultra-sound techniques to determine sex of the foetus. As unborn children, females face covert violence in terms of sex-selection and overt violence in terms of female foeticide after the use of sex selective abortion techniques. As girls under five years of age, women in India face neglect in terms of medical care and education, sexual abuse and physical violence. As adolescent and adult women in the reproductive age group, they face early marriage, early pregnancy, sexual violence, domestic violence, dowry harassment, torture in case of infertility – if they fail to produce a son.

Population Control Policies

There is a serious need to examine population policies and global funding from the perspective of medical market and marketization of the nation states in the context of newly emerging culture of daily changes of sponsors. Financial economists have reigned supreme to generate moment-to-moment existence among population so that they can get an unending supply of cannon fodder for the NRT experimentation. Budgetary provision on health has a hidden agenda of NRT. The victims are not given scientific details and by labelling them as parasites and beneficiaries, their consent is not sought. It has burdened women with backbreaking miseries. The nation-states have been coached to implement the use of NRT in secrecy – in line with the programmes executed by G8 countries in Thailand, Indonesia, Philippines, and Bangladesh. To achieve population stabilization, 2.1 per cent growth rate of population and net reproduction rate (NRR) of one (i.e., mother should be replaced by one daughter only) are envisaged. These have inherent sexist bias because it desires birth of one daughter and 1.1 sons. Those who support sex determination and sex pre-selection view these tests as helpful to achieve NRR 1. Recent study of Haryana revealed that out of 160 mothers and grandmothers interviewed by AIIMS (All India Institute of Medical Sciences) study team, 40 per cent supported sex determination on the ground that it contributed to population control and prevented families from having series of females in an attempt that a male was born (Bardia et al., 2004).

Gendered Power Relations and NRTs

Search for 'perfect' baby through genetic screening, ante natal sex determination tests, pre-implantation diagnosis, commercialization of sperm and/or egg donation, commercialization of motherhood and hormonal contraceptives raise many socio-legal and ethical questions.

Division of labour among women to control women's sexuality, fertility and labour by utilizing homophobia and pitting women of different race, religions, age and looks to suit the interest of NRT will serve the interest of patriarchy, medical mafia, pharmaceutical industries, scientists and technodocs at the cost of vulnerable human beings as raw material. If the NGOs do not want to get criminalized, they must dissociate from NRTs and divert the funding for public health, library, education, skill building and employment generation as a long-term investment and channelize their energies towards formation of self-help groups.

It is important to understand that reproduction has an individual and a social dimension. While examining birth control practices, an individual is a unit of analysis. While examining the population control policies we have to analyse pros and cons of NRTs, national governments, population control organizations, multinational pharmaceutical industries, public and private funded bodies, medical researchers and health workers who shape women's 'choices' – women's autonomy or control at micro and macro levels. Thus choices are not made in vacuum. NRTs as a choice for some women (educated career women) can become coercion for others (powerless and less articulate women). Hence it is important to be vigilant about power relations determined by race, age, class, and gender while examining implications of NRT on different stake groups.

Initiatives by the State and NGOs

PNDT Act was enacted in 1994 by the Centre followed by similar Acts by several state governments and union territories of India during 1988 (after Maharashtra legislation to regulate prenatal sex determination tests), as a result of pressure created by Forum Against Sex Determination and Sex Pre-Selection. But there was a gross violation of this central legislation. In response to the public interest petition filed by Dr Sabu George, Centre for Inquiry into Health and Allied Themes, Mumbai and Mahila Sarvangeen Utkarsh Mandal (MASUM) fought on their behalf by the Lawyers Collective Delhi (Basu, 2003), the Supreme Court of India gave a directive on 4 May 2001 to all state governments to make an effective and prompt implementation of the Pre-Natal Diagnostics Techniques (Regulation and Prevention of Misuse) Act (enacted in 1994 and brought into operation from 1 January 1996). Now, it stands renamed as 'The Pre-Conception and Pre-Natal Diagnostic Techniques (Prohibition of Sex Selection) Act'.

Recently enacted Prenatal Diagnostic Techniques (Prohibition of Sex Selection) Act, 2003 tightens the screws on sex selection at pre-conception stage and puts in place a string of checks and balance to ensure that the act is effective. The Pre-Natal Diagnostics Techniques (Regulation and Prevention of Misuse) Amendment Act, 2002 received the assent of the President of India on 17 January 2003. The Act provides 'for the prohibition of sex selection, before or after conception, and for regulation of pre-natal diagnostic techniques for the purposes of detecting genetic abnormalities or metabolic disorders or sex-linked disorders and for the prevention of their misuse for sex determination leading to female foeticide and for matters connected therewith or incidental thereto'. Under the Act, the person who seeks help for sex selection can face, at first conviction, imprisonment for a three year period and be required to pay a fine of ₹ 50,000. The State Medical Council can suspend the registration of the doctor involved in such malpractice and, at the stage of conviction, can remove his/her name from the register of the council.

Conclusion

We need to counter those who believe that it is better to kill a female foetus than to give birth to an unwanted female child. Their logic eliminates the victim of male chauvinism, does not empower her. The techno-doctors do not challenge anti-women practices such as dowry, instead display an advertisement, 'Better ₹ 5,000 now than ₹ 5 lakhs later', i.e., it is better to spend ₹ 5,000 for female foeticide than spending ₹ 5 lakhs as dowry for a grown up daughter. By this logic, it is better to kill poor people or third world masses rather than let them suffer in poverty and deprivation. This logic also presumes that social evils like dowry are God given and that we cannot do anything about them. Hence victimize the victim. Investing in daughter's education, health and dignified life to make her self-dependent are far more humane and realistic ways than brutalizing pregnant mother and her would-be daughter. Recently series of incidents in which educated women have got their grooms arrested at the time of wedding ceremony for demand and harassment for dowry, is a very encouraging step in the direction of empowerment of girls. Massive and supportive media publicity has empowered young women from different parts of the country to cancel marriages involving dowry harassment. They have provided new role models. There is a need to clarify the gender-just position from the anti-abortionist position. 'Women should have a right to their bodies and unconditional access to abortion is not in conflict with the claim that sex selection and sex selective abortions are unethical. It is not the abortion which makes the act unethical, but the idea of sex selection' (Madhiwalla, 2001). We have a great task of changing the mindset of doctors and clients, to create a socio-cultural milieu that is conducive for girl child's survival and monitor the activities of commercial minded techno-doctors thriving on sexist prejudices. Then only we will be able to halt the process of declining sex ratio resulting into the phenomenon of missing girls. To stop a gender imbalanced society we will have to convince doctors and clients, state and civil society that 'daughters are not for slaughter'.

References

Abraham, Ammu. 1985. 'Larsen and Turbo Seminar on Amniocentesis', *Women's Centre Newsletter*, Vol. 1, No. 4, October, Bombay.

Abraham, Ammu and Sonal Shukla. 1983. 'Sex Determination Tests', *Women's Centre Newsletter*, Vol. 1, No. 4, Bombay.

Bandewar, Sunita. 2003. 'Abortion Services and Providers' Perceptions: Gender Dimensions', *Economic and Political Weekly*, Vol. XXXVIII, No. 21, 24 May.

Bardhan, Pranab. 1982. 'Little Girls and Death in India', *Economic and Political Weekly*, Vol. 17, No. 36, September.

Bardia, A., E. Paul, S.K. Kapoor and K. Anand. 2004. 'Declining Sex Ratio: Role of Society, Technology and Government Regulation in Haryana: A Comprehensive Study', Comprehensive Rural Health Services Project, All India Institute of Medical Sciences, New Delhi.

Basu, Asmita. 2003. 'Sex Selective Abortions', *Lawyers Collective*, Vol. 18, No. 11, November, pp. 20–23.

Bose, Ashish. 2001. 'Without My Daughter: Killing Fields of the Mind', *The Times of India*, 25 April.

Chhachhi and Sathyamla. 1983. 'Sex Determination Tests', *Women's Centre Newsletter*, Vol. 1, No. 4, Bombay.

Census Reports, Ministry of Home Affairs, Government of India, Various Years.

George, Sabu and Ranbir S. Dahiya. 1998. 'Female Foeticide in Rural Haryana', *Economic and Political Weekly*, Vol. XXXIII, No. 32, 8–14 August.

Handbook on PNDT Act, 1994, Department of Family Welfare, Government of India, for use by Appropriate Authorities in States/Union Territories, New Delhi, 2002.

Holmes, Helen Bequart and B. Betty Hoskins. 1984. 'Pre-natal and Pre-conception Sex Choice Technologies: A Path to Femicide', paper presented at the International Interdisciplinary Congress on Women, the Netherlands.

Jeffery, Roger, Patricia Jeffery and Andrew Lyon. 1984. 'Female Infanticide and Amniocentesis', *Social Science and Medicine*, Vol. 19, No. 11, UK, pp. 1207–12.

Junhong, Chu. 2001. 'Prenatal Sex Determination and Sex-Selective Abortion in Rural Central China', *Population and Development Review*, Vol. 27, No. 2, June, pp. 259–81.

Kulkarni, Sanjeev. 1986. 'Prenatal SD Tests and Female Foeticide in Bombay City: A Study', Foundation for Research in Community Health, Bombay.

Kumar, Dharma. 1983. 'Amniocentesis Again', *Economic and Political Weekly*, Vol. XVIII, No. 24, 11 June.

Madhiwalla, Neha. 2001. 'Sex Selection: Ethics in the Context of Development', *Issues in Medical Ethics*, Vol. 9, No. 4, October–December.

Patanki, M.H., D.D. Banker, K.V. Kulkarni, and K.P. Patil. 1979. 'Prenatal Sex-prediction by Amniocentesis: Our Experience of 600 Cases', paper presented at the First Asian Congress of Induced Abortion and Voluntary Sterilization, March, Bombay.

Patel, Vibhuti. 2003. 'Locating the Context of Declining Sex Ratio and New Reproductive Technologies', *VIKALP – Alternatives*, Vikas Adhyayan Kendra, Mumbai.

——. 2003. 'Sons are Rising: Daughters are Setting', *Humanscape*, Vol. 10, No. 9, 2 September.

Rapp, Rayna. 1984. 'The Ethics of Choice', *Ms. Magazine*, April, USA.

Sheth, Shirish. 1984. 'Place of Prenatal Sex Determination', Larson and Turbo Seminar, September, Bombay.

Singh, Gurmeet and Sunita Jain. 1983. 'Opinion of Men and Women Regarding Amniocentesis', College of Home Science, Punjab Agricultural University, Ludhiana.

Wichterrich, Christa. 1988. 'From the Struggle against 'Overpopulation' to the Industrialization of Human Production', *Reproductive and Genetic Engineering – Journal of International Feminist Analysis (RAGE)*, Vol. 1, No. 1, pp. 21–30.

5

Gender Mainstreaming in Urban Administration

A.K. Singh

Women empowerment is the buzzword now-a-days. No country can afford development without considering women who constitute about half of its population. However, development has bypassed women in India despite worshipping and paying regards to women in mythology and historical texts. Gender disparities vary vastly across cultural, geographical and historical context. India is a large country with vast economic and socio-cultural diversity in its varied regions. The development issues related to women in a large country like India will not only be inappropriate but some times even misleading. Women-specific and women-related legislations have been enacted to safeguard the rights and interests of women, besides protecting against discrimination, violence, and atrocities and also to prevent socially undesirable practices. In past, the Government of India has undertaken a large number of schemes aimed at the socio-economic development of women under various Five-Year Plans.

Development of women in the First Five-Year Plan (1951–56) was clubbed with the welfare of disadvantaged group like destitute, disabled, aged, etc. The Second to Fifth Five-Year Plans (1956–79) continued to reflect the same welfare approach besides giving priority to women's education and launching measures to improve maternal and child health services, supplementary feeding for children, expectant and nursing mothers. Sixth Five-Year Plan (1980–85) had marked a clear shift in its approach, from welfare to development oriented plans towards women. The Seventh Five-Year Plan (1985–90) aimed at raising women's economic and social status and bringing them into the mainstream of the national development. The Eighth Five-Year Plan (1992–97) focused on human development with special reference to women. The Ninth Five-Year Plan (1997–2002) made significant changes in the conceptual strategy of planning for women development. The Tenth Five-Year Plan (2002–07) continued with its strategy of empowering women as agent of social change and development.

The vision of the Eleventh Five-Year Plan (2007–12) is to end the multifaceted exclusions and discriminations faced by women, to ensure that every woman is able to develop her full potential and share the benefits of the economic growth and prosperity (Chart 1).

Chart 1

Gender Development in Indian Planning

First Five-Year Plan (1951–56)	Development of women was clubbed with the welfare of the disadvantaged groups like destitute, disabled, aged, etc.
Second to Fifth Five-Year Plan (1956–79)	Welfare approach, besides giving priority to women's education, improved maternal and child health services, supplementary feeding for children and expectant and nursing mothers.
Sixth Five-Year Plan (1980–85)	Shift in the approach from 'welfare' to 'development' of women. Multi-disciplinary approach with thrust on health, education and employment.
Seventh Five-Year Plan (1985–90)	Aimed at raising women's economic and social status and bringing them into the mainstream of national development. The thrust was on generation of both skilled and unskilled employment through proper education and vocational training.
Eighth Five-Year Plan (1992–97)	Emphasis on the development of women.
Ninth Five-Year Plan (1997–2002)	Attempted 'Empowerment of Women'. The Plan also aimed at 'convergence of existing services' available in both women-specific and women-related sectors.
Tenth Five-Year Plan (2002–07)	Continued with the strategy of 'Empowering Women' as an agent of social change and development through Social Empowerment, Economic Empowerment and Gender Justice.
Eleventh Five-Year Plan (2007–12)	Emphasis on gender equity, gender budgeting and creation of environment free from all forms of violence against women.

Source: Compiled by the author.

There are several dimensions of gender development. These mainly include social, economic, political, and legal dimensions. Women's development has come a long way from the earlier welfare orientation approach in which women were taken as vulnerable sections of the population, whose situation could be ameliorated through the provision of support services like health, nutrition and child care. The present approach of empowerment looks at unequal gender and power relations and use conscientization, mobilization, solidarity, and collective action as the solution (Chart 2).

Chart 2

Different Aspects of Gender Development

CULTURAL	*LEGAL*	*POLITICAL*	*ECONOMIC*	*SOCIAL*
• Respect of rights of indigenous and traditional people • Participation in local resource management • Inclusion of indigenous knowledge	• Awareness of rights • Decentra-lization • Mainstreaming gender perspectives • Decision-making	• Gender justice, elimination of all forms of gender discrim-ination	• Poverty eradication • Micro-credit • Women and economy • Globalization • Women and agriculture • Women and industry • Support services	• Education • Health • Nutrition • Drinking water • Sanitation • Housing and shelter • Environment

A large number of social, economic and political factors are found to continue the development of women in ethnologically diverse, socially complex and tradition-bound societies such as India. A latest study on gender development (2005) has revealed that Kerala, Tamil Nadu, Punjab, Gujarat, Karnataka, and Maharashtra are the leading states as far as overall gender development indicators are concerned.

There are marked demographic contrast between the northern, eastern and central parts of India on one hand and the rest of the country on the other. The educational backwardness has been reported high in Bihar, West Bengal and Rajasthan while health indicators show that Bihar, Assam, Uttar Pradesh and Madhya Pradesh are backward states. The social status of women has also found to be poor in Andhra Pradesh, Assam, Rajasthan, and Bihar. Similarly, the economic status of women is found to be poor in Maharashtra, Odisha, Kerala and Rajasthan. As far as the leadership is concerned, Uttar Pradesh is ahead of state like Kerala. However, SHGs (self-help groups) per lakh females were reported high in Andhra Pradesh, Tamil Nadu, Karnataka, Kerala, and Odisha.

Indian women are at the crossroads of their destiny. There is a great upsurge in consciousness about their rights among all sections and classes of society in the country. There has been tremendous increase in developmental activities for women since the 1980s with a great leap forward in the 1990s. Women constitute 48.2 per cent of the country's population. However, development process has bypassed women. Their holistic development in terms of materials, resources, programmes, and policies is the broad mandate of working of Ministry of Women and Child Development, Government of India.

The Department of Women and Child Development was set up in the year 1985 as the national machinery for advancement of the women in the country. In the view of increasing importance of women empowerment, the Government of India converted the department into full-fledged ministry in the year 2006 and has implemented a number of programmes for women empowerment.

The Government of India has also adopted National Policy for Empowerment of Women, 2001 which aimed at bringing about the advancement, development and empowerment of women and to eliminate all forms of discrimination against women and to ensure their active participation in all space of public life and activities. The gender budgeting is also widely accepted as a powerful tool for empowerment of women. The Government of India is focusing on mainstreaming gender budgeting initiatives and bringing the subject at centre stage.

Gender Mainstreaming in Urban Sector

The bulk of public expenditure and policy concerns lie in gender neutral sectors like power, defence, petroleum, transport, etc., and the implications for women in these sectors are not recognized. It is increasingly being felt that unless gender concerns are mainstreamed in these sectors, public expenditure will always be skewed disadvantageously towards women. Hence, there is imperative need for gender mainstreaming. The importance of gender budgeting has been stressed time and again in different forums.

Women being underrepresented in planning process, the Jawahar Lal Nehru Urban Renewal Mission (JNNURM) provides an opportunity to build gender fair and inclusive cities. It seeks to promote planned urban development and equitable cities. Though, urban space, infrastructure and services which contribute to cities economic development, however men and women perceive their utility differently. Infrastructure development is not gender neutral. Lack of basic services affects both men and women; however women in cities especially in low income communities and slums are more severely affected by inadequate and poor services. In absence of access to toilets, women are forced to defecate in open which is unsafe and undignified while it is also a serious health and environmental threat. Women have traditionally been excluded from land ownership and it has contributed more marginalization of women as they are insecure and live in poverty. Women either do not get wages or earn less than men. Because of their low earnings they cannot afford to buy a house or land for construction of house. Since, women often lack education and technical skills; they tend to be predominantly in informal economy. The informal sector is under regulated and social safety network is lacking. Among the poor, forced evictions from illegal spaces (slums) are a major cause of insecurity. The demolitions of slums not only destruct homes, but also destroy the informal livelihoods. The women being the most vulnerable and disadvantaged group, are mostly affected by such evictions. Women living in slums and low income groups also face problem of domestic violence as the family income is very low to sustain the family. Women and children experience domestic violence through physical abuse, sexual assault and threats. Urban violence against women can be attributed due to lack of their power that comes from non-ownership of property and shelter. Urban women are also more dependent on public transport to move in the city however, men usually own personal transport. Women use transport differently from men based on the type of work they do. Urban women are bearing more burdens of diseases. Urban poor women are more anemic and morbidity rate among them is higher. Thus, the Ministry of Urban Development and Ministry of Housing and Urban Poverty Alleviation need to set out a clear urban gender policy that will provide the framework for the gender integration. A gender policy must have four key components:

(i) Bring a gender perspective into all aspects of planning, policy and legislation and activities that are within the domain of the Ministries.
(ii) Create an enabling environment for women and thus to realize their full human rights in cities and particularly for women belonging to poor and marginalized groups.
(iii) Outline sustainable mechanism for the equal participation of all including poor women in city development.
(iv) Promote equitable access and control over the urban resources for women and men.

Gender mainstreaming is about promoting inclusive and participatory planning and development of the cities. Women empowerment is essential for inclusive development. Women empowerment through mobilizing and organizing in groups that promote micro-finance and ensure their participation in development planning and livelihoods is imperative. Public private partnership with civil society's involvement for gender equality is an effective instrument for improving basic services to urban poor including women.

Box 1

Good Practices of Gender Mainstreaming

CURE: The Crosscutting Agra Programme implemented with the support of Agra Nagar Nigam, UP and USAID aimed at improving sanitation in selected low income communities and enhancing livelihood opportunities for young people and women. Center for Urban and Regional Excellence (CURE) facilitated the process of community mobilization, organization and inclusive planning. A Women's Toilet Saving Group helped women to build up a lump-sum investment required for the personal toilets. Credit was also provided through a Community Credit Facility. The project initiative led to the empowerment of women from low resource communities with capacities to address their livelihood needs on sustainable basis.

Community Led Sanitation Programme-Sangli: The community led sanitation programme in Sangli in Maharashtra has assisted 3,500 households across twelve slums in accessing adequate sanitation facilities. The initiative is a partnership between Municipal Corporation, USAID and Shelter Associates. The project has helped built community toilet blocks in phased manner, share toilets and in-house toilets. Women were closely engaged in designing the toilets and in Sanitation Committees for operation and management. Access to toilets has improved the environment, and increased the confidence level among women to manage facilities.

Housing for Slum Dwellers-Mumbai: Resettlement of slum dwellers living on relevant tracks in Mumbai was initiated through a partnership between the Urban Transport Project, National Slum Dwellers Federation, Mahila Milan Women's Organization and Society for Promotion of Area Resource Centers. Nearly 11,000 families were provided free and permanent housing small multi story apartments with about 6000 families in transit accommodation.

Women Take Charge of Toilets-Pune: A partnership between the municipal government, NGOs, CBOs helped to construct over 400 community toilet blocks which resulted in improved sanitation facility for more than five lakh poor people. SPARC, NSDF and Mahila Milan and Organizations of Slum and Pavement Women setup Savings and Credit groups and bid for the construction of the toilets. The women developed confidence, land to negotiate with local bureaucracy, monitored costs, challenges, social gender prejudices and overcame the reluctance on the part of government staff to deal with women.

Sanjha Prayas-Delhi: Sanjha Prayas is a programme for participatory urban governance which aims at extending the Bhagidari initiative in the slums. The programme was implemented by Centre for Urban and

Cont'd...

...Cont'd

Regional Excellence in partnership with slum dwellers, especially women, reaching out to nearly 1,50,000 people in 30 slum and resettlement areas to address their needs for basic municipal and social services, housing and livelihoods.

Water Kiosk-Delhi: Center for Urban and Regional Excellence (CURE) in partnership with the Energy Research Institute and a private partner, helped set up a women managed, commercially viable, water kiosk to improved access to good quality drinking water. The project was under taken in Kalandar colony, a slum settlement with over 10,000 people. CURE designed and executed a community mobilization process that engaged women in planning, management and operation of the water kiosk as a community enterprise.

Community-led Total Sanitation-Kalyani, West Bengal: Kolkata Urban Services for Poor project experienced with an innovative approach to reduce open defecation in Kalyani municipality in West Bengal. A series of training and awareness building activities was initiated for partnership building with NGOs, field facilitates, women community leaders, ward councillors and municipal officers for mobilizing community to construct personal toilets and improving sanitary conditions.

Parivartan: Ahmedabad Municipal Corporation in collaboration with industrial house, local community and civil society organizations launched Parivartan programme for upgrading slums. SAATH, a local NGO mobilized communities, especially women to identify their need and enabled them to participate in design and implementation process. SEWA helped women access credit to pay for their share of the cost.

This is high time for the Ministry to develop its gender policies for an integrated national urban policy. A review is required for all the urban policies and programmes from a gender perspective to make these gender equitable and pro-poor. Gender analysis involves an examination of gender issues across sectors using gender disaggregated data, looking at indicators separately for men and women, their differences, needs and priorities. Integrating gender concerns in urban development will be successful only when the administrators, municipal officers, people's representatives and other concerned persons are well convinced of the need for gender mainstreaming. Therefore capacity building of people's representative and concerned municipal officers and city managers is imperative to promote the concept of gender budgeting in urban local bodies (ULBs).

Though, initiatives from government and outside of the government have been taken for gender budgeting, however, only a few departments and ministries have adopted the gender budgeting analysis. There is imperative need for crucial interaction between analysis and the structures of gender that currently exist in society as well as with the elements necessary for transforming gender relations. The serious efforts are required for opening a meaningful dialogue with policy makers and other key players to make the appropriate for adopting the gender budget analysis.

Rationale for Gender Mainstreaming

(i) Women and men contribute to city development and have a right to equal access to basic services and resources.

(ii) Women and men access urban services in different ways.

(iii) Infrastructure development is not gender neutral.

(iv) JNNURM is an opportunity to integrate gender into urban policy, programme, planning, and development.

(v) More men than women use the motorized road. More women use smaller roads. Similarly women are more dependent on public transport while men usually own their personal vehicles for city transport.

(vi) Women have less access to technology such as mobile phones and the need is that they should be able to move around safely in cities.

(vii) Women are primarily responsible for water collection and storage. The public services based on user charges must be made gender friendly.

(viii) Women in slum settlements need access to toilets as the absence of toilet facility to them creates problems of security, safety and environmental health hazards.

(ix) Women use home for productive activities besides performing their household activities thus housing conditions matter more for women than for men.

(x) A few women own properties, hence, property tax regime tends to be male oriented. Women headed households may find it difficult to pay property taxes unless there are gender friendly provisions.

(xi) Women have low level of education and knowledge of computers therefore their access to e-Governance is critical.

(xii) Women councillors need more orientation and capacity building regarding different issues of urban development and governance in order to enhance their role in urban governance and management.

(xiii) Women's groups engaged in thrift and credit activities and self employment may be given opportunity to share the responsibility of urban sanitation and managing solid wastes.

(xiv) SHG-based micro-financing is an effective instrument for empowering poor women living in slum and low income groups.

(xv) Gender analysis of policies, programmes, schemes, and projects in urban sector oriented towards women empowerment is imperative.

Women's Participation in Local Government

The Constitution of India has made provision of establishment of local self-governments in order to decentralize the planning process and governance. The 73rd and 74th Constitution Amendment Acts were introduced which made provisions for three-tier system of decentralized governance. Women's role in decision-making is one of the most important questions for consideration in the movement for their empowerment. The 73rd and 74th amendments (1992) to the Indian Constitution have served as a major breakthrough towards ensuring women's equal access and increased participation in political power structure. There are about one million elected women representatives in panchayats and municipal bodies in India. The number of women representatives in urban local bodies (ULBs) of the selected states is shown in Table 1. It is estimated that elected women in all the three categories of ULBs account for 22,622.

Table 1
Number of Elected Women in ULBs

States	*Total*	*SC*	*ST*	*Chairpersons*
Uttar Pradesh	2,400	802	0	245
Bihar	1,388	143	1	NA
Orissa	654	NA	NA	34
Chhattisgarh	1,010	NA	NA	NA
Uttarakhand	236	NA	NA	21

Source: RCUES, 2010 Lucknow.

The Constitutional Amendment Acts also ensured the provision of reservation of women in local governments. One-third seats were reserved in urban local bodies also. A few states such as Bihar, Madhya Pradesh and Rajasthan have also made provision for 50 per cent reservation for women in local governments. Thus, the gender mainstreaming in decentralized governance has been initiated. Moreover, women's share in policy perspective and resources allocation in urban sector has been reported to be very low. With the launch of JNNURM and other infrastructure programmes and schemes, gender mainstreaming is getting momentum. JNNURM and reforms agenda seek to improve the effectiveness, accountability, efficiency, sustainability and service equity in cities. It also aims to reduce class and gender fragmentation by making socio-political and economic institutions, processes and resource allocations more equitable. Thus, gender based urban development is about promoting cities that respond, equally to men and women. Urban women experience cities differently and thus meeting their needs becomes critical.

Involvement of women in the political arena and in decision-making process is an important tool for empowerment as well as monitoring standards of political performance at local level. However, some of the major constraints prevent women from effective participation at local level. These include:

(i) Lack of orientation/training in urban development issues and municipal administration.
(ii) Lack of knowledge/orientation about municipal Acts, rules and regulations as well as various development programmes and schemes.
(iii) Lack of experience for dealing with multidimensional urban development issues and civic affairs.
(iv) Lack of knowledge about technical inputs related to municipal service delivery mechanism.
(v) Lack of support from male colleagues and municipal officers in the municipal affairs and urban development issues.
(vi) Lack of cooperation from municipal officials regarding the allocation of budgets at ward level and managing municipal affairs.
(vii) Lack of party support and poor organizational support and infrastructure.
(viii) Fear and insecurity and also lack of confidence in public speaking and handling municipal affairs.
(ix) Dual responsibility of managing home and taking charge of official duties.
(x) Criminalization of politics and corruption involve in municipal affairs.

In order to orient and provide training to women representatives in urban administration and municipal affairs, more than 60 organizations in India organize programmes for the capacity building of elected women representatives. Most of the organizations are working at the state level. The Government of India under the Ministry of Urban Development provides financial support to the organizations and academic institutions for organizing training and orientation programmes for elected women representatives. However, 50 per cent of the financial support was supposed to be mobilized from the concerned state. Now, the Ministry has changed the norms and provides 100 per cent funding to the organizations for conducting training programmes and orientation to the elected women representatives, however, state consent is required. Similarly, the Ministry of Housing and Urban Poverty Alleviation, Government of India has also made provision to provide training and orientation to be elected representatives for orienting urban poverty alleviation programmes in each state through Regional Centre for Urban and Environmental Studies located at Lucknow, New Delhi, Mumbai and Hyderabad. The Department of Urban Development in various states has initiated several capacity building or training initiatives to train women working at various levels of municipal administration. The National Academy of Administration, Mussoorie is actively involved in training senior government officers. The Academy has also set up a National Centre for Gender Training and Research to further issues related to women and development. The Ministry of Women and Child Development, Government of India, in association with concerned state governments is also organizing training, orientation programmes and workshops for the orientation on gender budgeting and gender sensitization. The Ministry of Housing and Urban Poverty Alleviation, Government of India, has also made provisions for 30 per cent reservation in skill training, Urban Self-Employment Programme, besides, exclusively Urban Women Self-Help Programme under Revamped Swarn Jayanti Swarozgar Yojana (SJSRY). The Women Self-Help Programmes have two main components, viz., women self-employment and thrift and credit societies that promote women self-employment and micro financing for their empowerment. The revised guidelines of SJSRY make provisions that there will be no project limit for financing the self-employment projects while women will get subsidy upto ₹ 3,00,000 or 35 per cent of the project under Urban Women Self-Help Programme. The women Self-Help Groups (SHGs) are also encouraged through revolving fund in the tune of ₹ 2,000 per women member for initiating income generating activities.

Gender Perspective in Municipal Budget

There are three major sources of income for ULBs. These are state and central governments allocation, state and centrally sponsored schemes; revenue obtained through local taxes, fees and user charges; and funds obtained from Central and State Finance Commissions. Besides international donor agencies like World Bank, Asian Development Bank, Japan Bank for International Cooperation, Department of International Development (DFID), etc., also provide financial support for municipalities for specific development projects in urban areas. Women's groups have been focusing on micro economies involved in dealing with problems faced by women at grassroots level such as drinking water, health, garbage disposal, etc. The decision-makers in ULBs need to address the following issues:

(i) How to bridge the gap between notional allocation and actual allocation.
(ii) Accounting, auditing and record keeping of gender disaggregated data and allocation.
(iii) How to achieve physical and financial performance of programmes and schemes.
(iv) Implementation of welfare and other developmental programmes and schemes for the urban poor.
(v) Gender based profiling of municipal expenditure.
(vi) Micro level planning with participatory approach for assessing micro level needs.
(vii) Micro level initiatives for gender equity and capacity building of women.
(viii) Synergy in allocation for resources across levels of governance, programmes and departments.
(ix) Gender responsive administration and resource mapping for creating employment opportunities and empowering women.
(x) Redesigning and prioritizing of resources for gender equity women empowerment in urban areas.
(xi) Addressing constraints, challenges and problems in gender mainstreaming.

Gender and the Norms of Good Urban Governance

The campaign for good urban governance is underpinned by seven interrelated norms: sustainability, decentralization, equity, efficiency, transparency and accountability, civic engagement and citizenship, and security. While each of these is applicable to both men and women, there are specific gender aspects that need to be highlighted.

Sustainability

Women play a critical role in urban life, with extensive responsibilities for their families' welfare. Sustainability is a cornerstone of future planning in the cities and consultations with all stakeholders in cities. Environmental planning and management have been identified as a prerequisite for sustainability. At times women's livelihood strategies and efforts to provide their households with basic necessities bring them into conflict with local government. It is essential that urban poor women's constraints are recognized and worked with, through supportive partnerships with local authorities.

Decentralization

Decentralization presents the opportunity for greater involvement of women in planning and consultation processes, and also has the potential for a more gender conscious allocation of local resources. Local authorities are closest to their citizens and hence in the best position to involve women in the decision-making process and in consultation. The decentralization of authority and resources is also an important means of improving stakeholder participation. However, struggles around resources at the local level may exclude women rather than to encourage them into the political process.

Equity

Equity in the city implies representation as well as access to resources. Equity of access to decision-making and the basic necessities of urban life are basic to good urban governance. Yet there are countless ways in which income or social status affects people's ability to participate in city life and access its resources. Even when resources are available, public expenditure may be under-allocated in gender terms. Women's rights to representation, as well as to basic services and other urban resources, cannot be denied.

Efficiency

The role women play in the urban economy is often not recognized because much of it takes place in the informal economy or hidden from view as home-working. Cities need to be efficient in terms of finances and administration. This means regulating and coordinating local authorities' management, and targeting finances for effective performance. In order to ensure this women and men have to be able to contribute optimally to their own survival and the economy. A key challenge is to make visible and valued the contribution of women as well as men to the efficient operation of cities. Efficiency is compromised when women and the poor are not involved in decision-making and policy choices.

Transparency and Accountability

Women must be in a position to access, interpret and comment upon local government performance. Transparency and accountability depends upon municipal administration and politics being open to public scrutiny. Communication needs to be accessible to people who cannot handle complex documents, to those not used to engaging in public debate, and to working parents with limited time – all factors affecting women more than men.

Civic Engagement and Citizenship

Governments and international agencies alike have increasingly appreciated the importance of women's grassroots organizations in advocating for services and providing infrastructure and basic services for themselves in the absence of provision from other sources. It is the responsibility of local authorities to encourage the full engagement of women. It is also in their interests to do so to ensure the effective functioning of urban institutions and community based organizations.

Security of Individuals and Their Environment

Insecure and even hostile urban environment can be perpetuated by local authorities' inattention to planning for women's security both domestically and in public places. Security of individuals and their environment is not confined to cities. It is a matter of growing urgency as unsafe cities restrict access and mobility for their citizens, especially women. Violence against women is just as likely to happen in the home as in public spaces. If women leave abusive relationships, they invariably lose their homes and security as well. Thus violence and the fear of violence prevent women from full and equal participation in the social life of their community and threaten our understanding of what should be the democratic functioning of our society.

Gender Budgeting Initiatives

In 1984, Austria introduced the first gender budgeting initiative. Taking budgets as essential instruments for promoting gender equality, pioneering analysis of the impact of public budgets on gender relations was carried out. The Australian example was not only crucial in raising awareness, but its approach served as an important point of reference for later gender budgeting initiatives. British Women's Budget Group, consisting of experts from universities, unions and non-governmental organizations (NGOs) is publishing comments on national budget since 1989. Their focus is on assessing taxes and transfers, but they also refer constantly to the importance of engendering economic policies. In 1993, the Women's International League for Peace and Freedom established a gender budgeting initiative in Canada. In 1995, South Africa's Women's Budget Initiatives established after the first democratic elections. By 2002, there were over 60 countries around the world that had experience of gender budget.

Over the last two decades, India's planning process has increasingly recognized the need to address gender inequalities. Formal earmarking of funds for women began with Women's Component Plants in 1997–98, however, gender sensitivity in allocation of resources started with the Seventh Plan. The plan documents have over the years reflected the evolving trends in gender matters.

Budgetary allocation for social services expenditure for capacity building, reduction of domestic drudgery and better quality of life for women is need of hour. Education, health, crèche, working women's hostel, housing, nutrition, water supply, drainage, sanitation, public toilets, fuel and energy, waste management, Public transport are some of the major areas of social services expenditure by which women are likely to get more benefits. Women also need self-help groups based credit for self-employment. Similarly, training programmes vocational and skill improvement training in prospective areas like bio-technology, information technology, etc., will create employment opportunities for women. Marketing facilities for women entrepreneurs and the implementation of National Street Vendor Policy will provide additional benefits to women for promoting self-employment ventures. Thus, it is imperative to create Women Development Cell in each urban local body for gender responsive budgeting and gender based profiling of municipal expenditure. This cell is also likely to address the gender issues and concerns in urban areas.

Gender budgeting as a tool is used for achieving gender equality and particularly correct the planning and investment distortions within government spending. Gender budgeting is likely to help to

(i) Balance gender needs through appropriate budget in financial systems.

(ii) To ensure pro-poor urban expenditure in areas such as water supply, sanitation-provision of sewerage and toilets, infrastructure development, storm water drainage, solid waste management, provision of low cost public transport, development of roads, provision of economic infrastructure, etc.

(iii) To provide for human-specific urban expenditure that are targeted to include women's requirements in the provision of housing, markets, buses, parks, and recreation centres.

Gender auditing tools have been developed by United Nations Development Programme (UNDP) that recommend a participative process for gender budgeting and for development of gender sensitive urban expenditure policy and guidelines. A tool kit has also been developed by United States Agency for International Development (USAID) for identifying gender needs in planning the successfully tested mechanism for gender based planning. The tools for gender inclusion in budgeting and urban planning process include:

(i) Spatial maps to assess women's access to physical, social, economic infrastructure to help develop a mix of macro and micro level plans.

(ii) Gender profiling a public expenditure, with impact assessment studies to understand gender based spending.
(iii) Gender based auditing and beneficiary assessments.

Conclusion

Gender budgeting refers to the systematic examination of the budget programmes and policies for the impact on women. Studies show that programmes and policies design to improve women's economic opportunities lead to higher rates of economic growth. Gender budgeting has gained prominence in recent years as it has become one of the most effective instruments of women empowerment. Gender budgeting seeks to mainstream gender analysis of issues within government policies, promote greater accountability for the commitments of governments to gender equality and influence budgets and policies. Gender budgeting framework include the following approaches:

(i) Undertake a policy appraisal to identified gender issues and resource allocations, and how policy will affect prevailing in equalities.
(ii) Evaluate the policies, programmes and schemes through using survey and other techniques that how they have affected beneficiaries.
(iii) Evaluate public expenditure incidence and gender based profiling of public expenditure.
(iv) Examine the impact of budget, resources and policies and programmes on women.
(v) Prepare a budget statement and disseminate the results.

The public expenditure is classified into three major categories: gender-specific expenditure, expenditures that promote gender equality within the public services, mainstreaming expenditure. Gender budgeting seeks to integrate gender considerations into the government budget process; however it is not confined to the government budget only. It is basically an instrument for empowering women and addressing their concerns and needs. Though gender budgeting in urban sector is limited, however, gender mainstreaming, engendering urban development and gender budgeting is imperative in urban sector in order to address the needs of urban women and their empowerment.

References

Bannerjee, Nirmala and P. Roy. 2003. *Gender in Fiscal Policies: A Case of West Bengal*, Snapshot of Gender Budget Initiatives in South Asia, UNIFEM, New Delhi.

Beall, J. 1995. *Urban Governance: Why Gender Matters*, Gender in Development Monograph Series No. 1, United Nations Development Programme, New York.

——. 1997. 'Participation in the City: A Gender Perspective', in Beall (ed.), *A City for All: Valuing Difference and Working with Diversity*, Zed Books, London, pp. 38–48.

Beneria, L. 1995. 'Towards a Greater Integration of Gender in Economics', *World Development*, Vol. 23, No. 11, November.

Bridge. 2002. *Cutting Edge Pack on Gender and Budgets*, Institute of Development Studies, University of Sussex, Brighton.

Budlander, D. 2000. 'The Political Economy of Women's Budgets in the South', *World Development*, Vol. 28, No. 7, July.

Chakravarty, Lekha. 2003. *Macro Scan of Union Budget 2003 in India: A Glimpse through Gender Lens*, UNIFEM, New Delhi.

Chant, S. 1997. *Gender, Urban Development and Housing*, UNDP Publication Series for Habitat II, Vol. 2, United Nations Development Programme, New York.

Gender Budget Initiatives: Strategies, Concepts and Experiences. 2001. UNIFEM-IDRC-Commonwealth Secretariat, Brussels, October.

Hamadeh-Banerjee, L. and P. Oquist. 2000. *Overview: Women's Political Participation and Good Governance: 21st Century Challenges*, United Nations Development Programme, New York, pp. 1–7.

Kapdi, N.Y. 2008. *Gender Budgeting in Urban Local Bodies in Training Module on Urban Poverty Alleviation*, RCUES, Mumbai.

Lahiri, Ashok et al. 2003. *Gender Budgeting in India*, Money Series No. 3, UNICEF-NIPFP, New Delhi.

Machado, L.M.V. 1994. 'Continuity of Urban Movements: The Participation of Low-income Women in the Health Movement of the Jardim Nordeste Area in Sao Paulo, Brazil, 1976–1986', paper presented at the International Seminar on Gender, Urbanisation and Environment, Nairobi, Kenya, June 11–17.

Mehta, A. et al. 2004. *The Budget: A Gender and Poverty Sensitive Perspective*, National Commission for Women, New Delhi.

Michaud, A. 2000. *Canada: Is there a Connection between Moving about Freely and Good Urban Governance?*, Women in Urban Governance, UNCHS (Habitat), Nairobi.

Planning Commission. 2006. Approach Paper to the Eleventh Five-Year Plan, New Delhi.

Sarraf, E. 2003. 'Gender Responsive Government Budgeting', IMF Working Paper, Washington.

Sharp, R. 2003. *Budgeting for Equity: Gender Budget Initiatives within a Framework of Performance Oriented Budgeting*, UNICEF, New York.

World Bank. 2001. *World Bank Policy Research Report 2001: Engendering Development through Gender Equality in Rights, Resources and Voice*, Oxford University Press, New York.

6

Conceptualization and Manifestation of Women Empowerment

Shyam Kartik Mishra

The charter of the United Nations signed in 1945 was the first agreement by the world community that proclaimed gender equality as a fundamental right. Gender equality and empowerment of women is now recognized globally as a key element to achieve progress in all spheres of life. Empowerment is also one of the eight Millennium Development Goals (MDGs) to which world leaders agreed at the Millennium Summit held in year 2000 in New York.

Initially, mainstream development agencies concerned with women ignored the language of empowerment, but as top-down development failed to alleviate poverty in the 1990s, especially among women, the discourse began to change. Empowerment entered the lexicon of mainstream women/gender and development discourse leading to emergence of intensified need to conceptualize the term more precisely and accurately. A brief endeavour has been made in the article to survey the efforts made to conceptualize the term 'women empowerment' and also to identify the indicators that manifest this term and facilitate empirical researches in this field.

Empowerment and Power

The dictionary definition of 'empower' is to 'enable' or 'give power to'. Most social scientists use it to mean 'power as in the probability that one actor within a social relationship will be in a position to carry out his/her own will despite resistance, regardless of the basis on which this probability rests'.

To Parpart et al. (2002) in order to think about empowerment in new ways, we need to explore its diverse and complex history. While Paulo Freire (1973) did not use the term, his emphasis on education as a means for conscientizing and inspiring individual and group challenges to social inequality provided an important backdrop for social activists concerned with empowering the poor and marginalized (Stromquist, 1995). Intellectuals and activists in the South, and to a lesser extent the North, drew on Freire and others to expand the concept of empowerment. Social activists concerned with poverty issues saw empowerment as a local, grassroots endeavour, designed to inspire the poor to challenge the status quo. On the other hand, business and personnel managers generally thought of empowerment as a means for improving productivity within established structures. Mainstream development agencies adopted this interpretation in the 1990s, when they too began to use the language of empowerment, participation and people's development. Thus, empowerment seems to fit many shoes.

How can we explain this seeming paradox? How can empowerment have such different meanings and consequences? The explanation may lie in the fluidity of the term 'power'. To empower implies the ability to exert power over, to make things happen. It is an action verb that suggests the ability to change the world, to overcome opposition. It has a transformatory sound, an implicit promise of change, often for the better. Consequently, empowerment has often been the watchword of crusaders trying to make the world a better, more equitable place. But this change is often seen as requiring a revolution or, at the very least, fundamental social transformation (Wolf, 1999; Scott, 1990). Others hold a more benign view of power, one that emphasizes the potential for rational discussion and evolutionary change within modern societies. Associated with liberal arguments about modernization and democracy, this approach assumes that even marginalized people can bring about change by mobilizing to convince the powerful of the need for change. While apparently different, both perspectives are captured by the notion that power is largely the ability to exert power over institutions, resources and people.

Michel Foucault moves the analysis further. Rejecting the notion that power is something held by individuals or groups (and not others), he argues that it permeates society. It is fluid, relational and exists only in the everyday relationships of people, both individually and in institutions. Such power can lead to repressive practices that are expressed in disciplined bodies, actions and thoughts/discourses. While much of Foucault's work has centered on the disciplinary, disempowering nature of modern power, he recognizes that relations of power inspire resistance as well (Foucault, 1979; McNay, 1992). In this regard, we find Akhil Gupta and James Ferguson's reading of Foucault useful, especially their argument that Foucault did not see resistance in a disembodied duel with power, but rather as a complex interaction. People are empowered and changed through resisting disciplinary power relations, but this very action/agency may also strengthen their incorporation into the status quo. While this analysis illuminates the workings of power (and empowerment) at the individual and institutional level, Foucault has less to say about the impact of larger political and economic structures. Moreover, his analysis is relentlessly European and male-focused. A more feminist and global analysis is required if we are to rethink women's empowerment in comparative perspective.

Power, Power Relations and Inequality

Most scholars involved in the study of power relations in society agree that there has been little agreement on defining power, and much less on how to measure power. However, all agree on the fact that power is a universal phenomenon and that access to power is unevenly distributed in society (Reddy, 1986). Exercising power involves some sort of coercion, persuasion or some kind of control on human behaviour depending on the social order and power configuration in communities. The following definitions of power illustrate this phenomenon:

Weber (cited in Bendix, 1962) defined power as, 'the probability that one actor within a social relationship will be in a position to carry out at his own will, despite resistance, regardless of the basis on which probability rests'. Dahl (1957) defined power as, 'A has power on B to the extent that he can get B to do something that he would not otherwise do'. Lynd (1957) narrated thus, 'Organized power exists ... always and everywhere, in societies large or small, primitive or modern .... Because it performs the necessary functions of establishing and maintaining the version of order by which a given time and place lives' (cited in Reddy, 1986).

Power is relational. Power operates at different levels – within a person, between individuals and between groups. There are several types of power relations in society. Rowlands (1995) described these as 'power to', 'power over' and 'power with'.

'Power to' is the ability to change the conditions of one's existence. It signifies the position of relatively powerful and as a way forward for the relatively powerless, for development of capacities to exert increased control over and/or to change their conditions of existence.

'Power over' indicates control over other people. It implies that an increase in power of one group or individual diminishes the power of others.

'Power with' is the ability to achieve control through alliances and joint action with others. It implies that increase of power of some people does not diminish that of others power (Rowlands, 1995).

Power has material dimensions too. It may be in form of access to resources, levels of poverty, and the range of choices and constraints affecting people's ability to achieve their aspirations. There are certain values that are shared by individuals, families, communities and those who are subordinated, such as gender, age and ethnic discriminations operating through many levels of social organizations/interactions. Those values, structures and processes are important to be investigated before arriving at suitable empowerment strategies (Thomas et al., 1998). Wilk (1999) adds that power, albeit hard to measure inequality in it, is basic to understand society. Folbre (1994) proposes the dismantling of inequitable power structures, stressing particularly those based on gender, race, class, age, nation, etc.

Pragmatic Conceptualization of Empowerment

While empowerment has been extensively talked about and practiced in various settings, the exact meaning of 'empowerment' does not seem to be well considered. Empowerment clearly has to do with power. Empowering an individual/group means enabling the individual/group to direct their own life and reach a stage where they are more likely to succeed in whatever they attempt to do. Empowerment is an ongoing process and not an end by itself. The processes involved in empowering are:

(i) Growth in people's awareness and confidence;
(ii) Ability to articulate problems;
(iii) Gaining access to resources and public facilities; and
(iv) Negotiating over relations between different social groups (Reddy, 2002).

Empowering may be understood as 'enabling people, especially women to acquire and possess power resources, in order, for them to make decisions on their own or resist decisions that are made by others which affect them. A person may be said to be powerful when he/she has control over a greater or equal proportion of power resources in society. The extent of possession of various power resources, such as, personal wealth, assets, land, skills, education, information, knowledge, social status, position held, leadership traits, capabilities for mobilization and maneuverability, etc., determine the degree of decision-making power' (Reddy and Suma, 1987). Disadvantaged women, especially in rural areas, possess least proportion of these resources and as a result they are powerless and dependent on the powerful and wealthy.

Collective empowerment refers to individuals in groups and communities. For instance, affirmative action seeking to empower those previously excluded from the mainstream of development (Blacks, slaves, women, handicapped and other disadvantaged). Groups or communities act together in order to gain access to policy- and decision-making arenas where their future and their quality of life are determined (Sadan and Arza, 1996). The work of Haan (1998) has also been influential in broadening understanding of empowerment and deprivation. He argued that poverty led to denial of rights and opportunities to poor for full participation in society. To arrest this kind of social exclusion, there was a need for improving their capabilities and entitlements.

Empowerment in competence is another concept discussed in the management context, which refers to the process of developing skills, knowledge and attitudes required to carry out tasks successfully and efficiently. By developing capabilities of people their job competence could be improved. In the context of development administration, the capacities we might want to improve include that of the development managers, field workers, implementing institutions/organizations and those of the beneficiaries.

Women Empowerment

In a further elaboration of the concept of female power, Safilios-Rothschild (1982) identifies two types of power – that which is derived from men and power that is derived independent of men. The former consists of the power that women may enjoy because of who their fathers and husbands are. The latter includes women's ability to control decisions about their productive and economic activities, including freedom of movement and control over the resulting wage or income; and ability to have an important say in decisions that affect their lives. It must be clarified that female power in this instance is not used in terms of 'power over' but in the sense of 'power to'. 'Power to' is the ability to perform or produce, and implies also the freedom and resources to do so whereas 'power over' refers to domination and control. Viewed in these terms, female power is very similar to the concept of female autonomy used in many studies. Autonomy has been defined as 'the ability .... To obtain information and use it as the basis for making decisions about ones private concerns and those of one's intimates' (Dyson and Moore, 1983).

Women Empowerment and Feminism

Since the 1980s, feminists have in fact contributed important insight to these debates. Most feminists have started from querying the concept of power as simply power over people and resources. An arena of politics that has been particularly important for understanding the concept of public power as power over has been that of the state. Feminist scholars have addressed this issue in terms of both the institutional power of the state to privilege some (male) interests over other (female) ones and its capacity to maintain gender inequalities. They have also examined the question of state power in the context of the state's monopoly of violence and its claim to the legitimate use of this violence. Third World feminists in particular have sought to engage with state-based resources and agencies, and to theorize from their experiences of such engagements (Agnihotri and Mazumdar, 1995; Parpart and Staudt, 1989; Rai and Lievesley, 1996). Attempting to address some of the differences among feminist analyses of state-based power, Tetreault, among others, has sought to explore whether state/institutions can become 'authorized' as opposed to being in power by demonstrating 'over and over' the 'hard resources' of 'expertise, eloquence, judgement and competence' (Tetreault and Teske, 2000). In doing so she has sought to reinforce Hannah Arendt's distinction between power and authority, and ultimately a feminist vision of public power. Others have rejected the domain of state power, seeing it as unimportant to feminist politics (Allen, 1990). Participation in institutional and public political life is therefore empowering for some and disempowering for others.

Individual and collective participation has been an important foundational concept for analysing empowerment. Participation in challenges to hegemonic systems and discourses has often inspired both greater self-understanding and political action in women's private and public lives. Involvement in the politics of subversion is thus empowering in itself, even if it fails to transform immediately dominant power relations. As Patricia Hill Collins points out, 'change can also occur in the private, personal space of an individual woman's consciousness. Equally fundamental, this type of change is also empowering'. However, feminist scholars have been worried about the differential burdens of participation (Phillips, 1999). Working class women and women from some ethnic and religious groups do not have the resources of time and money to be empowered through participation in collective action. In other words, the cost of their participation is disproportionately high. From a different perspective Third World and black feminist and activists have also reminded us that individual conscientization does not necessarily lead to progressive politics. The language of women's empowerment has been used by right-wing political groups and parties to inspire Hindu women to resist the 'pseudo-secularism' of the male, Westernized elites who have granted Muslim and other minorities 'concessions' not available to the Hindu majority (Butalia and Sarkar, 1996). While this rhetoric has inspired Hindu women's agency in defence of the dharma (faith), such empowerment obviously poses important questions for other communities, as well as for Hindu women who do not subscribe to this interpretation of empowerment.

At the level of individual development, Amartya Sen's work on human capabilities stresses empowerment as both a means and an end. It is a process of developing individual capacities through gaining education and skills in order to empower individuals to fight for a better quality of life (1990, 1995). Sen sees poverty as an indication of the inability of people to meet their basic needs, whether physical or more intangible, through participation, empowerment and community life (Dreze and Sen, 1989). Sen criticizes development economics for emphasizing quantity, such as longevity, rather than the quality of lives led (Crocker, 1995). He points out that women in particular face social as well as physical problems and that 'the remedies sought have to take note of the nature of the constraints involved and extent to which they can be removed' (Dreze and Sen, 1989). While one may quarrel with Sen's lack of attention to the political processes required for equitable resource distribution, he raises some important issues for the study of empowerment. However, he too assumes that human empowerment is best carried out at the local communities where most people live their lives (Rai, 2002). Though Sen's focus on capabilities provides a framework for the study of empowerment, feminists need to be wary of his argument about the universal right to development and his lack of attention to the political processes required for equitable resource distribution that could lead to general empowerment.

Naila Kabeer (1994) also insists on the centrality of empowerment for the struggle to achieve gender equality. Drawing on the work of Lukes (1974), she criticizes the liberal and Marxist emphases on power over resources, institutions and decision-making. Adding to Lukes'

(1974) argument that power also consists of being able to control discussions/discourses and agendas, she argues, however, for a more feminist approach to power, one that emphasizes the transformative potential of power within. This power is rooted in self-understanding that can inspire women (and some men) to recognize and challenge gender inequality in the home and the community. Like Batliwala (1994), she emphasizes collective, grassroots participatory action – the power to work with others 'to control resources, to determine agendas and to make decisions'. More concerned with action than theory, she continues to explore practical, measurable ways to empower women, especially at the local level (Kabeer, 1999).

J. Rowlands (1997, 1998) brings a broader analytical perspective to the discussion of gender and empowerment. Drawing on Foucault and feminist writings, she argues that 'empowerment is more than participation in decision-making; it must also include the processes that lead people to perceive themselves as able and entitled to make decisions'. It is personal, relational and collective. She recognizes that empowerment is not just a gender issue but also a development issue affecting women and men. While she acknowledges the complexity and difficulties of empowerment as a concept and a practice, she remains convinced that the key to empowerment lied in mobilizing marginalized people, especially women. She cautions, however, that empowerment is a process rather than an end product, neither easily defined nor measured. At the same time, she believes 'there is a core to the empowerment process ... which consists of increases in self-confidence and self-esteem, a sense of agency and of 'self' in a wider context, and a sense of *degnidad* (being worthy of having a right to respect from others)'.

This seeming congruence of policy and approach obscures the difficulties faced by those trying to understand, implement and measure women's empowerment. While the very instability of the term has its advantages – for empowerment varies by context and condition – that same fluidity impedes our understanding and implementation of empowerment. Some practitioners and scholars focus on personal empowerment. Indeed, Caroline Moser places self-reliance and internal strength at the center of empowerment. For her, empowerment is the ability 'to determine choices in life and to influence the direction of change, through the ability to gain control over crucial material and non-material resources'. Others emphasize collective empowerment, noting the fragility of individual efforts (Kabeer, 1994). Always concerned with transforming ideals into practice, Moser (1993) remains skeptical about the willingness of mainstream development agencies to embrace the grassroots, participatory small-scale methods of the empowerment approach in a meaningful way.

To Stromquist (1995), empowerment consists of four dimensions, each equally important but none sufficient by itself to enable women to act on their own behalf. These are the cognitive (critical understanding of one's reality), the psychological (feeling of self-esteem), the political (awareness of power inequalities and the ability to organize and mobilize) and the economic (capacity to generate independent income).

The concept of empowerment has special resonance within the women's movement today. Although its origins are unclear, the evidence points to an Asian rather than a Western inception, perhaps best reflected in the publication by Gita Sen and Karen Grown, *Development, Crisis, and Alternatives,* widely distributed at the Third World Women's Conference at Nairobi in 1985. An exhaustive interrogation of the ideas and actions in the USA's feminist movement reveals no such concept in almost 40 years of the movement's efforts to reframe and advance the condition of women in society. Contrary to popular belief, the concept of empowerment did not formally originate with Freire. His ideas of conscientization are totally compatible with the notion of empowerment, but conscientization (or deep awareness of one's socio-political environment) is really a precursor to the development of empowering skills and feelings. However, Hill (2007) opines, 'As feminist economists, we can draw on analysis of power and relevant insights from all disciplines to develop an approach to human empowerment that ties social outcomes to actual institutional arrangement.'

Manifestation/Measurement of Women Empowerment

In considering the measures of empowerment, it is important to consider the question of what constitutes 'women's empowerment' in order to bring out the kinds of sensitivity involved in gender issues and to focus on the female side of the gender equation. How do we decide how empowered a woman or a group of women are? What are its appropriate measures? Do frequently used socio-economic measures or indicators such as education, income and labour force participation adequately describe or capture the concept of empowerment?

Kabeer (1999) brought out certain widely used indicators for measuring women's agency and achievement, the two vital components of empowerment as follows:

Measuring 'Agency'

Indicators which focus explicitly on the measurement of agency include measures of both positive as well as negative agency: women's mobility in the public domain, their participation in public action, the incidence of male violence and so on. However, the form of agency which appears most frequently in measurement efforts, and hence the one we will be focusing on here, relates to decision-making agency. This is not surprising since decision-making in some form is at the heart of some of the best known attempts to conceptualize power (Lukes, 1974; McElroy, 1992). Measures of decision-making are usually based on responses to questions asking women about their roles in relation to specific decisions, with answers sometimes combined into a single index and sometimes presented separately. Below I have summarized some examples of decisions which typically appear in measurement efforts and the geographical context covered:

Typical Decisions in Decision-making Indicators

Egypt: Household budget; food cooked; visits; children's education; children's health; use of family planning methods (Kishor, 1997).

India: Purchase of food; purchase of major household goods; purchase of small items of jewellery; course of action if child falls ill; disciplining the child; decisions about children's education and type of school (Jejeebhoy, 1997). Degree of marital control exercised by husband; experience of physical, sexual and emotional violence; control over women's earnings and extent of autonomy and decision-making power (NFHS-3).

Nigeria: Household purchases; whether wife works; how to spend husband's income; number of children to have; whether to buy and sell land; whether to use family planning; whether to send children to school, how much education; when sons and when daughters marry; whether to take sick children to doctor and how to rear children (Kritz, Makinwa and Gurak, 1997).

Zimbabwe: Wife working outside; making a major purchase; the number of children (Becker, 1997).

Nepal: What food to buy; the decision by women to work outside; major market transactions; and the number of children to have (Morgan and Niraula, 1995).

Iran: Food purchase; inputs, labour and sale in agricultural production and other income-earning activities; sale and purchase of assets, children's education; seeking healthcare for children (Razavi, 1992).

Pakistan: Purchase of food; number of children; schooling of children; children's marriage; major household purchases; women's work outside the home; sale and purchase of livestock; household expenses; purchase of clothes, jewellery and gifts for wife's relatives (Sathar and Kazi, 1997).

Bangladesh: Ability to make small and large consumer purchases; house repair; taking in livestock for raising; leasing in of land; purchase of major assets (Hashemi et al., 1996). Children's education; visits to friends and relatives; household purchases; healthcare matters (Cleland and Van Ginneken, 1994).

Measuring Achievement

Direct Evidence of Empowerment

Devaluation of women: reports of domestic violence; dowry paid at marriage.

Women's emancipation: belief in daughter's education; freedom of movement.

Reported sharing of roles and decision-making: egalitarian gender roles; egalitarian decision-making.

Equality in marriage: fewer grounds reported for justified divorce by husbands, equality of grounds reported for divorce by husband or wife.

Financial autonomy: currently controls her earnings; her earnings as share of household income.

Sources of Employment

Participation in the modern sector: index of assets owned; female education.

Lifetime exposure to employment: worked before marriage; controlled earnings before marriage.

Setting Indicators

Family structure amenable to empowerment: does not now or previously live with in-laws.

Marital advantage: small age difference between spouses; chose husband.

Traditional marriage: large educational difference with husband; did not choose husband.

Bardhan (2003) described different aspects of women empowerment and some important indicators there of as shown in Box 1:

Box 1

1. Socio-economic	*2. Socio-cultural and gender relations (human agency)*
Ownership of property (land, house, animals, jewellery, machines, etc.)	Participation in decision-making
Employment/income	Spouse age difference
Education level	Husband/wife communication
	Age at first marriage and choice of life partner
	Formal/informal association with support groups or kin

Bajpai and Mishra (2007) identified the variables/indicators of women empowered and their interface as mentioned in Chart 1:

Chart 1

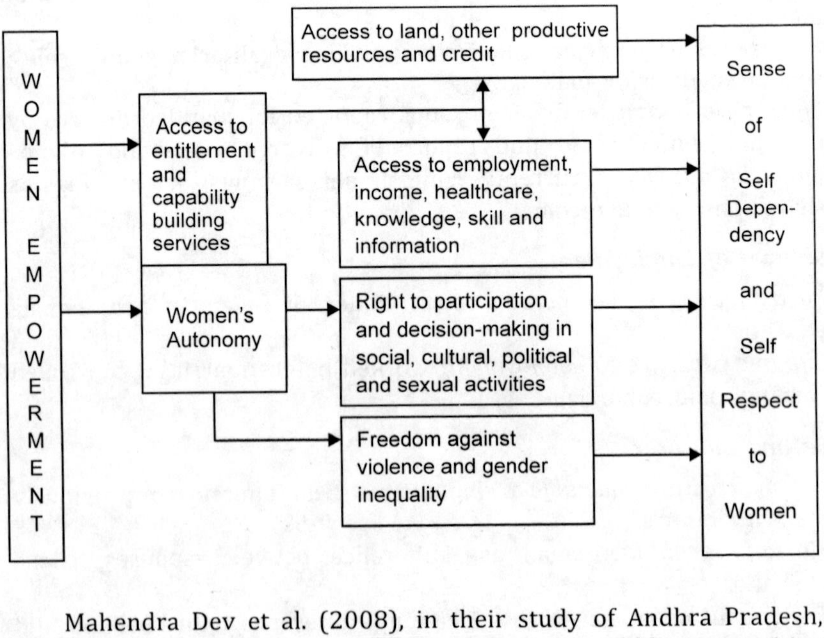

Mahendra Dev et al. (2008), in their study of Andhra Pradesh, observe that advances in women empowerment would have a positive spill over impact on child well-being. To them, there are four types of women empowerment, namely, maternal education, economic empowerment, intra household decision-making power and community level empowerment which have the aforesaid effect.

The Issue in Debate

Despite disagreement on issues of origin, definition, indicators, and measurement related to term 'empowerment', there is global consensus, irrespective of discipline, that access to power is unevenly distributed within and between the classes of human society. Therefore, in-depth study of both causes and remedies of impoverishment either of an individual or a class draws upon empowerment. Being the subject (women empowerment) multidisciplinary, its study remained more of academic nature and significance to the discipline concerned. However, if it is to serve the purpose of having some policy implications for the upliftment of ever deprived class, i.e., female interdisciplinary aspect (socio-politico-economic interface) has to be evolved and developed for conceptualization and manifestation of the term women empowerment.

References

Agnihotri, I. and V. Mazumdar. 1995. 'Changing Terms of Political Discourse: Women's Movement in India 1970s–1990s', *Economic and Political Weekly*, Vol. 29, pp. 1869–78.

Allen, J. 1990. 'Does Feminism Need a Theory of the State?', in S. Watson (ed.), *Playing the State*, Verso, London.

Bajpai, A.D.N. and S.K. Mishra. 2007. *Women Empowerment and Reproductive Behaviour*, Classical Publishing Company, New Delhi, p. 24.

Batliwala, S. 1994. 'The Meaning of Women's Empowerment: New Concepts from Action', in G. Sen et al. (eds), *Population Policies Reconsidered: Health, Empowerment and Rights*, Harvard University Press, Cambridge, pp. 127–38.

Becker, S. 1997. 'Incorporating Women's Empowerment in Studies of Reproductive Health: An Example from Zimbabwe', paper presented in the Seminar on Female Empowerment and Demographic Processes, Lund, 20–24 April.

Bendix, J. 1962. *Max Weber Typology of Leadership: Sources of Authority*, Anchor Books, New York.

Butalia, U. and T. Sarkar (eds). 1996. *Women and Right-Wing Movement: Indian Experiences*, Zed Books, London.

Cleland, J.G. and J.K. Van Ginneken. 1994. 'Maternal Education and Child Survival in Developing Countries: The Search for Pathways of Influence', *Social Science and Medicine*, Vol. 77, pp. 1357–68.

Crocker, D.A. 1995. 'Functioning and Capability: The Foundation of Sen's and Nussbaum's Developed Ethic', in J. Glover and M. Nussbaum (eds), *Women, Culture and Development: A Study of Human Capabilities*, Clarendon Press, Oxford.

Dahl, R.A. 1957. 'The Concept of Power', *Behavioural Science*, Vol. 2, July, pp. 201–15.

Dreze, Jean and Amartya Sen. 1989. *Hunger and Public Action*, Clarendon Press, Oxford.

Dyson, T. and M. Moore. 1983. 'On Kinship Structure, Female Autonomy and Demographic Behaviour in India', *Population and Development Review*, Vol. 9, pp. 35–60.

Folbre, Nancy. 1994. *Who Pays for the Kids*? Routledge, New York.

Foucault, Michel. 1979, *Discipline and Punish: The Birth of the Prison*, Harmondsworth.

Freire, Paulo. 1973. *Education for Critical Consciousness*, Seabury Press, New Haan York.

Haan, A. 1998. 'Social Exclusion: An Alternative Concept for the Study of Deprivation', *IDS Bulletin*, Vol. 29, No. 1, pp. 10–19.

Hashemi, S.M., S.R. Schuler and A.P. Riley. 1996. 'Rural Credit Programme and Women's Empowerment in Bangladesh', *World Development*, Vol. 24, No. 4, pp. 635–53.

Hill, Marianne T. 2007. 'Development as Empowerment', in Bina Agarwal, Jane Humphries and Ingrid Robeyns (eds), *Amartya Sens's Work and Ideas: A Gender Perspective*, Routledge, New York, p. 147.

Jejeebhoy, Shirin J. 1997. 'Wife Beating in Rural India: A Husband's Right?', *Economic and Political Weekly*, Vol. 33, No. 15, pp. 855–62.

Kabeer, N. 1994. *Reversed Realities: Gender Hierarchies in Development Thought*, Verso, London.

Kabeer, N. 1999. 'Resources, Agency, Achievements: Reflections on the Measurement of Women's Empowerment', *Development and Change*, Vol. 30, No. 3, July, pp. 435–64.

Kishor, S. 1997. 'Empowerment of Women in Egypt and Links to the Survival of Health of their Infants', paper presented at the Seminar on Female Empowerment and Demographic Processes, Lund, 20–24 April.

Kritz, P., M.M. Makinwa and D.T. Gurak. 1997. 'Wife's Empowerment and Fertility in Nigeria: The Role of Context', paper presented at the Seminar on Female Empowerment and Demographic Processes, Lund, 20–24 April.

Lukes, S. 1974. *View Power: A Radical*, Macmillan, London.

Lynd, R. 1957. 'Power in American Society as Resource and Problem', in Arthur Kornhauser (ed.), *Problem and Power in American Democracy*, Wayne State University Press, Detroit.

MacKinnon, C. 1987. *Feminism Unmodified: Discourses on Life and Law*, Harvard University Press, Cambridge.

Mahendra Dev, S. et al. 2008. 'Women Empowerment and Human Development in Andhra Pradesh: An Empirical Analysis', paper presented at the

Conference on Measuring Human Development, organized by University of Maryland and NCAER, New Delhi, 16–18 May.

McElroy, M. 1992. 'The Policy Implications of Family Bargaining and Marriage Markets', in L. Haddad, J. Hodinatt and H. Alderman (eds), *Intra-household Resource Allocation in Developing Countries: Methods, Models and Policy*, John Hopkins University Press, Baltimore, pp. 53–74.

McNay, K. 1992. *Foucault, Feminism and Power: Gender and the Self*, North East University Press, Boston.

Morgan, P. and B. Niraula. 1995. 'Gender Inequality and Fertility in Two Nepali Villages', *Population and Development Review*, Vol. 21, No. 3, pp. 541–61.

Moser, C. 1993. *Gender Planning and Development: Theory, Practice and Training*, Routledge, London.

Narayan, Deepa. 2001. 'Role of Empowerment in Poverty Reduction', presentation at the World Bank, 5 July.

National Family Health Survey NFHS–3, 2005–06. Vol. I, IIPS, Mumbai, India.

National Policy for the Empowerment of Women. 2001. Department of Women and Child Development, Government of India, New Delhi.

Parpart, J. and K. Staudt. 1989. *Women and State in Africa*, Lynne Rienner Press, Boulder.

Parpart, Jane L., Shirin M. Rai and Kathleen Staudt (eds). 2002. *Rethinking Empowerment: Gender and Development in Global/Local World*, Routledge, London.

Phillips, Anne. 1999. *Which Equalities Matter?*, Polity Press, Cambridge.

Pradhan, Bina. 2003. 'Measuring Empowerment: A Methodological Approach', *Development*, Vol. 42, No. 2, June.

Rai, S. and G. Lievesley. 1996. *Women and the State: International Perspectives*, Taylor and Francis, London.

Rai, Shirin. 2002. *Gender and International Political Economy: From Nationalism to Globalisation*, Polity Press, Cambridge.

Razavi, S. 1992. Agrarian Change and Gender Power: A Comparative Study in South Eastern Iran, D. Phil. Dissertation, St. Antony College, Oxford University.

Reddy, G.N. 1986. *Social Mobilisation and Empowerment of Women: A Case of Peddamany and Alaram Village*, Multi-country Study Mission Report, Asian Productivity Organisation, Japan.

Reddy, G.N. 2002. 'Empowering Women through Self Help Groups and Micro-Credit: The Care of NIRD Action Research Projects', *Journal of Rural Development*, Vol. 21, No. 4, pp. 511–35.

Reddy, G.N. and N.R. Suma. 1987. *Women and Child Development: Some Contemporary Issues*, Chugh Publication, Allahabad.

Rowlands, J. 1997. *Questioning Empowerment*, Oxfam Publications, Oxford.

Rowlands, J. 1998. 'A Word of the Times, But What Does it Mean? Empowerment in the Discourse and Practice of Development', in H. Afshar (ed.), *Women and Empowerment*, St. Martin's Press, New York.

Rowlands, S. 1995. 'Empowerment Examined', *Development in Practice*, Vol. 5, No. 2, pp. 101–17.

Sadan, E. and C. Arza. 1996. 'Process-Focused and Product-Focused Community Planning: Two Variations on Empowering Professional Practice', *Community Development Journal*, Vol. 32, No. 1, 3–16 January.

Safilios-Rothschild, C. 1982. 'Female Power, Autonomy and Demographic Change in the Third World', in C. Hohn and R. Mackensen (eds), *Determinants of Fertility: Theories Re-examined*, Groom Helm, London.

Sathar, Z.A. and S. Kazi. 1997. *Women's Autonomy, Livelihood and Fertility: A Study of Rural Punjab*, Pakistan Institute of Development Studies, Islamabad.

Scott, J. 1990. *Dominance and Arts of Resistance*, Yale University Press, New Haven.

Sen, Amartya. 1990. 'Gender and Cooperative Conflict', in I. Tinker (ed.), *Persistent Inequalities*, Oxford University Press, Oxford, pp. 123–49.

Sen, Amartya. 1995. 'Gender Inequality and Theories of Justice', in J. Glover and M. Nussbaum (eds), *Women, Culture and Development*, Oxford University Press, Oxford.

Sen, Amartya. 2002. 'Education as a Means for Empowering Women', in Jane L. Parpart et al. (eds), *Rethinking Empowerment*, Routledge, New York, pp. 23–37.

Stromquist, N. 1995. *Literacy for Citizenship: Gender and Grassroots Dynamics in Brazil*, State University of New York Press, Albany.

Tetreault, M.A. and R.L.: Teske. 2000. *Conscious Acts and the Politics of Social Change: Feminist Approach to Social Community and Power*, Vol. 1, University of South Carolina Press, Columbia, p. 276.

Thomas, A., J. Chataway and W. Marc. 1998. *Finding Out Fast*, Sage Publications, London.

Wilk, Richard. 1999. 'Quality of Life and Anthropological Perspective', *Feminist Economics*, Vol. 5, No. 2, pp. 91–93.

Wolf, Eric. 1999. *Envisioning Power: Ideologies of Dominance and Crisis*, University of California Press, Berkeley.

World Development Report 2000. *Attacking Poverty*, World Bank, Washington, DC.

7

Women Employment

A Comparative Analysis of Scheduled Castes and Other Social Groups in Uttar Pradesh

Rajendra P. Mamgain

The role of women in overall development of humankind is well acknowledged, particularly in the upbringing of their families. However, most of their work particularly of home care such as cooking, fetching water, child care, washing clothes and many related chores, is generally regarded as unproductive through a narrow lens of defining work (Sharma, 1985). This has also been contested by several scholars in the past (see Sen, 2010). Without going into debate of what is work and what is non-work, particularly in the case of women, we would confine ourselves to the general definition of a work and worker, as is being followed by National Sample Survey Organization (NSSO) in its quinquennial surveys on employment and unemployment. NSSO defines 'work' as 'engagement of a person in any gainful economic activity during a reference period'. Accordingly, a person is enumerated as worker when she or he is engaged in a gainful economic activity for a given period of time. Three reference periods are used by NSSO to ascertain the activity of a person, i.e., Usual Status (US) with a reference period one year preceding of the date of survey, Current Weekly Status (CWS) with reference period last one week preceding the date of survey, and Current Daily Status (CDS) with daily activity status of a person during all the seven days in a week preceding the date of survey.

According to this criterion, the participation of women in work turn to much lower than their male counterparts and almost remained stagnant over the years. Several reasons are given for the low participation of women in work, such as economic distress, educational improvement and social customs. It is observed that demographic variables such as age, child care responsibilities and mental status have significant negative effects on the work participation of women. This is true both for rural and urban areas (World Bank, 2010). Interestingly, it is also observed that participation of women in the labour force tends to decline with the improvement in their educational levels. Rural women tend to face a greater 'education penalty' than urban women. It is also found that women tend to withdraw from the labour market with the improvement in their household income. It is observed that the probability of women participation in workforce is lower with the higher incomes of their husbands (ibid.). In the absence of regular wage employment, educated women tend to report themselves unemployed rather than accepting low status jobs. Cultural barriers also impede women's participation in the labour market.

With this brief background the article attempts to examine the pattern of women's participation in work in a most populous state of Uttar Pradesh in a comparative framework with all India.

Economy of Uttar Pradesh

Uttar Pradesh (UP) is the most populous state of India. The economy of the state has witnessed a structural change over a period of time. The contribution of the state in the Gross Domestic Product (GDP) of India in 2009–10 was about 8.0 per cent. As per the advance estimates released by State Planning Institute, Uttar Pradesh for the year 2008–09, services sector is the largest contributor to the Gross State Domestic Product (GSDP) in the state with 47.1 per cent followed by agriculture with 31.70 per cent and industry with 21.20 per cent. Unlike the national pattern, the structure of GSDP in the state witnessed slower diversification from agricultural to non-agricultural sector during the period 1993–94 to 2008–09. Though the economy of Uttar Pradesh is second largest, next to Maharashtra in terms of GSDP, it ranks at the bottom in per capita income with the exception of Bihar. The per capita Net State Domestic Product (NSDP) of the state is ₹ 12,637 in 2008–09 compared to the prices of the year which is less than half of the all-India per capita net 1999–2000 national income for the same year.

There has been a slow growth in per capita income in the state as compared to several Indian states and national average. As a result, the gap in per capita income has widened over the years. The gap in per capita NSDP in Uttar Pradesh with respect to India increased from nearly 39 percentage points in 1999–2000 to over 50 per cent in 2008–09 (Table 1). This increase in the gap in income levels in the state also indicates increasing inter-state income inequalities in India. This has been recently highlighted by several scholars in policy documents. Planning Commission in its Mid-Term Review brings forth the challenge of increasing inequalities including income across the Indian states and among various social groups in the country. It underlined the need to re-look at the growth strategy which is more widespread (Planning Commission, 2010). It will be seen in the later part of the article how an overwhelmingly large majority of workforce dependent on agriculture have lowest level of earning in Uttar Pradesh and how there is a strong pattern of increasing difference over the years in per worker earnings between agricultural and non-agricultural sector.

Table 1

Relative Share of Uttar Pradesh in NSDP

Year	*NSDP (₹ Crore)*			*Per Capita NSDP (₹)*		
	Uttar Pradesh	*India*	*% share of UP in India*	*Uttar Pradesh*	*India*	*As % of India*
1999–2000	1,75,159	17,86,526	9.8	9,749	15,881	61.39
2004–05	2,10,462	23,88,768	8.81	10,421	19,331	53.91
2008–09	2,76,677	33,39,375	8.29	12,637	25,494	49.57

Source: Central Statistical Organization 2011.

Demographic and Social Profile

With a population of 199.58 million in 2011, Uttar Pradesh is the most populous state of the Indian union, accounting for 16.5 per cent population of the country. Women constitute about 47.6 per cent of population in the state. Like-wise all India pattern, the decadal growth of population in the state decelerated from 25.80 per cent during 1991–2001 to 20.09 per cent during 2001–11. The sex ratio defined as number of women per 1,000 men has marginally improved from 898 in 2001 to 908 in 2011 in the state (GoI-RGI, 2011). However, the sex ratio is comparatively much lower in Uttar Pradesh than the national average of 940 in 2011. The low sex ratio in the state also indicates higher mortality rate among females. The life expectancy among females is lower by one year (59.3) as compared to their male counterparts in the state. This is unlike the national pattern where life expectancy for females is higher than males. The lower life expectancy of females has implications for their low participation in the workforce also.

With a female literacy rate of over 59 per cent, Uttar Pradesh ranks 31 among the 35 states/UT in Indian union. There is still a gender gap of nearly 20 percentage points in literacy in the state. However, the Population Census 2011 shows significant improvement in the literacy rates both in Uttar Pradesh and India over the past decade.

In terms of social composition of population in 2001, Scheduled Castes constitute 21.15 per cent of the state's population. Nearly 18.5 per cent of population is Muslim and an overwhelming majority of 80.6 per cent of population is Hindu according to 2001 census.

Participation of Women in Work

Here focus is on women's work participation across various economic categories of households and also across social groups, specifically Scheduled Castes (SCs) and other than Scheduled Castes and Scheduled Tribes (non-SCs/STs).

According to NSSO quinquennial surveys on employment and unemployment, over 15 per cent of women population in Uttar Pradesh is economically active in 2009–10. This is much lower than the national figure of 22 per cent. This is popularly known as work participation rate (WPR) (Table 2). As is well known, WPR for women is far lower than males, both in Uttar Pradesh and rest of India. This pattern is almost similar across all states, regions and across various social groups in India.

Table 2

Work Participation Rates in Uttar Pradesh and India (%)

Year	*Uttar Pradesh*		*India*	
	Male	*Female*	*Male*	*Female*
1993–94	51.5	18.2	54.5	28.0
1999–2000	49.8	17.1	52.7	25.3
2004–05	50.1	21.5	54.7	28.0
2009–10	50.2	15.3	54.6	22.0

Source: NSSO Rounds on Employment and Unemployment.

The NSSO data shows a continuous decline in the participation of women in work both in Uttar Pradesh and India since 1993–94 with an exception for the period 2004–05. The possible explanations for this long-run decline in women's WPRs are: (i) increasing participation of women in education, (ii) increase in household income resulting in women's withdrawal from the labour force, and (iii) socio-cultural factors inhibiting participation in work, Neff et al. (2012) argue that while education can be an explanatory factor in rural areas for decline in women's WPRs, same is not true in urban areas. Rather, they found a significant evidence of decline in women WPR due to improvement in household incomes, suggesting reduction in distress induced WPRs.

Pattern of WPRs by Type of Household

NSSO categorizes sample households according to their main economic activity, both for rural and urban areas. In rural areas five categories of such households include the following: (a) self-employed in agriculture, (b) self-employed in non-agriculture, (c) agriculture labour, (d) other labour, and (e) others (include none of the above as major activity). In urban areas, households are categorized into following major economic activities: (a) self-employed, (b) regular earnings, (c) casual labour, and (d) others. Analysis of WPRs of women across these various types of households brings forth following interesting features (see Table 3a and 3b):

(i) There has been a sharp decline in women's WPRs in rural agricultural wage labour households in Uttar Pradesh during the period 1993–94 to 2009–10. Similar pattern is observed for women belonging to other labour households in the rural areas of the state.

(ii) The WPRs of women belonging to self-employed households, both in agriculture and non-agriculture, remained almost constant around 19 per cent since 1993–94 in Uttar Pradesh. This thereby, suggesting sustained demand for female labour in such households mostly as unpaid family workers. This may be even at zero marginal productivities.

(iii) While women WPR is lowest at 7.9 per cent among 'other' households in rural Uttar Pradesh, it also declined rapidly over the period 1993–94 to 2009–10.

(iv) While women's WPR is much less in urban areas than rural ones, their participation in self-employed households declined between 1999–2000 to 2009–10 after remaining almost constant during the earlier period, 1993–94 to 1999–2000.

(v) Women's WPR steadily declined among urban labour households in Uttar Pradesh as well as at all-India level.

(vi) Despite belonging to similar economic category of households, women's WPRs differ significantly when juxtaposed with their social groups. This is more revealing in rural areas of the state across all economic categories of households as compared to national pattern.

In brief, women do participate in higher proportion in casual wage labour households, both in rural and urban areas and same is in Uttar Pradesh and rest of India; their participation tended to decline over the years. The reasons for such decline are mentioned earlier, and we would confine our analysis to highlight trends in women's WPRs in Uttar Pradesh and India in a comparative way to draw conclusions.

Table 3a

Female WPRs by Type of Household in Uttar Pradesh (%)

Type of Household	*1993–94*			*1999–2000*			*2009–10*		
	SC	*Non-SC/ST*	*Total*	*SC*	*Non-SC/ST*	*Total*	*SC*	*Non-SC/ST*	*Total*
Rural self-employed in non-agriculture	21.9	18.0	18.8	23.2	16.5	18.0	18.1	16.7	17.0
Rural agriculture labour	34.5	22.1	28.9	30.6	20.6	26.1	28.2	12.0	18.7
Rural other labour	27.1	19.7	23.1	23.4	13.3	17.8	15.7	16.3	15.9
Rural self-employed in agriculture	27.7	17.4	19.0	24.6	18.3	19.3	26.2	18.4	19.6
Rural others	27.6	13.3	17.6	13.8	11.7	12.1	10.5	7.1	7.9
Urban self-employed	11.9	10.1	10.3	17.5	10.0	10.7	12.6	7.4	7.9
Urban regular salaried earning	11.3	7.8	8.3	10.6	6.5	7.2	11.8	8.8	9.2
Urban casual labour	20.8	15.9	17.6	13.5	9.0	10.5	7.5	9.6	9.1
Urban others	9.4	3.5	4.1	13.5	5.1	6.2	0.0	2.1	1.9
Total (rural +urban)	27.2	15.7	18.2	23.9	15.1	17.1	19.1	14.2	15.3

Table 3b

Female WPRs by Type of Household in India (%)

Type of Household	*1993–94*			*1999–2000*			*2009–10*		
	SC	*Non-SC/ST*	*Total*	*SC*	*Non-SC/ST*	*Total*	*SC*	*Non-SC/ST*	*Total*
Rural self-employed in non-agriculture	29.4	25.4	26.1	27.4	21.8	22.9	20.2	18.7	19.0
Rural agriculture labour	41.2	40.8	40.9	38.3	38.2	38.3	33.7	34.0	33.9
Rural other labour	34.1	34.5	34.4	28.3	26.9	27.3	22.8	24.4	23.8
Rural self-employed in agriculture	31.9	31.8	31.8	30.4	30.2	30.2	28.4	27.4	27.5
Rural others	21.1	17.2	18.0	16.2	15.7	15.8	13.2	12.4	12.6
Urban self-employed	19.1	14.7	15.1	19.0	13.1	13.7	16.6	12.2	12.7
Urban regular salaried earning	14.7	13.0	13.2	13.6	12.0	12.3	16.6	14.1	14.4
Urban casual labour	29.8	25.9	27.0	26.7	20.7	22.3	22.9	18.9	20.0
Urban others	7.5	6.3	6.4	10.5	6.1	6.6	5.7	3.8	4.1
Total (rural +urban)	32.4	27.0	28.0	29.6	24.2	25.3	24.5	21.4	22.0

Source: Calculated from NSSO Unit Level Data on Employment and Unemployment (Various Rounds).

WPRs Across Social Groups

The social background of women is an important variable determining their participation in the work. It is generally argued that women belonging to SC and ST communities do not hesitate in participating in the labour market unlike other women. The lack of productive assets and sole dependence on their physical labour in case of most of the SC households, it is a sheer economic necessity to participate in work by household members on a large number irrespective of their gender consideration. For SCs the cultural barriers, thus, are not that severe as in the case of Muslims or other Hindu women. In fact it is argued that many of the SC women have come out of the cultural barriers in their entry to work.

The juxtaposition of social background of women with the economic category of their households brings out following important trends (Table 3a and 3b):

(i) WPRs among SC women are much higher than non-SC/ST women both in Uttar Pradesh and India. During 2009–10, the WPRs among SC women in the state are lower by 5.4 percentage points than national average.

(ii) While there has been a faster deceleration in WPRs of SC women in Uttar Pradesh from 27.2 per cent in 1993–94 to 19.1 per cent in 2009–10, the WPRs among non-SC/ST women remained between 15.7 per cent and 14.2 per cent during the period under reference. Thus, the gap in WPRs between SCs and non-SC/ST women tended to decrease over the years.

(iii) The rapid decline in WPRs of SC women has been witnessed among casual wage labour households, both in rural and urban areas of the state.

(iv) If regular salaried employment is an indicator of decent work and relatively better incomes for a household, the work participation of women in such households is expected to be comparatively lower than other households which have to participate in casual wage work due to distress situations. This is clearly observed in urban areas of India, both for SCs and other social groups. However, it does not necessarily hold true for Uttar Pradesh. A high WPR of 12.5 per cent is observed in SC households belonging to economic category of regular salaried employment households in the state; whereas the participation is low at 7.5 per cent among SC women belonging to economic category of casual wage labour households in the urban areas of the state during the year 2009–10. Thus, this pattern does not support the hypothesis that women withdraw from the workforce once their household income improves, particularly in urban areas of the state, irrespective of their social background.

WPRs by MPCE Quintiles

It will be interesting to examine the pattern of participation of women in work across various income groups of households in Uttar Pradesh. Since income data for households are not available, the monthly per capita expenditure (MPCE) is generally taken as a proxy of household income, despite its several well known limitations. Several attributes of employment can be studied across these MPCE quintiles. Here we have analysed the pattern of women WPRs across various MPCE quintiles. The pattern of WPRs across MPCE quintiles shows an expected 'U' shape curve, i.e., women are compelled to work in larger number in low income households due to distress situations. They gradually withdraw from the workforce to look after their families once their incomes improve. They again tend to participate in higher proportion once their

Table 4

WPRs by MPCE Quintiles (%)

MPCE quintile group	*1993–94*			*1999–2000*			*2009–10*		
	SC	*Non-SC/ST*	*Total*	*SC*	*Non-SC/ST*	*Total*	*SC*	*Non-SC/ST*	*Total*
Uttar Pradesh									
0–20	28.5	16.3	20.4	23.8	14.4	17.4	19.2	13.3	15.0
20–40	26.1	16.7	19.1	24.9	15.9	18.3	21.0	13.7	15.8
40–60	25.4	15.7	17.7	24.5	15.8	17.7	17.8	13.8	14.7
60–80	27.3	14.3	16.2	22.9	15.6	16.9	16.0	14.4	14.6
80–100	28.8	15.4	16.7	22.1	13.5	14.6	19.8	16.9	17.3
Total	27.2	15.7	18.2	23.9	15.1	17.1	19.1	14.2	15.3
India									
0–20	31.9	28.6	29.4	29.0	25.1	26.2	21.2	19.8	20.2
20–40	31.9	27.2	28.2	28.9	24.5	25.5	23.5	19.5	20.4
40–60	32.4	26.8	27.8	28.9	23.7	24.7	25.1	20.8	21.6
60–80	32.7	26.1	27.1	31.4	24.3	25.4	26.6	22.2	22.9
80–100	34.2	26.5	27.3	31.0	23.6	24.4	30.2	24.6	25.3
Total	32.4	27.0	28.0	29.6	24.2	25.3	24.5	21.4	22.0

Source: Calculated from NSSO Unit Level Data on Employment and Unemployment (Various Rounds).

household attains higher household incomes. This pattern has emerged more clearly in 2009–10 than earlier period of 1993–94 and 1999–2000 for Uttar Pradesh. However, the all-India pattern somehow differs completely, i.e., with increase in household income, women WPRs tend to increase (Table 4). This pattern is also seen in case of SC and other households as well. This analysis of WPRs clearly shows the crucial role of women in supporting the household income.

Regional Variations in WPRs

NSSO has divided Uttar Pradesh into five regions. It is possible to make a comparable analysis of each region on various parameters for which data is available. We have analysed the pattern of WPRs among women across NSSO regions within Uttar Pradesh. The WPR among women is lowest at 7.4 per cent in the southern upper Ganga plains of the state. The second lowest WPR is in northern upper Ganga plains at 8.9 per cent (Table 5). A highest WPR of over 26 per cent is seen among women in southern region of the state. The next highest WPR is in eastern region. These show wide regional variations in WPRs of women in the state of Uttar Pradesh.

Table 5

Regional Pattern of Women's WPRs in Uttar Pradesh, 2009–10 (%)

NSSO Region	*SC*	*Non-SC/ST*	*Total*
Northern upper Ganga plains	5.3	9.8	8.9
Central	19.6	12.0	14.3
Eastern	27.7	20.0	21.8
Southern	30.9	24.3	26.1
Southern upper Ganga plains	7.2	7.5	7.4
Total	19.1	14.2	15.3

Source: NSSO 66th Round Unit Level Data, 2009–10.

The WPRs among SC women also vary across five regions of the state. It is lowest in northern upper Ganga plains region at 5.3 per cent and 7.2 per cent in southern upper Ganga plains, respectively. Interestingly, it is only in the northern upper Ganga plains where WPRs for SC women are almost half than non-SC/ST women in the region. In rest of the four regions, SC women have much higher WPRs than non-SC/ST women. The reasons for low WPRs among SC women and also for other women in upper Ganga plains include relatively better household incomes for SCs and others in this region, and a strong cultural factor such as *purdah* system which restricts the participation of women in work. Here, the behaviour towards women work appears to be common irrespective of the social class of a household. However, there is a need to explore reasons for such huge differences in WPRs in the state.

Structure of Women Employment

Employed persons are generally categorized into three groups in terms of status of their employment, i.e., self-employed including those working as unpaid family workers, regular salaried workers and casual wage workers. The latter two categories do also form as wage employment. Here we have again divided self-employment into two sub-groups, i.e., self-employed in agriculture and allied activities and self-employed in non-agriculture. Similarly, casual wage labour is divided into agriculture and non-agriculture wage labour. Regular salaried workers are also divided into public and private sector of their employment. This detailed classification helps one understand the nature and quality of employment available to women in the state.

Broadly speaking, self-employment is a predominant form of employment for women workers in Uttar Pradesh as well as in India. More than three-fourths of women are self-employed in Uttar Pradesh in 2009–10. This is much higher than the national average of 53.3 per cent. Casual wage employment is the next dominant source of employment. Regular wage employment has the lowest share in total employment of women. In the following sections we have discussed the trends in self-employment, casual wage employment and regular salaried employment for women separately while keeping in view the above mentioned six sub-divisions of category of employment in mind.

Trends in Regular Salaried Employment

While the regular wage salaried work is considered as a most stable source of employment, the other forms of employment such as casual wage work and self-employed are mostly irregular in their availability and inconsistent in term of income earnings. There is a huge deficit of regular salaried employment in India. Only 16 per cent of the Indian workforce is working in regular salaried jobs. This ratio is much lower for women workforce. In 2009–10, nearly 11 per cent of women are working in regular salaried jobs in the country. The corresponding figure for Uttar Pradesh is less than half at 5.3 per cent. A further bifurcation of regular salaried employment into public and private sector shows the higher share of public sector in women' employment in Uttar Pradesh, thus, indicating limited employment opportunities for the women of the state in private sector's regular salaried jobs. On the other hand, the situation is just reverse as private sector being a major employer for salaried jobs at national level (Table 6). Similarly, the percentage share of SC women in regular salaried jobs in Uttar Pradesh is much less at 4.3 per cent in their total employment as compared to other women (5.7%) during the year 2009–10. Public sector is also main provider of salaried jobs to SC women in the state.

The share of salaried jobs for women in Uttar Pradesh nearly doubled from just 2.8 per cent in 1993–94 to 5.3 per cent in 2009–10. Similar trend has been noticed at national level (Table 6). Much of the increase in regular salaried jobs of women in the state is led by a sizeable growth of employment opportunities for them in the public sector. This has been observed for women belonging to both SCs and non-SC/STs social groups. The relative contribution of private sector in regular salaried employment creation for women has, in fact, marginally decreased from 2.9 per cent in 1999–2000 to 2.2 per cent in 2009–10 for Uttar Pradesh (Table 6).

Table 6

Changes in the Status of Employment of Women Workers (%)

Status of Employment	*1993–94*			*1999–2000*			*2009–10*		
	SC	*Non-SC/ST*	*Total*	*SC*	*Non-SC/ST*	*Total*	*SC*	*Non-SC/ST*	*Total*
				Uttar Pradesh					
Self-employed in agriculture	47.7	71.0	63.4	45.7	68.0	60.8	51.7	66.8	62.4
Self-employed in non-agriculture	7.5	15.2	12.7	10.5	16.8	14.8	6.4	17.0	13.9
Regular salaried jobs in public sector	—	—	—	1.3	1.7	1.5	2.6	3.3	3.1
Regular salaried jobs in private sector	—	—	—	1.7	3.4	2.9	1.7	2.4	2.2
Regular salaried (Public + Private)	1.4	3.5	2.8	3.0	5.1	4.4	4.3	5.7	5.3
Casual wage labour-Agriculture	40.2	8.5	18.9	37.7	8.9	18.2	31.5	8.0	14.9
Casual wage labour-Non-agriculture	3.2	1.8	2.3	3.1	1.2	1.9	6.0	2.5	3.5
Total	100.0	100.0	100.0	100.0	100.0	100.0	100.0	100.0	100.0

Cont'd...

...Cont'd

					India				
Self-employed in agriculture	29.3	50.4	46.0	26.7	47.2	42.6	26.6	43.2	39.6
Self-employed in non-agriculture	8.4	11.8	11.1	10.4	13.4	12.7	11.4	14.3	13.7
Regular salaried jobs in public sector	—	—	—	1.8	2.9	2.7	3.4	4.2	4.0
Regular salaried jobs in private sector	—	—	—	4.2	5.5	5.2	6.5	7.1	6.9
Regular salaried (Public + Private)	4.5	6.9	6.4	6.0	8.4	7.9	9.8	11.3	11.0
Casual wage labour-Agri culture	51.8	25.9	31.3	50.7	26.9	32.3	41.1	23.4	27.3
Casual wage labour-Non-agriculture	6.0	4.9	5.2	6.2	4.1	4.6	11.0	7.8	8.5
Total	100.0	100.0	100.0	100.0	100.0	100.0	100.0	100.0	100.0

Source: Calculated from NSSO Unit Level Data on Employment and Unemployment (Various Rounds).

Trends in Casual Wage Employment

About 18.4 per cent of women workers in Uttar Pradesh are working as casual wage labour, largely in agriculture. This is almost half the proportion of casual wage labour at all-India level (Table 6). Yet another distinguishing feature relates to steady decline in the share of casual wage employment of women in Uttar Pradesh, particularly since 1999–2000 by nearly two percentage points in 2009–10. At the national level, the share almost remained same at about 36 per cent since 1993–94. In brief, women workers in Uttar Pradesh are comparatively less vulnerable from the bouts of casual wage employment than their counterparts at the national level. It is intriguing that despite the low levels of income for workers in Uttar Pradesh, the participation of women in casual wage labour is lower. This may be due to restrictions in their entry to casual wage works or lack of such wage employment opportunities in the state. The mix of these two factors may be reinforcing their lower participation in the work in the state.

The situation of SC women workers is worrisome as about 38 per cent among them work as casual wage labour and only 32 per cent working as agriculture wage labour in Uttar Pradesh (Table 6). At all-India level, a highest 52 per cent of SC women workers are casual wage workers in 2009–10. The corresponding share of their counterparts belonging to non-SC/ST social groups is much less in casual wage works. This depicts the vulnerability of SC households to uncertainty in their employment, earnings and higher chances of their exploitation.

There is a gradual decline in the share of casual wage work for SC women workforce since 1993–94 both in Uttar Pradesh and India. On the other side, the share of casual wage workers among women from other caste households almost remained same both in Uttar Pradesh and India over the period 1993–94 to 2009–10. This feature of casual wage employment particularly across social groups would need an in-depth investigation which could shed light on whether overall employment situation is improving for women in Uttar Pradesh in the form of declining dependence on casual wage labour, or they are now growingly facing discrimination in getting such casual wage employment as reflected in almost constant share of other caste women in casual wage labour.

Trends in Self-employment

Self-employment is a predominant form of work both for men and women in India. Over two-thirds of women workers are self-employed in Uttar Pradesh. Only 62.4 per cent of women workers in the state are self-employed in agriculture. At the national level, women have been able to diversify their employment at a faster pace as nearly 40 per cent of them are self-employed in agriculture. About 14 per cent women workers are self-employed in non-agricultural sector both in Uttar Pradesh and rest of India in 2009–10 (Table 6). Due to lack of productive assets like and among SC households, their proportion as self-employed is much low than other caste groups.

The decline in the share of SC women in casual wage labour is compensated by the corresponding increase in their share as self-employed, particularly in agriculture. This could be possible as several of SC households have engaged themselves in share cropping in several parts of Uttar Pradesh and they report themselves as self-employed in agriculture. However, their share in non-agricultural self-employment tended to decline since 1999–2000 in the state (Table 6).

To sum up, while women are gradually withdrawing from work over the years, there has certainly been improvement in their status of employment in Uttar Pradesh. Their large dependence on casual wage employment, particularly among SC households, has gradually reduced over the years. They are now increasingly participating in their educational development. The recent trends in women's WPR at national level challenge the conventional hypothesis that participation of women belonging to poor households is higher which gradually declines with the increasing income levels. However, it still holds true in case of Uttar Pradesh and SC households.

Educational Level of Women Workers

Education is an important factor in determining the nature of employment and level of earnings in the labour market. Studies have shown that probability of workers in better paid occupations is higher for better educated workers as compared to illiterate or semi-literate workers. It is also shown how caste acts as an important factor in determining the labour market outcomes in terms of employment and earnings.

There are glaring differences in the educational level of males and females both in Uttar Pradesh and rest of India. According to latest 2011 Population Census, there is a gender gap of 20 percentage points in the literacy rates in the state. Over 59 per cent of females and 79.2 per cent of males are literate in the state. The corresponding female literacy rate for India is much higher at 65.5 per cent and that for males, 82.1 per cent.

The NSSO data shows a very low percentage of educated (high secondary and above) among female workers as compared to males both in Uttar Pradesh as well as in India. Nearly one-tenth of women workforce is educated in Uttar Pradesh. The corresponding figure at all-India level is much higher over 14 per cent in 2009–10. Nearly two-thirds of the women workforce in the state is illiterate as against a national figure of 52.3 per cent during the year 2009–10 (Table 7).

Table 7

Educational Levels of Women Workers (%), 2009–10

Educational Level	*Uttar Pradesh*			*India*		
	SC	*Non-SC/ST*	*Total*	*SC*	*Non-SC/ST*	*Total*
Illiterate	77.2	63.2	67.3	61.7	49.6	52.3
Primary and below primary	10.6	17.3	15.4	20.7	23.0	22.5
Middle	7.3	8.3	8.0	9.2	11.6	11.1
Secondary	1.6	3.6	3.0	4.3	5.8	5.5
Higher secondary	1.0	2.5	2.0	1.6	3.2	2.8
Diploma/certificate	0.0	0.1	0.1	0.5	0.8	0.8
Graduate and above	2.2	5.1	4.3	2.0	6.0	5.1
Total	100.0	100.0	100.0	100.0	100.0	100.0

Source: NSSO 66th Round Unit Level Data, 2009–10.

There is a significant difference in the educational levels of women workers across their social groups. Over three-fourths of SC women workforce is illiterate as compared to 63.2 per cent of other caste women. Thus, the percentage of educated women is least among SC and highest among other groups (Table 7).

Perhaps very low educational level of an overwhelming large majority of female population is a matter of serious concern, particularly for states like Uttar Pradesh where employment fetches abysmally low earning for females, thus perpetuating widespread poverty and inequality in the state.

Yet another distinct feature of India labour market is discrimination based on caste and religion despite the higher educational attainment, thus resulting in high incidence of unemployment. A study by Indian Institute of Dalit Studies (IIDS, 2007) shows a huge discrimination in the Indian urban labour market despite having a relatively better educational qualification of marginalized groups such as SCs and Muslims while seeking jobs in the labour market.

Per Worker Productivity

Per worker productivity is measured through dividing GSDP for each industry group by number of workers in that group. The data, thus do not allow us to measure gender-wise productivity. However, the aggregate value of per worker GSDP across industry groups throw valuable information (Table 8).

Table 8

Per Worker Productivity at 1999–2000 Prices (in ₹)

Sectors	*Uttar Pradesh*		*India*		*CAGR (1994–2005)*	
	1993–94	*2004–05*	*1993–94*	*2004–05*	*UP*	*India*
Agriculture, forestry and fishing	15,915	17,360	16,388	20,022	0.79	1.84
Mining and quarrying	1,40,933	1,77,704	1,73,696	3,06,266	2.13	5.29
Manufacturing	37,063	36,191	88,097	1,34,512	−0.22	3.92
Electricity, gas and water supply	3,82,989	14,55,328	5,11,199	10,51,833	12.90	6.78
Construction	60,223	23,850	1,05,957	96,717	−8.08	−0.83
Trade, hotels and restaurants	53,217	41,398	1,20,932	1,79,685	−2.26	3.67
Transport, storage and communication	71,704	91,800	1,94,265	2,94,386	2.27	3.85
Financing, insurance, real estate	4,32,048	4,05,445	17,48,357	19,96,489	−0.58	1.21
Community, social and personal services	43,253	82,737	1,08,227	2,20,944	6.07	6.70
Total	29,276	34,948	42,761	71,854	1.62	4.83

Source: Calculated from NSSO data on Employment and CSO data on GDP/GSDP.

There are significant inter-industry differentials in per capita GSDP both in Uttar Pradesh and India. Agriculture sector has the lowest per capita GSDP among all industry groups at ₹ 17,360 in 2004–05 in Uttar Pradesh. Construction is yet another sector next to agriculture with low per worker GSDP at ₹ 23,850 in 2004–05. Similar pattern is observed at all-India level. A more perturbing pattern is a very low growth in per worker GSDP as compared to all-India growth, i.e., 1.62 per cent as compared to 4.8 per cent during the period 1993–94 to 2004–05.

Though per worker GSDP is lowest in agriculture both in UP and rest of India, its annual growth has been less than half compared to the growth at national level. In fact, growth of per worker GSDP has been negative in manufacturing, trade, finance and insurance, and construction in Uttar Pradesh. The decline in real per worker GSDP in these sectors during 1993–94 to 2004–05 also imply increasing vulnerability of workers to fluctuating productivity levels. In other words, structural shifts in employment from agriculture to industry are accompanied by declining productivity levels in non-agricultural sectors like manufacturing, construction and trade – the marginal productivity of labour in these sectors tending towards zero.

Thus, for a vast majority of 80 per cent of women workers who are engaged in agricultural sector, their earnings are abysmally low in comparison to those workers employed in other industries. This is more so for women workers belonging to SC and OBC households.

Working Poor

The low levels of productivity is also reflected in widespread poverty among workers. Over one-fourth of workers in Uttar Pradesh are living below poverty line income – termed as working poor. A highest 34.6 per cent of SC workers are working poor in the state. The percentage of such workers is lowest at 15.4 per cent in other social groups (Table 9). As mentioned earlier, a large majority of SC workers work as casual wage labour in agriculture.

Table 9

Percentage of Poor among Workers, 2004–05

Group	*Uttar Pradesh*	*India*
ST	28.84	37.6
SC	34.58	29.5
OBC	26.39	20.9
Others	15.43	12.6
Rural	25.10	21.4
Urban	30.70	23.6
Total	26.08	21.9

Source: Calculated from NSSO Unit Level Data on Employment and Unemployment.

Interestingly, the percentage of 'working poor' is comparatively high in urban areas, both in Uttar Pradesh and rest of India. This also implies that agriculture, despite having lowest per worker GSDP acts as a cushion to those who are self-employed in it from widespread poverty conditions in comparison to other workers such as agricultural labour and non-agricultural wage labour and those self-employed in non-agriculture (Planning Commission, 2008).

Education emerges as a crucial instrument for diversification in occupation, raising income levels and reduction in poverty levels. Studies indicate a strong negative correlation between educational attainment and poverty levels (Mathur and Mamgain, 2004).

In fact, poverty levels are almost four times higher among illiterates as compared to persons with higher education. Nearly 60 per cent of poor belong to the category of illiterates (Planning Commission, 2008).

Summing up

The lower participation of women in work outside home in Uttar Pradesh in comparison to several states and national average indicates fewer employment opportunities for women. Their lower participation is partly due to social customs. It is observed that work participation rate of SC women is highest both in Uttar Pradesh and India who do not have social restrictions on their participation in work. However, this is true for southern and central regions of Uttar Pradesh and certainly not relevant to Gangetic regions where customs prevail upon the participation of women in work even in the case of SC women. It is also observed that their higher participation in work is also associated with the high incidence of poverty among them in the state. The 'U' shaped curve of women's WPRs in Uttar Pradesh reveals the general pattern of women's work participation. However, such pattern is gradually disappearing at the national level and a new pattern of increasing women's WPRs with increasing household income strongly emerges. This also shows a significant contribution of women in household incomes.

The structure of women employment is highly tilted towards agriculture and there are very limited employment opportunities for women outside agriculture. This is more so for the SC women who are largely working as casual wage labour in agriculture. However, there are positive developments in the structure of employment of women. Their share is gradually declining in casual wage works and increasing in regular salaried jobs as well as in self-employment. This becomes more pronounced in case of SC women in Uttar Pradesh. The rapid withdrawal of women in casual wage works and consequent decline in their overall work participation also shows the reduction in their vulnerabilities and increase in incomes of their households. Larger participation in government wage programmes may have positive impact on household incomes and thus reduction in distress induced participation.

They also lag much behind in terms of their human capital endowments as compared to their male counterparts. The situation of SC women is again worst on this count which underscores the need to improve their educational levels through focused state sponsored initiatives in a time bound manner. They cannot be left to the vagaries of the market forces which will again exclude them from the mainstream development. There is a need to initiate intensive skill development programmes for both men and women of the state to improve their employability and productivity. Accelerating the growth process is necessary for the state of Uttar Pradesh to catch up with other Indian states, but at the same time the growth has to be accompanied by reduction in disparities in development across various social groups and regions in the state.

References

CSO. 2011. Gross State Domestic Product at Factor Cost, Uttar Pradesh, Central Statistical Organisation, *http://mospi.nic.in/rept_pubn/sdp199_ 2000/ GSDP_ UttarPradesh.pdf,* accessed on 12 May 2012.

Dreze, Jean and Amartya Sen. 1995. *India: Economic Development and Social Opportunity*, Oxford University Press, New Delhi.

Government of India-RGI. 2011. Population Census of India 2011, Occasional Paper No. 1, Office of the Registrar General of India, New Delhi.

IIDS. 2007. *Labour Market Discrimination and Urban Sector*, Research Series: Social Exclusion, Indian Institute of Dalit Studies, New Delhi, Vol. 1, No. 1.

Mathur, Ashok and R.P. Mamgain. 2004. 'Human Capital Stocks, Their Level of Utilisation and Economic Development in India', *The Indian Journal of Labour Economics*, Vol. 47, No. 4.

Neff, Daniel, Kunal Sen and Veronika Kling. 2012. 'The Puzzling Decline in Rural Women's Labour Force Participation in India: A Re-examination', *The Indian Journal of Labour Economics* (Forthcoming Issue).

Planning Commission. 2008. *Human Development Report, Uttar Pradesh*, Government of Uttar Pradesh, Lucknow.

——. 2010. Mid-Term Appraisal of Eleventh Five-Year Plan, New Delhi.

Sen, Gita. 2010. 'Beyond a Segmented Economics of Work', *The Indian Journal of Labour Economics*, Vol. 53, No. 1.

Sharma, Kumud. 1985. 'Interaction between Policy Assumptions and Rural Women's Work: A Case Study', Centre for Women's Development Study, New Delhi, *http//www.cwds.ac.in/occasionalpapers.htm.*

Sudarshan, Ratna M. and Shrayana Bhattacharya. 2008. 'Through the Magnifying Glass: Women's Work and Labour Force Participation in Urban Delhi', ILO Asia Pacific Working Paper Series.

World Bank. 2010. *India's Employment Challenge: Creating Jobs, Helping Workers*, Oxford University Press, New Delhi.

8

Social Demography

Gender Perspectives and Prospectives

P.S. Tripathi and Mukulika Hitkari

Social Demography: Incorporators and Indicators

Demographic indicator like urban female health parity syndrome is an essential requisite in the area of gender development. Although rural trends are still way behind in exhibiting their impacting awareness, development strategies describing parameters of demographic trends conceptually refer to attainment of non-discriminating gender prospects; welfare, extension and accessibility of improved maternal health services and socio-economic demographic indicators inclusive of nutrition, life expectancy at birth, crude death rate, crude birth rate, sex ratio, fertility, literacy, population, maternal mortality rate and infant mortality rate.

These indicative trends are discussed in a limited but adequate space. The increased life expectancy and uneven performance between fertility rates and mortality rates have posed dual challenges to simultaneously improve both primary and secondary healthcare services. Due to certain social and cultural norms and prevalence of wide illiteracy, the conservative and rigid piece of mind governing the marital reproductive as well as nutritional behaviour of women is still and has mostly spread its tentacles time and again. The National Family Health Survey-3, 2005–06 estimates that overall teenage pregnancy (15–19 years) is 16 per cent in India (IIPS and Macro International, 2007). This phenomenon results in increased infant as well as mortality rates. Startlingly, the mortality pattern universally exhibits sex differential favouring women, i.e., most findings relate to the fact that females live longer than males despite maternal mortality rates being high in populated areas, high fertility and sub-optimal nutrition conditions mainly in rural living.

Actual infrastructural development firmly and foundationally rests on parameter of GDI (Gender Development Index). Obviously, if this parameter falls short, actual infrastructural development is sure to founder in the perspective of female healthcare services. It is one of the few countries in the world where urban women and men have nearly the same LEB (life expectancy at birth). The inevitable fact of typical female advantage in life expectancy is not visible in India. In other words, Indian women have high mortality rates particularly during childhood and in their reproductive years.

The Indian population is passing through a nutritional transition phase coupled with high prevalence of low birth weight, morbidity, infant mortality, and poor maternal nutrition. Again, programmes like Integrated Child Development Scheme, Iodine Deficiency Control Programme, Child Survival Programme and Mid-day Meal Programme have resulted in much below expectation levels. However, the Tenth and Eleventh Five-Year Plans accord greater focus to nutritional education coupled with coherence of food security and nutritional security (Twelfth Five-Year Plan) for generating to greater awareness among girls and mothers towards healthcare. Uttar Pradesh ranks second only to Bihar in terms of malnutrition of children below five years – a non-abstracted miserable condition, more existing in southern and central regions of Uttar Pradesh. Two facts can be highlighted: First, nutritional level is strongly correlated with mother's education. As per National Family Health Survey-3 (NFHS-3), children of illiterate mothers are twice as more stunted and thrice as more undernourished as those of at least high school passed out mothers. Secondly, nutritional status has undergone inter-state variations and discrepancies in a stimulus concern to socio-economic development.

One of the basic demographic characteristics of the population is the sex composition which plays a vital role in shaping society and economy. This social demographic trait is affected by the differentials in mortality conditions of males and females, sex selective migration and sex ratio at birth. As a matter of fundamental observance, it is the female community which has since times of social anonymity borne the brunt of adversity of gender inequity. Kerala stands exception to the gender inequity happening with its sex ratio to be placed at 1,058 females per 1,000 males in 2010–11. The rapid spread of the use of ultrasounds and amniocentesis for sex determination followed by sex selective induced abortions has created a situation of daughter drought with tragic consequences. In this global context, media and communications can render a most effective part in generating multi-sphere and requisite awareness – thereby contributing towards a significant outcome.

Pertinently, two questions need careful perusal for an insight into the quality of life and sustained human development. First, is this the sign of socio-economic development in a globally competitive scenario? Secondly, without gender development issue, can a nation resort to sustainable development? These prospective high points in the domain of social demography still await debates as also a great extent of coordination along with concerted action and transforming perceptions in solving gender issues.

Another issue is fertility. Fertility is coherently intertwined with women's health issue. Various health challenges are time and again confronted by Indian women fraternity. Notably, large differences in fertility levels manifest in determinants like differences in state/region, education, religion, caste, and place of residence. The disparity is clearly visible. Uttar Pradesh being the most populous state has a total fertility rate of over five children per woman whereas Kerala with high levels of female education and autonomy has a fertility rate of under two. But, among all, education and health (as indicators of social infrastructure) are the most important variables which affect fertility. To control the escalating population, the buzzing call is to create awareness among female fraternity regarding reproductive rights – such education being of crucial importance for better prospective purposes.

Emanating from the above, female education is a crucial element in economic and social development. Higher levels of literacy and education lead to greater awareness and contributions – also being generally associated with modernization, urbanization, industrialization, etc., development of flexible attitudes. Female education needs to have a focus at the very inceptional stages where literacy plays a major assisting role in moulding girl child into an aware, responsible and self-reliant being – demanding and contributing towards economic growth. With female education being the focal concern, high levels of infant mortality combined with strong son preference are motivating factors leading to population growth even in major cities – thereby eroding mothers nutritional status. Perceptibly, this trend is almost equally prominent in both rural and urban areas. Population policy estimates relate to increasing awareness about legal age at marriage for females from 27 per cent to 80 per cent by 2011. Requisitely, population stabilization cannot be achieved without carefully addressing the health issues related to women fraternity. However, the main thrust is to be laid on reduction of infant mortality and maternal mortality rates and expecting a positive impact about healthy minds. Furthermore, approaching the interlinked aspect of maternal mortality rate and mortality, the fact undeniably remains that over 1,00,000 Indian women die each year from pregnancy-related causes as also being anaemic. The WHO and UNICEF estimate that even in Asia, India's maternal mortality rate is comparatively lower than the ratios of Bangladesh and Nepal but higher than those for Sri Lanka and Pakistan. The question to gravely ponder is whether is this empowerment? If no, then serious note needs to be heeded to maternal mortality rate. In developing countries like India, this situation is influenced by differences in socio-economic status of women; variations relating to access to maternal and child health services among states, educational levels; place of residence; less graded nutritional intake; type of assistance; inter-state discrepancies persist; early marriage; early motherhoods; gender discrimination. When analysed on the basis of religion, sex, place, literacy, etc., three major formulations have come to light in this highly less researched upon area. The first significant fact stays that literacy rate is directly proportional to gender empowerment. Emanatingly, second persisting fact is that sex ratio plays a major determinant in and for gender empowerment. Thirdly, awareness towards enhancement of women participation and involvement at social, economic and political levels.

To accord final shape to the demographic indicators discussed herein, the infant mortality rate is considered to be the most important measure of how well the government distributes available resources for health, education, socio-economic status of women, and public spending. There lies no second thought to the fact that most often in rural areas, health of families and communities are generally tied to the health of women, e.g., their illness or death has serious and far-reaching consequences for her family; bearing its linkage primarily with three crucial areas, viz., maternal education, mother's age linked with fertility, and maternal and child nutrition. The population policy stringently emphasizes on elimination of severe malnutrition among children by 2011. The most crucial area is of infant mortality, directly correlated with maternal health and manifesting in latter's nutritional care. Thus, substantially, the social demography syndrome envisages key issues dealing with socio-economic indicators, status of gender equity and welfare as the central point of a nation's development for which the concerned authorities have to work not only in coordination and cohesion; but also with an effective spirit of participation and contributory approach towards long run awareness generation coupled with building up female capabilities.

Gender Disparities and Persisting Challenges

Health-related challenges still exist. Against the scenario of preceding Plan periods – even inclusive of Twelfth Five-Year Plan – consistent efforts are being pursued challengingly in the direction of gender empowerment and gender development. Improvements in women's health realized in recent years are at times exposed to threat or have been reversed owing to crisis, war, economic stability or some pandemic. Essentiality of basic healthcare, family planning and obstetric services are in contrary to the arising question of unavailability. 'Gender equitable approaches' to health are imperative in enabling full female participation in the planning and delivery of health services. As custodians of family health, women play a critical role in sustaining and maintaining overall well-being. Starting with the transformation of thoughts and bent of mind of their individual self, women in cities can effort to extend their participatory role in educating and generating awareness to their counterparts in rural areas for positive outcomes in domain of gender development. But in this step towards initiating gender-based concerns, certain alarming contents need to be considered as challenges to be overcome:

(i) Every year about 10 million women endure life-threatening complications during motherhood.

(ii) Poverty poses a major threat to her normal sense, thereby, losing the ability to provide sustenance for herself and children.

(iii) Causes affecting maternal mortality rate (as discussed earlier) account for major proportion of female ill health and deficient intake.

(iv) Millennium Development Goals (MDGs) challengingly focus on reducing the maternal mortality rate by 75 per cent between 1990–2015 and ensuring universal access to reproductive health by 2015.

(v) Food and Nutritional Insecurity in this global scenario has further worsened matters.

Numerous studies undertaken (referring to Indian Institute of Population Sciences and World Bank) indicate that malnutrition poses a health concerning challenge, with its negative impact being compounded by heavy work demands, poverty, childbearing and rearing, by special nutritional needs of women. According to NFHS–3, mother's education is highly co-related with level of malnutrition among children. Again, urban-rural comparative analysis indicates that inadequate facilities result in reluctance of health providers to render non-impeded service coupled with non-alignment among functions, capacity and resources. Empowerment with its major thrust on indicator charts like female education and malnutrition are not providing the desired results as a subsequent significant outcome. For, example, in the case of Uttar Pradesh, the per capita additional resource requirement for providing nutritional supplements in the State in 2009–10 has been estimated at about ₹ 190. In other words, imperfections or deficiencies in health and nutritional functional system poses a graded challenge towards positive social demographic trends which need to be unobtrusive in respect of women's healthcare but is still way behind the desired targets. It has to be established that pursuance of gender disparities in urbanized populated areas poses to a major challenge towards gender equity and welfare. Emphasis on population stabilization and improvement of the health status of the people with focus on health concerns of womenfolk and children (as per the Population Policy) are prerequisites to adequate Physical Quality of Life Index and Human Development Index so as to ensure access to the process to sustainable development.

In this context, a major aspect relatively justifying healthcare is to focus on FLE (family life education) which would cover planning for one's future, imparting adolescent education, gender roles and responsible parenthood. It has been evidently found (by a survey study undertaken for millennium cities in 2008–09) that the health of Indian women has its firm linkage or is intrinsically linked to their status in society. Either their contributions are overlooked or they are viewed as economic burdens. As focused upon time and again, the issue co-existingly remains that running effects bear a transitivity effect, i.e., destitution or ill health, lacuna in services and deficient malnutritional status have severe repercussions not only in the case of women but also their family and children. It is for this purpose that family life education proves to be indispensable. The crucial issue needs to be relevantly linked to adequate health resources in lieu of social betterment, assessing constraints to health and reprioritizing resources so as to benefit the sphere of maternal healthcare. More so, focus on education of girls is another challenging area which could result in significant spin of improvements in terms of outcomes pertaining women health issues.

National Rural Health Mission (NRHM) was launched as a major health pilot project on 5 August 2005 seeking to achieve goals set forth by

the end of Eleventh Five-Year Plan by the coordinated efforts of various departments with its thrust concerns, viz.:

(i) Reduction of infant mortality rate and maternal mortality rate by 50 per cent.
(ii) Universalize access to public health services.
(iii) Education and health awareness towards womenfolk.
(iv) Assuring gender and demographic balance.
(v) Promoting healthy lifestyle.

But in the wake of Twelfth Five-Year Plan, treading road to gains seems to be quite beyond reach. Hence, challenges demand serious tackles and implementation towards socio-economic development and gender equity. Furthermore, it is an undeniable fact that health issues become vitally important and get a boost if women are allowed to serve as major decision-makers coupled with increase in participatory levels of adherence to non-discrimination. Nutritional inequalities eventually manifest in gender inequities and result in impeding socio-economic development. That is why education has a strong correlation with gender equity and welfare in a demographic set-up.

State Demographic Profile

The less expected average level of social demographic status in the most populous state in the country, i.e., Uttar Pradesh (UP) manifests itself in the demographic profile of the state where gender-biased attitude still prevail, all the more evident among rural womenfolk. It is only due to lack of awareness that fertility rate (in rural areas) is 4.13 whereas 2.95 (in urban areas). Referring to the data available for some status file in UP, the following projections for 2016 are ascertained in Table 1:

Table 1

Projections for Uttar Pradesh for 2016

Indicator	*2001*	*2011*	*2016*
Population (million)	171.2	198.8	209.7
Fertility Goal	4.0	2.6	2.1
Crude Birth Rate	28.2	21.6	18.8
Crude Death Rate	11.2	9.5	9.0
Infant Mortality Rate	79.7	67.0	60.8

Source: Ministry of Family Welfare, Government of Uttar Pradesh, 2008.

Such reflections indicate that the targets appear to be promising towards demographic developments but needs an enforcement. With accelerating population to be controlled, sharp reduction in fertility rates is projected. Crude death rate and crude birth rate for UP would decline to 9 and 18.8 respectively but infant mortality rate still needs a sharp reduction as it depends on mother's nutrition, health, attitude, and marriageable age too.

UP has a large unmet need for maternal services and concerned strategies to be adopted which pose a formidable challenge to gender development aspect. This is primarily due to gaps in the existing health infrastructure and services and the lack of outreach to remote areas with less privileged segments. One of the main challenges for the family welfare programme in UP is to expand coverage and accessibility of services by improving their quality. The strategies to be focused also include government's role in its endeavour to identify the strengths of the programme and build on them simultaneously removing weaknesses that impede policy implementation. Another major headway dilates to capacity build up in the state for the delivery of 'quality RCHS (Reproductive and Child Health Services)'. Therefore, women's health issue would be redundant if the Human Resource Development aspect is supplicating by not considered through training programme, skill enhancement and thrust on female health education.

On giving a careful glance at the 'Nutritional Profile of UP', prospective trends start dimming in lieu of the alarming facts coming to light:

(i) Every sixth malnourished child in India lives in UP.
(ii) UP ranks second with respect to prevalence of malnutrition amongst children under three years.
(iii) About 56 per cent children born to illiterate mothers are underweight.
(iv) Every second adolescent girl is anaemic (a gender discriminatory feature).
(v) About 64 per cent girls get married by 18 years resulting in higher maternal mortality rate and infant mortality rate.
(vi) Less than 3 per cent mothers receive the minimum full dosage of iron tablets.
(vii) Only one in 16 children receive one dose of Vitamin A supplement.
(viii) Only 23 per cent mothers undergo health check up after delivery.

In this pretext, it becomes judiciously imperative to endeavour in the direction of maintaining gender parities as well as a socio-economic standing in the infrastructurally surviving Uttar Pradesh. Moreover, the sorry plight of such a federal status raises innumerable questions on grounds of gender stability and sustainability.

By another analysis, the 'Draft Uttar Pradesh Human Development Report' (DUPHDR) mentions that combined losses due to high mortality rates and disability (as measured by Disability Life Adjusted years which form the scale of measurement for health services) are very high in UP. The World Bank Study, 2000 made a startling revelation that Uttar Pradesh at 273.2 Disability Adjusted Life Years (DALYs) has the highest loss rates among all states. Nevertheless, the overwhelming causes can relevantly be attributed to communicable diseases, malnutrition and prenatal conditions in Uttar Pradesh.

Gender Perspective – Pertaining to Liberalization and Empowerment

Increasing power for production coupled with rising consumption, in liberalized market happenings, has led to stemming of anxiousness to meet social and economic international standards; thereby creating enthusiasm for Economics of Womanpower, considered a byproduct of changing emphasis in economic science. The focal thrust in the current global scenario incorporates gender perspective in policies and plans, gender auditing, and finally making women 'visible' and 'heard' on all platforms, viz., domestic, social, national, and international. Significantly, realization to empower oneself with awareness of rights manifests in the woman herself because others can merely help to create conditions which are favourable as well as support processes that work in this direction. To understand the above syndrome, women empowerment needs to be seen in a gender relational context, i.e., a clear vision of the relationships, roles, responsibilities and inequalities. Eventually, it is the prevailing social values and attitudes which model and define a woman's participatory role thus giving rise to differentials in access to resources and healthcare. The prime concerns of Indian thought are governed by principles of gender equality and 'protection of women's rights', also best expressed in the Indian Constitution.

Henceforth, the above framework witnessed perennial shifts in different decades from being 'welfare-oriented' in the 1970s (recognizing female participation in economic growth). The 1980s adopted a 'multidisciplinary approach' bearing a major emphasis on the three core sectors of health, education and environment. Recognizingly and emanatingly, the liberalized 1990s focused fundamentally on economic/financial independence and self-reliance of women by effective implementation of training-cum-employment-cum-income generation programmes. As a follow up to the recent preceding decade of 2000s, the prospects of authenticating the empowering process of women are assuming awareness regarding gender equity and contributory recognition skills. But, in this context, overcoming the problem of their status quo or physical quality of discriminative life requires a long term structural strategy to be seriously worked upon. Considering the empowerment process with the employment levels in a liberalized market-centric approach, infrastructural progress and socio-economic development together pertain to male and female participation in workforce in an almost equal measure. However, it is noteworthy that the employment of women does not always as well as necessarily lead to economic independence. In fact, social forces, norms and ethics, too, affect the empowering status of women.

Truly signifying the social demographic perspectives and prospective challengingly dealing with gender sensitivities, the female income-employment aspect corresponding with liberalization manifests in five of the main processes, to bring about changes in women's:

(i) mobility and social interaction;
(ii) labour patterns;
(iii) access to and control over resources;
(iv) control over decision-making; and
(v) promotion of educational significance.

The Constitution of India provides for removal of constraints towards granting equal rights and privileges without observing any content of gender inequities, no doubt, the womenfolk inevitably requiring greater measure of protection in developing countries. In a parlance, the contribution of women capabilities be non-discriminatingly assessed because their participation in most fronts, viz., economic, social, educational, political, cultural, etc., is a requisite depending on environ conditions including socio-economic indicators of human development, literacy levels, attitudes, and quality of life.

Gender Concerns: Defining Role of Non-Governmental Organizations and Self-Help Groups

Change is rightly considered to be an inevitable process in development making way into its acceptability by Indian womanhood on all fronts. But the core values, e.g., rigidity of traditions, discharging of responsibilities self-reliantly, shackles of obsolescence either have not changed or have changed imperceptibly. Nevertheless, such organizations and groups have an emphasizing role in creating an aura of awareness and trucing the conflict between the hardcore values and warranted externalities in the competitive era of globalization, thereby defining their contribution as a major step towards lending significance to gender pertinent concerns in a judicious mode. Gender demographics

encompasses or, rather, should incorporate a broader spectrum of women issues. But, less fortunately, the mass understandability confines itself to mere reservations, attitudes, economic independence, etc. However, the locus standi of self-entrepreneurship still needs to be explored towards a motivating insight into a robust developed society.

In the above pretext, three different approaches have been highlighted, each encompassing several relevant illustrations to be assigned significance to:

(i) Non-governmental organizations
(ii) Self-help groups
(iii) Individualistic approach – though performing collectively

Non-governmental Organizations (NGOs)

Some very important and interesting case studies have been researched upon which can verily serve as an inspirational source to the willing ones.

(i) **Premlata Das** (Socially oppressed): This organization now heads a residential school commendably for tribal girls in Odisha's backward Rayagada district.

(ii) The **Mann Deshi Mahila Sahakari Bank** (MDMSB): An all-women NGO group with 3,100 shareholders, over 25,000 customers, and 96 per cent recovery together with a federation of over 275 Self-Help Groups (SHGs) (100% recovery) is a glowing tribute to womanpower scripting a revolution in the nation. Though depositors are males too, yet finances are handled and imparted only by and through women. This proves to be a citing example of leadership development skills.

(iii) **Viji Srinivasan**: She is a role model working for empowerment of marginalized, vulnerable and socially oppressed women in rural Bihar and Jharkhand. She started 'GOGOBAISI' (tribal word for women empowerment) to hone their creative skills and trying to uplift their living standards. Successfully running NGO called 'ADITHI' (Agriculture, Dairy, Industries, Tree Plantation, Handicrafts and Integration of Women) since over two decades, it is committedly involved in around two and a half dozen projects, employs approximately 34,000 women; also credited to develop 568 SHGs with a mission to promote education and self-dependence.

Self-Help Groups

(i) First and foremost, Kanpur city is a living and strengthening example with 64 SHGs being run under the aegis of 'Lok Vikas

Mandal'. Each group constitutes around 30 women (employing around 1,920 women in total). Their activities include small and retail businesses stimulating self-employment.

(ii) Veena Devi, the elected Mukhiya of Loharpur Panchayat in Naiwada, Bihar, is acclaimed to be the first and best to work towards infrastructural betterment in the concerned region as also significantly creating awareness relating to gender parity issues, nutrition and literacy. She has been acknowledged by the government time and again.

(iii) In the transforming face of social demography, the successful working of SHGs in Chitrakoot endeavouringly justify the progress in both society and economy; where the rural women have ventured into journalism – the targeted domain being to generate awaringly guided views on health, education and polity. Here, the female editorial team of 'Khabar Lahariya', a fortnightly rural newspaper, is produced by a group of a dozen predominantly Dalit and Kol women (who were initially deemed to be a victim of social oppression) and sold in nearly 200 villages with a print run of 1,500.

(iv) Shortlisting the last example present in north-eastern states like Manipur not only that the women's markets have been a cradle of every mass movement but also such groups are consistently trying to play a defining role in the direction of gender non-discrimination coupled with improving the Human Development Index with a special focus on girls.

Individualisitic Approach

Gender-oriented concerns analysed under the prospective profile of social demography can fully and judiciously justify their status quo stand only if women empowerment is understood and implemented to its optimum level. In this correlation, it becomes important to highlight their outstanding contributions on all fronts which are enough to provide a stimulus to those willing to explore themselves even in the face of rigidities and socio-economic disparities.

Sarladevi from Allahabad founded the 'Bharat Sri Mahamandal' Association for women which imparts knowledge related to upliftment of women and necessity of education. Ranging from *Judit Polgar* (chess), only woman in the history of any sport to enjoy success against top 10 men players; to *Padma Bandopadhyaya*, first woman in India to become Air Marshall in the world's fourth largest Air Force; and bio-revolutionist *Kiran Mazumdar Shaw* to world's most powerful businesswoman (investment banker) *Naina Lal Kidwai* who has spearheaded schemes for micro-lending in villages and sponsored earth renewal through water harvesting, women, some hailing from low income backgrounds have efforted to make their presence felt in multifarious spheres of life ranging from rustic level heads of panchayats to bureaucrats, corporates, defence, industry, agriculture, etc. Also, *Manita Kurl* of Mahailgaila in Nawanshahr district is the only first woman commission agent in Punjab proving herself in an unconventional career of farming, being a torchbearer with a positive change in mindset. This radical change is productively in line with the liberalized process in India, thus opening the gates of exchange, understanding and knowledge to the external society. This socio-economic aspect obviously amounts to self-realization of women empowerment. But, the hardcore fact remains that these are just a counted few citations – who can channelize and decentralize their resources to provide encouraging boost and motivation to the attitudes of the willing female folk to integrally confront the persisting adversities and firmly make their mindsets flexible in justified and adequate support of female rights since their inceptional stages.

In a parlance, it can be evidently stated that the spirit of developmental change in the real sense of the term rests in the committed efforts of women. Then only true meaning can be lent to the demographic prospectives and sustainability.

Suggestive Facts

In lieu of the fact that states with the highest prevalence of child malnutrition have the lowest coverage and receive low finding for it, the Integrated Child Development Service (ICDS) was given due importance and consideration which significantly aims to provide child growth monitoring, child and adolescent education along with some basic health services to young children and pregnant women. An evaluation of constraints, challenges and related formulation of strategies concerning the domain of child and women health; restructuring the existing primary healthcare system to parallel itself to needs of lesser privileged womenfolk – to make it more accountable by issuing identification; establishing institutional frameworks for improved quality of governance of health in the backdrop of urbanized trends; investment in technology and human resources for generating positive awareness towards improving demographic indicators; and above all, the recognition of the centrality of women and child health in poverty alleviation, reduction in mortality rates, improved life quality and overall economic development.

An acknowledged fact is the exigency for ensuring research and analytical study on gender issues – with special reference to the urban women health sector to serve as the pivotal point in setting a precedent and according due relevance to the concept of Human Development Index or gender empowerment. There is scope and space for lots to be channelizingly and resourcefully implemented. But this to be made an indispensable requisite in a decentralized manner as far as educational concerns are considered, i.e., at the secondary and higher education levels as an awaring learning process.

Nation-building is a multidimensional exercise – calling for an integrated approach to the perspectives and prospectives of gender issues under social demography. Special education and Public Information Efforts can promote gender equities with respect to nutrition, healthcare, education, and social, economic and political activity as well as equitable inheritance rights. Evidently, the imperativeness is to get rid of time-abused practices in favour of time-honoured ones.

Undoubtedly, discrimination serves as a major impediment against women which, as a repercussion, violates their human rights – thus jeopardizing development. There is massive evidence that empowering and investing in women definitely brings in huge development dividends. For instance, girl education is the single most effective way of tackling poverty. It increases life expectancy, reduces family size, improves child survival, raises productivity and enables women to make their voice standing in all spheres coupled with ensuring a sustainable demographic cycle. This empowerment in political, social, educational, economic, and health status is a highly significant end in attaining sustainable development – although as a long run measure.

The fact cannot be ruled out that India (of the 20th and 21st centuries) is among the few developing countries where equality and improvement in status quo of female folk are considered to be inevitable goals of development and social policy. Thus, in evaluating the domain of social demography, overall socio-economic change towards liberalized growth assumes relevance, which eventually encompasses woman's accessibility to economic resources, public participation, decision-making and, above all, impetus to education and mass communication for 'longer period success' of human development targets. In this perspective, various studies have revealed the fact that population and development programmes are most effective when steps have simultaneously been taken to improve the status of women. For this, formulation of a human resource development strategy towards women is an exigency also calling for timely implementation too.

Thus, the very parameters of demographic trends need be appropriately harmonized and co-ordinated effectively for improved results in the critical domain of Gender Development Studies. Policies should not merely prove to be just paper formulations as is the general case often but actual programming, implementation and reprioritizing of resources towards gender development is a major global call - calling serious attention in the current competitive wake especially in developing nations like India - where social demography standards need to be taken pragmatic care of.

References

Bhalla, A.S. 1995. *Uneven Development in the Third World: A Study of China and India*, Macmillan, Basingstoke, UK.

Country Health System Profile, 2002. *Report of the UN World Conference on Women*, organized under the aegis of United States International Development Agency.

India Registrar General Reports, 2000–08. New Delhi.

International Institute for Population Sciences (IIPS) and Macro International. *National Family Health Survey (NFHS-3), 2005–06: India*, Vol. 1.

International Institute for Population Sciences, 2007. Mumbai.

Kaur, Ravindar. 2004. 'Sensing the Future: Female Literacy on the Rise in All Communities', *Times of India*, December.

National Family Health Survey Reports, 2004–07.

Report of Uttar Pradesh Ministry of Family Welfare, 2008.

State Population Policy, Government of Uttar Pradesh, 2002.

United Nations Children's Fund (UNICEF) Reports, 2002–08. *The Progress of Indian States*, New Delhi.

United Nations Development Report, 2007–08.

Venkatasubramaniam, K. 2004. 'Health System Reforms', *Yojana*, Vol. 48, No. 1, January, pp. 11–18.

World Health Organization (WHO), 2000 onwards. 'Revised Estimates of Maternal and Child Mortality: A New Approach by WHO and UNICEF', Geneva.

9

Mental Health of Women

Manju Agrawal, Meeta Malhotra and
Anupama Srivastava

Women are integral to all aspects of society. Their multiple roles lead to work overload, role conflict, etc., and may at times render them at greater risk of mental health problems than men. Women bear the burden of responsibility associated with being wives, mother and caregivers to others. According to World Health Organization (1998), women are becoming an essential part of the labour force and they are the prime source of income in one quarter to one third of households. Women's mental health is not something that is paid a lot of attention. It is low on the priority list of women themselves, who always put their family and home and the needs of others first, before attending to their own. As a result, women's mental health does not receive adequate attention. The body of literature in gender analysis points to three common roles of females: reproductive, productive and community.

Reproductive roles: These are the roles that procreate and sustain the human race, e.g., reproducing children, rearing responsibilities, caring for the sick, and other domestic roles. These are usually maintenance roles without any monetary value attached to them. These roles are considered unproductive work as performing these roles is not recognized as 'work'. These tasks are not reflected in any country's Gross Domestic Product or Gross National Product.

Productive roles: These are the roles that generate food and wealth. It comprises work done by both women and men that generate income (in cash and/or in kind) and have an exchange value.

Community roles: These are roles for the whole community welfare such as cleaning water sources, attending funerals, carrying out religious activities, attending local council meetings and weddings, etc. Community roles are those undertaken primarily by women at the community level to maintain scarce resources of collective consumption such as water, healthcare and education.

Both men and women play multiple roles, however the major difference is that men typically play their roles sequentially, and focus on single role, while women do multi-tasking, balancing the demands of each within their limited time constraints. Since women tend to assume multiple roles, it is important to take these into account when planning mental health interventions for them.

This article focuses on the status of mental health of women, possible factors associated with mental health of women, gender differences in the mental illness and policy implications.

Gender acquired risks are many. Many of them arise from women's greater vulnerability to poverty, discrimination and lower socio-economic status. The social gradient in health is gender biased. Women constitute around 70 per cent of the world's poor and earn significantly less than men when in paid work (WHO, 1998). Many of the negative experiences and exposures to mental health risk factors that lead to and maintain the psychological disorders in which women predominate involve serious violations of their rights as human beings including their sexual and reproductive rights. Women perform 66 per cent of the world's work, produce 50 per cent of the food, but earn 10 per cent of the income and own 1 per cent of the property (UNICEF, 2007). In some regions, women provide 70 per cent of agricultural labour, produce more than 90 per cent of the food, and yet are nowhere represented in budget deliberations (World Economic Forum, 2005). Other socio-demographic factors like lack of formal education, being married, occupations of daily wage labourers, being homemaker (not working outside) have been found to be the most significant predictors of mental health problems in women (Davar, 1999; Patel et al., 1999; Sachi Devi, 2003; Vindhya et al., 2001). Gender-based differences may emanate from a biomedical (genetic, hormonal, anatomical, physiological); psychosocial (personality coping, symptom reporting); and epidemiological (population-based) factors. Among women the biological causes of psychiatric disorders are mainly rooted in menstruation, childbirth and menopause (Kohen, 2001). The social trends show that domestic violence, subordinate social status, constant responsibility for the care of others and little decision-making power push women towards considerable social and psychological disadvantage. Further, in countries like India, due to preference for male children, females may receive less care, nutrition and emotional support. Low income and income inequality and other forms of discrimination at workplace have adverse effect on their mental health. Globalization has further added to the economic vulnerability of women. There is strong evidence that globalization and large-scale restructuring has increased income inequalities, difficulties and harsh impacts on the lives of people, particularly on women. As a result, gender is an important determinant of mental health and mental illness.

Gender differences are quite prominent in the rates of common mental disorders: depression, anxiety and somatic complaints. Women have been found to be two to three times more likely to suffer from common mental disorder than men (Davar, 1995; Patel et al., 1999). A number of researches have well documented the finding that women are more likely than men to experience depressive disorders (Choi, 2001; Weissman et al., 1984, 1991). Similarly, anxiety disorders are more prevalent among women than among men, and women with anxiety disorders are more likely than men to exhibit morbid depression (Pigott, 2003). The diagnosis of panic disorder with agoraphobia and generalized anxiety disorder (GAD) are two to three times more common among women (Bourdon et al., 1988; Robins et al., 1984; Schneier et al., 1992) and social phobia is three to four times as common among women than in men. Also eating disorders such as anorexia nervosa, bulimia nervosa, etc., are primarily seen among women (Leach, 1995).

According to Kohen (2001), there may not be significant differences in prevalence of major psychiatric morbidity such as schizophrenia, bipolar affective disorder and other psychoses between male and female patients, but differences in clinical symptomatology and long-term management issues need to be taken into consideration. For example, in schizophrenia gender differences in age of onset of symptoms have been observed. Men were found to have an earlier onset of symptoms than women and poorer premorbid psychosocial development and functioning (Piccinelli and Homen, 1997). Some researchers report a higher frequency of hallucinations or more positive psychotic symptoms in women as compared to men (Lindamer et al., 1999). When schizophrenia coexists with homelessness, women have been found to suffer from higher rates of sexual and physical victimization, and more morbid anxiety, depression and medical illness than men (Brunette and Drake, 1998). In the case of bipolar disorder, women are more likely to have rapid cycling, show more morbidity (Leibenluft, 1996) and have a greater likelihood of being hospitalized during the manic phase of the disorder (Hendrick, Altshuler and Gitlin, 2000).

Gender-Based Violence and Mental Health

The prevalence of violence against women is disturbingly high (WHO, 1998). Violence against women can take three forms – physical (slapping, pushing, etc.) psychological (insults, humiliation, etc.) and sexual violence (forced sex, rape, etc.). The National Family Health Survey–3 revealed that more than a third of women in India have been physically mistreated by their husbands or other family members (IIPS, 2007). Some community-based surveys have revealed that physical violence has been experienced by 16–48 per cent of females in different settings in India (Babu and Kar, 2009; INCLEN, 2000; Jejeebhoy, 1998; Verma and Collumbien, 2003; Visaria, 2000). The studies available on psychological violence and sexual violence are limited. Some of the community-based studies suggested that psychological violence ranges from 23–72 per cent (Babu and Kar, 2009; Duvvury, Nayak and Allendorf, 2002; INCLEN, 2000; Jejeebhoy, 1998; Visaria, 2000). Fifteen per cent of total sample of women in a multi-site study reported one or more incidents of forced sex (INCLEN, 2000). A study conducted in Kheda district, Gujarat, revealed that 20 per cent of the women reporting physical violence described abuse of a sexual nature (Visaria, 1999). A few studies based on samples of men revealed that 9 per cent (Martin et al., 1999), 12–26 per cent (Stephenson et al., 2006) and 50 per cent (Duvvury, Nayak and Allendorf, 2002) reported committing sexual violence. It is important to point out here that majority of the studies in India have been carried out on the samples of married women and a few studies are based on reporting by men.

Acts of violence against women include dowry deaths, wife battering, female foeticide and infanticide, sexual violence, trafficking in girls, etc. These factors adversely affect a woman's right to life, liberty and dignity, and thereby her mental health. Most of the research on gender based violence has focussed on the issue of domestic violence. In India, there has been a legislation against domestic violence in 2005, popularly known as the Protection of Women from Domestic Violence Act. Although legally, domestic violence is identified as a crime, public recognition of domestic violence as a criminal act is low due to the fact that there is widespread acceptance of violent behaviour as part of marital life and of male entitlement (International Council for Research on Women, 2002; Sriram, 2001). Cultural and social factors are interlinked with the propagation and tolerance of violent behaviour. Through the process of socialization, in India, men acquire stereotyped gender roles of domination and control, whereas women learn behaviours of submission, dependence and respect for authority.

Gender violence leads to shock, fear, denial, guilt, humiliation, anxiety, depression, post-traumatic stress disorder, and suicidal attempts (Purewal and Ganesh, 2000; Ramanathan, 1996; Roberts et al., 1998). Having noticed an increasing incidence of sexual violence against females, the researchers have proposed that female victims make up the single largest group of those suffering from post-traumatic stress disorder (Calhoun and Resnick, 1993).

Reproductive Health and Mental Illness among Women in Developing Countries

Vindhya (1999) on the basis of review of studies reported that frequency of mental illness among women is highest in the reproductive years, i.e., between 16 and 40 years. Wasserheit and Holmes (1992) reported that gynaecological morbidities including Reproductive Tract Infections (RTIs) are extremely common among women in resource poor countries of the world having potentially devastating effects on the health and social well-being of women and their children. Also the proportion of females at risk for gynaecological morbidity in the developing countries is increasing due to rapid urbanization and population growth. Jaswal (2001) in her study on low income urban women in Mumbai found a high association between gynaecological morbidity and common mental disorders. Gynaecological morbidity adversely affected the lives of these poor women in three areas – physical (causing weakness and fatigue), social (inability to participate in functions and ceremonies) and psychological (poor self-image and personal dignity). Some of the female-specific psychiatric disorders are:

Premenstrual Dysphoric Disorder (PMDD): In Diagnostic and Statistical Manual of Disorders (DSM IV), PMDD refers to the recurrent emotional and physical symptoms that occur in the last week of premenstrual cycle and remit in the first two days following the onset of menstruation. The diagnosis is made prospectively over two consecutive cycles. It is characterized by depressed mood, persistent anger, irritability, marked anxiety, affective liability, lack of energy and motivation, increased appetite and specific food cravings, hypersomnia or insomnia and physical symptoms such as tenderness, swelling and headaches. Banerjee et al. (2000) in their study to identify the prevalence of PMDD in Indian women found that 6.4 per cent of them met the diagnosis of PMDD.

Voluntary and Forced Abortion and Infertility: According to Zolese and Blacker (1992), abortion may be coupled with feelings of guilt that can lead to generalized anxiety, phobias and diagnosis of depression. Sex-selection tests and sex-selective abortions have become a curse to development indicators of India posing a threat to the entire fabric of social structure. Mothers agree to the family decision else they face dire consequences.

When infertility occurs in a couple especially in developing countries, the woman is held responsible and socially isolated. The causes of infertility in developing countries may be sexually transmitted diseases or toxic exposures in man or woman, infections due to poor obstetric and gynaecological practices or by untrained attendants in child birth and abortion (Paltiel, 1993). Infertility, in India, has very strong social stigma. It may lead to separation, divorce and marrying again without divorcing. The social and family environment for such women may be extremely oppressive with several mental health consequences.

Post-partum Psychiatric Problems: Pregnancy and childbirth have a huge psychological and physiological effect on women. The psychiatric disorders precipitated or triggered by pregnancy or childbirth have been acknowledged by American Psychiatric Association (1994). Based primarily on the work of the Task Force on DSM-IV (Purnine and Frank, 1996) the manual now has a course and specific designation 'post-partum onset' which can be applied to both psychotic and non-psychotic post-partum mental disorders. Thus major depressive disorders, bipolar disorders, schizo-affective disorders and psychotic disorders (not otherwise specified) will have the qualifier 'with post-partum onset'.

There are three types of post-partum disorders – post-partum blues, depression and psychosis. The mildest of the post-partum mood disturbances are the post-partum 'blues'. The symptoms of this syndrome begin within the first week following childbirth, peak on the fifth day and resolve by the twelfth day after child birth. It is characterized by dysphoria, crying, anxiety, insomnia, poor appetite and irritability. This mood disturbance consisting of post-partum blues is usually short-lived, usually self remitting and does not cause serious impairment to a woman's functioning (O'Hara et al., 1991). However, in some women, the disturbance may continue even after the initial post-partum period leading to post-partum depression (Cox et al., 1993). It is a more serious condition and results from the interplay of multiple biological and psycho-social factors. The biological causes include a sudden fall in oestrogen and progesterone levels, hypothyroidism and neurotransmitter changes in the brain linked to the hormonal changes (Brockington and Cox-Roper, 1988).

Post-partum depression may get exacerbated by cultural factors and subordinate position of women. Traditionally a post-partum woman in India is socially isolated and confined to usually a less ventilated room, lacking standards of hygiene. Men, not even husband is allowed to enter that room or spend much time there. In absence of social and psychological support in the situation the PPD takes a bad shape as observed. Chandran et al. (2002) observed 359 women of Tamil Nadu in the last trimester of pregnancy and in 6–12 weeks after delivery. The incidence of PPD was 11 per cent. The rate of PPD was linked with low income, birth of a daughter, relationship difficulties, and adverse life events during pregnancy and absence of practical help.

Post-partum psychosis is much rarer than PPD. It severely impairs the functioning of a woman and in most extreme cases there is high risk of suicide and infanticide (Millis and Kornblith, 1992).

Perimenopause and Menopause: Perimenopause is characterized by irregular ovulatory cycles and it describes the period just before the menopause, from the time when the hormonal and clinical features of approaching menopause begin until the end of first year after menopause (WHO, 1998). During perimenopause due to hormonal changes a woman may experience various physical and some mood symptoms like irritability, anxiety, difficulties in concentration, depressed mood, lack of energy, and poor sleep. Menopause is characterized by gradual oestrogen depletion. Although it is now well documented that menopause *per se* does not increase the risk for depression but it has been found that the physical and hormonal changes together with psycho-social stressors may increase the risk of affective symptomatology (Avis and McKinlay, 1995; Kaufert et al., 1992).

Globalization and Mental Health of Women

We have entered the era of globalization. One of the important factors in globalization is urbanization. Urbanization is the relative increase of the urban population as a proportion of the total population (Harpham et al., 1988). A number of studies have clearly documented the association between urbanization and poor mental health (Harpham and Blue, 1995). Walker argues that the by-products of multinational businesses, i.e., income and educational inequalities, economic insecurity, etc., have risen parallel with prevalence of depressive disorders.

A number of studies have established a link between rising income inequality and increasing rates of common mental disorders like depression, anxiety and somatic symptoms (Patel et al., 1999) increased rates of mortality from physical conditions (Lynch et al., 2000) and increased mental health-related mortality associated with substance use disorders and suicide (Lorant, 2000). The impact of globalization and structural adjustment programmes has been particularly severe on the poor countries. It also affects men and women in distinct ways due to separate roles they play, and the different constraints they face in responding to policy changes and shifts in relative prices (Kirmani and Munyakho, 1996). A reduction in social welfare expenditure and public sector jobs can cause the costs of healthcare, education and food grains to become unaffordable to the poor, a majority of whom are women (Bandarage, 1997). A study done in Goa (India), Harare (Zimbabwe), Santiago (Chile), Pelotas and Olinda (Brazil) the societies experiencing rise in income disparity due to rapid economic change revealed that female gender, low education and poverty were strongly associated with common mental disorders (Patel et al., 1999). The study clearly indicates that gender must be taken into account in looking at the way income disparities and poverty in society influence mental health. According to the WHO (1998), 'Women's health is inextricably linked to their status in society. It benefits from equality, and suffers from discrimination. Today, the status and well-being of countless millions of women world-wide remain tragically low' (WHO, 1998).

Marginalized Social Status and Mental Health

Socio-economic status also plays a significant role in women's mental health. Women even in countries like United States of America find access to healthcare comparatively lesser than men within the same social group (Krieger and Zierler, 1995). Low income earning mothers, especially lone mothers, have higher levels of depression than the general population (Macran, Clark and Joshi, 1996; Salsberry, Nickel, Polivka et al., 1999).

Women belonging to low income group are exposed to more threatening and more uncontrollable life events, such as the illness and death of children compared with the general population and they experience it more frequently. Women, especially if they belong to minority groups face more dangerous neighbourhoods, hazardous workplaces, greater job insecurity, violence and discrimination (Belle, 1990; Brown, 1998; Patel et al., 1999). The illiterate, poor, refugees, unemployed and women in low paying work or sex workers, household maids and beggars are most vulnerable to mental distress.

Thus, it can be concluded that poverty, domestic isolation, powerlessness and patriarchal oppression are all associated with higher prevalence of psychiatric morbidity in women. Considerable body of evidence points to the social origins of psychological distress for women. Sex bias also found in traditional patterns of infanticide and newly practised sex choices of foetuses, through selective abortion (WHO, 1995).

Gender Bias in Treatment and Healthcare

Bias in the treatment of female patients and the diagnosis of psychological disorders has been reported (Broverman et al., 1972). Women complain about lack of privacy, confidentiality and information about options and services available especially in many developing countries. Another problem that women face is that doctors either attribute different meanings to similar symptoms for presenting female and male patients (Malterud and Okkes, 1998) or attribute women's illnesses to psychiatric disorders and prescribe inappropriate medication (WHO, 1998). Gender inequalities, manifested through fertility, marriage, work norms, violence in marital relationships, and poor psychological health, have resulted in rural Indian women not seeking treatment for their symptoms and accepting high thresholds of suffering (Amin and Bentley, 2002).

Identification of psychological disorder is first step in improving the quality of care along with an effective treatment. Females are a significant predictor of being prescribed psychotropic drugs. Simoni-Wastila (2000) found that women are 48 per cent more likely to use any psychotropic medication than men after statistically controlling for demographics, health status, economic status, and diagnosis.

Implications for Policies and Programmes

A gender-sensitive approach to mental health provides guidance to the identification of appropriate responses from the mental healthcare system, as well as from public policy. Gender differences exist clearly, even where the socio-economic gradient may not be strong. Gender analysis improves understanding of the epidemiology of mental health problems, decisions and treatment of these problems in under-reported groups, and also increases potential for greater public participation in healthcare (Vlassoff and Moreno, 2002). For reducing gender inequalities in mental health, the life priorities and mental health concerns of women should be taken into account in the design and implementation of various policies and programmes (Avotri and Walters, 1999). There is also a need to adopt a psychosocial and public health approach to improve primary prevention and address gender-specific risk factors for common mental disorders that predominantly affect women as opposed to the emphasis on the biomedical model adopted by the National Mental Health Policy (1982) in India.

The increasing number of cases of sexual violence against women and their vulnerability to develop common mental disorders calls for low or preferably no cost gender sensitive counselling services by psychologists and social workers working in community based health services. Each primary health centre should have mental health desk at least for screening. Moreover, primary healthcare providers require training to detect and deal successfully with mental health problems resulting from gender violence especially domestic violence. Protection of Women from Domestic Violence Act, 2005 should be strictly enforced.

Health experts and development agencies should make an effort to devise interventions to improve reproductive health of women as association between gynaecological morbidity and mental illness has been reported. Female-specific psychiatric disorders and their socio-cultural correlates need attention from both the healthcare professionals and social scientists. Gender sensitive policies should also be planned to deal with some of the gender inequalities resulting from rising income disparities associated with globalization. Government should make an effort to ensure gender equitable distribution of benefits of globalization. Social security nets are especially important for mental health of women.

Lack of self-worth, competence and autonomy, low status due to low income, lack of physical, sexual and psychological safety and security are, for many women, reasons for risk in mental health. The pervasive violation of women's rights, including their reproductive rights, contributes directly to the growing burden of disability caused by poor mental health (WHO, 2006). Therefore, an inter-disciplinary action is needed to develop policies which protect and promote women's autonomy. Government should take steps to develop and integrate gender-relevant indicators in the existing national health policy, and to find mechanisms to monitor gender sensitivity in the health system.

Women's mental health affects not only family members but also others in society (Afifi, 2007). Their increasing presence in the workforce means that their mental health affects national productivity. Their social role as caregivers means that their mental health affects the mental health of their family members especially of children and elderly.

To reduce gender disparities in health, the provision of medical services alone is clearly not sufficient (Vlassoff and Moreno, 2002). In order to improve health through a gender lens it is necessary to improve access, affordability and appropriateness to the health services for women.

References

Ad Hoc Working Group on Women, Mental Health, Mental Illness and Addictions. Women, Mental Health and Mental Illness, and Addiction in Canada: An Overview, http://www.cwhn.ca/PDF/womenMentalHealth.pdf (accessed on 27 August 2006).

Afifi, M. 2007. 'Gender Differences in Mental Health', *Singapore Medical Journal*, Vol. 48, No. 5, p. 386.

Amin, A. and M.E. Bentley. 2002. 'The Influence of Gender on Rural Women's Illness Experiences and Health-Seeking Strategies for Gynaecological Symptoms', *Journal of Health Management*; Vol. 4, pp. 229–49.

Avis, N.E. and S.M. McKinlay. 1995. 'The Massachusetts Women's Health Study: An Epidemiologic Investigation of the Menopause', *Journal of the American Medical Women's Association*, Vol. 50, pp. 45–49.

Avotri, J.Y. and V. Walters. 1999. 'You Just Look at Our Work and See If You Have Any Freedom on Earth: Ghanaian Women's Accounts of their Work and Health', *Social Science and Medicine*, Vol. 48, pp. 1123–33.

Babu, B.V. and S.K. Kar. 2009. 'Domestic Violence Against Women in Eastern India: A Population-Based Study on Prevalence and Related Issues', *BMC Public Health*, Vol. 9, p. 129.

Bandarage, A. 1997. *Women, Population and Global Crisis*, Zed Books, London.

Banerjee, N., K.K. Roy and D. Takkar. 2000. 'Premenstrual Dysphoric Disorder: A Study from India', *International Journal of Fertility and Women's Medicine*, Vol. 45, No. 5, pp. 342–44.

Belle, D. 1990. 'Poverty and Women's Mental Health', *American Psychologist*, Vol. 45, pp. 385–89.

Bourdon, K., J. Boyd, D. Rae, et al. 1988. 'Gender Differences in Phobias: Results of the ECA Community Survey', *Journal of Anxiety Disorders*, Vol. 2, pp. 227–41.

Brockington, I.F. and A. Cox-Roper. 1988. 'The Nosology of Puerperal Mental Illness', in I.F. Brockington and R. Kumar (eds), *Motherhood and Mental Illness 2: Causes and Consequences*, Wright, London.

Broverman, I.K., S.R. Vogel, D.M. Broverman, F.E. Clarkson and P.S. Rosenkrantz. 1972. 'Sex-Role Stereotypes: A Current Appraisal', *Journal of Social Issues*, Vol. 28, pp. 59–78.

Brown, G.W. 1998. 'Genetic and Population Perspectives on Life events and Depression', *Social Psychiatry and Psychiatric Epidemiology*, Vol. 33, pp. 363–72.

Brunette, M. and R.E. Drake. 1998. 'Gender Differences in Homeless Persons with Schizophrenia and Substance Abuse', *Community Mental Health Journal*, Vol. 34, No. 6, pp. 627–42.

Calhoun, K.S. and P.A. Resnick. 1993. 'Post-Traumatic Stress Disorder', in D.H. Barlow (ed.), *Clinical Handbook of Psychological Disorders*, Guilford Press, New York, pp. 48–98.

Chandran, M., P. Tharyan, J. Muliyil and S. Abraham. 2002. 'Post-Partum Depression in a Cohort of Women from a Rural Area of Tamil Nadu, India: Incidence and Risk Factors', *British Journal of Psychiatry*, Vol. 181, pp. 499–504.

Choi, S.H. 2001. 'Changes in Premenstrual Symptoms in Women with Schizophrenia: A Prospective Study', *Psychosomatic Medicine*, Vol. 6, pp. 822–29.

Cox, J.L., D. Murray and G. Chapman. 1993. 'A Controlled Study of the Onset, Duration and Prevalence of Postnatal Depression', *British Journal of Psychiatry,* Vol. 163, pp. 27–31.

Davar, B.V. (ed.), 2001. *Mental Health from a Gender Perspective*, Sage Publications, New Delhi.

Davar, B.V. 1999. *Mental Health of Indian Women: A Feminist Agenda*, Sage Publications, New Delhi.

Duvvury, N., M. Nayak and K. Allendorf. 2002. Domestic Violence in India 4: Exploring Strategies, Promoting Dialogue, Men Masculinities and Domestic Violence in India: Summary Report of Four Studies, International Centre for Research on Women, Washington, DC.

Epidemiologie Sante Publique, Vol. 48, pp. 239–47.

Finkler, Kaya. 1985. 'Symptomatic Differences between the Sexes in Rural Mexico', *Culture, Medicine and Psychiatry*, Vol. 9, pp. 27–57.

Harpham, T. and I. Blue. 1995. *Urbanization and Mental Health in Developing Countries*, Avebury, Aldershot, Eng., Brookfield, Vt. USA.

Harpham, T., T. Lusty and P. Vaugham. 1988. *In the Shadow of the City-Community Health and the Urban Poor*, OUP, Oxford.

Hendrick, V., L.L. Altshuler and M.J. Gitlin. 2000. 'Gender and Bipolar Illness', *Journal of Clinical Psychiatry*, Vol. 61, pp. 393–96.

International Clinical Epidemiological Network. 2000. *Domestic Violence in India: A Summary Report of a Multi-Site Household Survey*, International Centre for Research on Women and the Centre for Development and Population Activities, Washington, DC, pp. 9–11.

International Council for Research on Women. 2002. *Men, Masculinity and Domestic Violence in India: A Summary Report of Four Studies*, Washington, DC.

International Institute for Population Sciences (IIPS) and Macro International. *National Family Health Survey (NFHS-3), 2005–06: India*, Vol. I.

International Institute for Population Sciences, 2007. Mumbai.

Jaswal, S. 2001. 'Gynaecological Morbidity and Common Mental Disorders in Low-income Urban Women in Mumbai', in B.V. Davar (ed.), *Mental Health from a Gender Perspective*, Sage Publications, New Delhi, pp. 138–54.

Jejeebhoy, S.L. 1998. 'Wife-beating in Rural India: A Husband's Right?', *Economic and Political Weekly*, Vol. 33, No. 15, pp. 855–62.

Kaufert, P.A., P. Gilbert and R. Tate. 1992. 'The Manitoba Project: A Re-examination of the Link between Menopause and Depression', *Maturitas*, Vol. 14, pp. 143–55.

Kirmani, M.N. and D. Munyakho. 1996. 'The Impact of Structural Adjustment Programmes on Women and AIDS', in L.D. Long and E.M. Ankrah (eds), *Women's Experience with HIV/AIDS: An International Perspective*, Columbia University Press, New York.

Kohen, D. 2001. 'Gender and Mental Health: Recognition of Unresolved Issues', *Advances in Psychiatric Treatment*, Vol. 7, pp. 3–4.

Krieger, N. and S. Zierler. 1995. 'Accounting for the Health of Women', *Current Issues in Public Health*, Vol. 1, pp. 251–56.

Leach, A.M. 1995. 'The Psycho Pharmacotherapy of Eating Disorders', *Psychiatry Annals*, Vol. 25, pp. 628–33.

Leibenluft, E. 1996. 'Women with Bipolar Illness: Clinical and Research Issues', *American Journal of Psychiatry*, Vol. 153, pp. 163–73.

Lindamer, L.A. et al. 1999. 'Gender-Related Clinical Differences in Older Patients with Schizophrenia', *Journal of Clinical Psychiatry*, Vol. 60, pp. 61–67.

Lorant, V. 2000. 'Inegalites Socio-Economiques de la Mortalite dans les Communes belges', *Revue Epidemiologie Sante Publique*, Vol. 48, pp. 239–47.

Lynch, J.W., G.D. Smith, G.A. Kaplan and J.S. House. 2000. 'Income Inequality and Mortality: Importance to Health of Individual Income, Psychosocial Environment, or Material Conditions', *British Medical Journal*, Vol. 320, pp. 1200–04.

Macran, S., L. Clarke and H. Joshi. 1996. 'Women's Health: Dimensions and Differentials', *Social Science and Medicine*, Vol. 42, No. 9, pp. 1203–16.

Malik, I.A., N. Bukhtiari and M.J.D. Good. 1992. 'Mothers' Fear of Child Death: A Study in Urban and Rural Communities in Northern Punjab, Pakistan', *Social Science and Medicine*, Vol. 35, pp. 1043–53.

Malterud, K. and I. Okkes. 1998. 'Gender Differences in General Practice Consultations: Methodological Challenges in Epidemiological Research, *Family Practice*, Vol. 15, pp. 404–10.

Martin, S.L., A.O. Tsui, K. Maitra and R. Marinshaw. 1999. 'Domestic Violence in Northern India', *American Journal of Epidemiology*, Vol. 150, No. 4, pp. 417–26.

Millis, J.B. and P.R. Kornblith. 1992. 'Fragile Beginnings: Identification and Treatment of Postpartum Depression', *Health and Social Work*, Vol. 17, pp. 192–99.

Naeem, S. 1992. 'Vulnerability Factors for Depression in Pakistani Women', *Journal of the Pakistan Medical Association*, June, pp. 137–38.

National Mental Health Policy Document. 1982. Directorate of Health, New Delhi.

Nations, K. Marilyn and Linda Rebhun. 1988. 'Angels with Wet Wings Won't Fly: Maternal Sentiment in Brazil and the Image of Neglect', *Culture, Medicine and Psychiatry*, Vol. 12, pp. 171–200.

O'Hara, M.W., J.A. Schlechte, D.A. Lewis, et al. 1991. 'Prospective Study of Postpartum Blues: Biologic and Psychosocial Factors', *Arch Gen Psychiatry*, Vol. 48, pp. 801–06.

Paltiel, F.L. 1993. 'Women's Mental Health: A Global Perspective', in M.A. Koblinsky, Timyan and J. Gay, *The Health of Women: A Global Perspective*, Westview Press, Boulder.

Papanek, H. 1998. 'To Each Less Than She Needs, from Each More Than She Can Do: Allocations, Entitlements and Value', in I. Tinker (ed.), *Persistent Inequalities: Women and World Development*, Oxford University Press, Oxford.

Patel, V., R. Araya, M. de Lima, A. Ludermir and C. Todd. 1999. 'Women, Poverty and Common Mental Disorders in Four Restructuring Societies', *Social Science and Medicine*, Vol. 49, No. 3, pp. 1461–71.

Piccinelli, M. and F.G. Homen. 1997. 'Gender Differences', in *The Epidemiology of Affective Disorders and Schizophrenia*, World Health Organization, Geneva.

Pigott, T.A. 2003. 'Anxiety Disorders in Women', *Psychiatric Clinics of North America*, Vol. 26, pp. 621–72.

Purewal, J. and I. Ganesh. 2000. 'Gender Violence, Trauma, and its Impact on Women's Mental Health', *The Indian Journal of Social Work*, Vol. 61, No. 7, pp. 542–57.

Purnine, D. and E. Frank. 1996. 'Should Postpartum Mood Disorders be Given a More Prominent or Distinct Place in DSM-IV?', in T.A. Widiger (ed.), *DSM-IV Sourcebook*, Vol. 2, American Psychological Association, Washington, DC, pp. 261–81.

Ramanathan, S. 1996. 'Violence against Women', *International Medical Journal*, Vol. 3, pp. 145–48.

Roberts, G.L, J.M. Lawrence, G.M. Williams, and B. Raphael. 1998. 'The Impact of Domestic Violence on Women's Mental Health', *Australian and New Zealand Journal of Public Health*, Vol. 22, pp. 796–801.

Robins, L.N., J.E. Helzer, M.M. Weissman, H. Orvaschel, E. Greenberg, J.D. Burke, Jr. and D.A. Regier. 1984. 'Lifetime Prevalence of Specific Psychiatric Disorders in Three Sites', *Archives of General Psychiatry*, Vol. 4, pp. 949–58.

Sachi Devi, K. 2003. 'Common Mental Disorders in Primary Health Care Settings: A Study of Socio Demographic Correlates', Unpublished Doctoral Dissertation, Andhra University, Visakhapatnam, India.

Salsberry, P.J., J.T. Nickel, B.J. Polivka, R.A. Kuthy, C. Slack and N. Shapiro. 1999. 'Self Reported Health Status of Low Income Mothers', *Image Journal of Nursing Scholarship*, Vol. 31, pp. 375–80.

Scheper-Hughes, Nancy. 1987. 'Culture, Scarcity and Maternal Thinking: Mother Love and Child Death in Northeast Brazil', in Scheper-Hughes (ed.), *Child Survival*, Reidel, Dordrecht, pp. 187–208.

Schneier, F.R., J. Johnson, C.D. Hornig et al. 1992. 'Social Phobia: Comorbidity and Morbidity in an Epidemiologic Sample', *Archives of General Psychiatry*, Vol. 49, pp. 282–88.

Sen, G., A. George and P. Ostlin. 2002. 'Engendering Health Equity: A Review of Research and Policy', Harvard Centre for Population and Development Studies, Working Paper Series 12, p. 13.

Simoni-Wastila, L. 2000. 'The Use of Abusable Prescription Drugs: The Role of Gender', *Journal of Women's Health and Gender Based Medicine*, Vol. 9, pp. 289–97.

Sriram, R. 2001. 'Violence in the Family: A View from Within', *The Indian Journal of Social Work*, Vol. 62, No. 7, pp. 379–96.

Stephenson, R., M.A. Koenig and S. Ahmed. 2006. 'Domestic Violence and Symptoms of Gynecologic Morbidity among Women in North India', *International Family Planning Perspectives*, Vol. 32, No. 4, pp. 201–08.

The Clothesource Digest of Sourcing Intelligence. 2008. Edition 12, Oxfordshire, Clothesource Limited.

UNICEF. 2007. 'Basic Education and Gender Equality: The Big Picture', *http://www.unicef.org/education/index_bigpicture.html* (accessed on 15 February 2011).

Verma, R.K. and M. Collumbien. 2003. 'Wife Beating and the Link with Poor Sexual Health and Risk Behaviour among Men in Urban Slums in India', *Journal of Comparative Family Studies*, Vol. 34, pp. 61–74.

Vindhya, U. 1999. 'Women's Mental Health: Psychological/Feminist Issues', in U.N. Dash and U. Jain (eds), *Perspectives on Psychology and Social Development*, Concept Publishing, New Delhi.

Vindhya, U., A. Kiranmayi and V. Vijayalakshmi. 2001. 'Women in Psychological Distress: Evidence from a Hospital-based Study', *Economic and Political Weekly*, Vol. 36, No. 25, pp. 4081–87.

Visaria, L. 1999. 'Violence Against Women in India: Evidence from Rural Gujarat', in *Domestic Violence in India: A Summary Report of Three Studies*, International Centre for Research on Women and the Centre for Development and Population Activities, Washington D.C.

Visaria, L. 2000. 'Violence against Women: A Field Study', *Economic and Political Weekly*, Vol. 35, No. 20, pp. 1742–51.

Vlassof, C. 1994. 'Gender Inequalities in Health in the Third World: Uncharted Ground', *Social Science and Medicine*, Vol. 39, No. 9, pp. 1249–59.

Vlassoff, C. and C. Garcia Moreno. 2002. 'Placing Gender at the Centre of Health Programming: Challenges and Limitations', *Social Science and Medicine*, Vol. 54, pp. 1713–23.

Wasserheit, J.N. and K.H. Holmes. 1992. 'Reproductive Tract Infections: Challenges for International Health Policy, Programmes and Research', in A. Germain, K. Holmes, P. Piot and J.N. Wasserheit (eds), *Reproductive Tract*

Infections: Global Impact and Priorities for Women's Reproductive Health, Plenum Press, New York, pp. 7–34.

Weissman, M., B.A. Prusoff, G.D. Gammon, K.R. Merikangas, J.F. Leckman and K.K. Kidd. 1984. 'Psychopathology in the Children (Age 6–18) of Depressed and Normal Parents', *Journal of the American Academy of Child Psychiatry*, Vol. 23, pp. 78–84.

Weissman, M., M. Bruce, P. Leaf, L. Florio and C. Holzer. 1991. 'Affective Disorders', in D.A. Regier and L.N. Robins (eds), *Psychiatric Disorders in America.* The Free Press, New York, pp. 53–80.

World Economic Forum. 2005. 'Women's Empowerment: Measuring the Global Gender Gap', Geneva.

World Health Organization. 'Gender and Women's Mental Health', www.who.int/mental_health/prevention/genderwomen/en/print.html (accessed on 27 August 2006).

World Health Organization. 'Gender Disparities in Mental Health', www.who.int/mental_health/ media/en/242.pdf (accessed on 27 August 2006).

World Health Organization. 1995. *Bridging the Gaps,* The World Health Report, Geneva.

World Health Organization. 1998. 'Gender and Health: Technical Paper', Report No. WHO/FRH/WHD/98.16, Geneva.

Zolese, G. and C.V.R. Blacker. 1992. 'The Psychological Complications of Therapeutic Abortion', *British Journal of Psychiatry*, Vol. 160, pp. 742–49.

10

Daughter Dispreference

Experiences from Rural Community in Uttar Pradesh

Roli Misra

Sex ratio is an important demographic indicator reflecting the socio-economic structure of any society. The decreasing child sex ratio (0–6 years) has been a concern in India's demography in recent times as this ratio has decreased markedly from 927 in 2001 to 914 in 2011 for the country as a whole. This decline is more for rural areas from 934 in 2001 to 919 in 2011 and for urban areas it is 906 in 2001 and 902 in 2011. Pravin Visaria's (1971) study was the first major effort to understand the phenomenon of skewing sex ratio. He concluded that higher female mortality in different age groups was responsible for low sex ratio. In present context with the avert of new technology the practice of female infanticide has been replaced by genocide of millions of women known as female foeticide – denying the girl its very right to take birth. The rapid spread of the use of ultrasounds and amniocentesis for sex determination followed by sex selective induced abortions has created a situation of daughter-drought with tragic consequences. Elisabeth Croll (2001) in *Endangered Daughters* valiantly confronts the horror of fewer women in Asia especially in China and India. She talks about Amartya Sen's 100 million missing girls from the population totals of Asian countries in particular. In the light of new modern technology the survival of daughters in now at a greater risk.

The *Atharvaveda* says, 'The birth of a daughter, grant it elsewhere, here grant a son'. This saying in the holy scripture sums up the mindset of the people in this subcontinent towards female children who are subjected to multifarious travails inflicted by the society on them. Whatever the natural biological laws of human reproduction had given mankind for balancing its natural sex ratio, they have been taken away by man-made laws, customs, traditions, religious beliefs and sophisticated medical technology, resulting in a lower status in society for girls as well as women. For too long have they been left on the back burner, facing discrimination throughout their entire journey from cradle to the grave. In particular, peculiar to South Asia, and certainly to India, tradition, values and customs encrusted over time have resulted in the insatiable desire for sons, with families having totally marginalized the joy and pleasure in giving birth to a baby girl (Walia, 2005). In some parts of the world, gender inequality is reflected in unusually high mortality rates of women and female children and a consequent preponderance of men in the total population. In an article in 1990, Amartya Sen noted the alarming fact that the sex ratio for female children in China, India and South Korea was actually deteriorating while the overall sex ratio for females in those countries had marginally improved.

India is in a transitional phase between the traditional and modern India, where old norms and expectations clash with modern ideas, in other words, India is experiencing a process of modernization with considerable changes in its social and economic institutions. With its relatively sustained, high rate of growth during recent years, rapidly expanding private and service sectors, rising demand for well-educated professionals and a growing middle class, India is undergoing far-reaching changes. The Green Revolution has contributed to large productivity gains, there has been a spread of cash economy, improvements in communications and transport; the media has grown in importance and there has been an increase of contract-based relationships replacing previous personalized patron-client ones. These changes have either directly or indirectly increased the value attached to the acquisition of basic levels of information and knowledge (Kabeer, 2000). It is against this background of a traditional society in transition, a situation of fluidity, the problem of daughter discrimination needs to be conceptualized.

Protecting Frameworks for the Girl Child

Indian Constitutional Mandate

The Indian Constitution has a framework within which ample provisions exist for the protection, development and welfare of children. The Constitution guarantees equality and prohibits discrimination on the grounds of sex. The right to equality (Article 14), right to life (Article 21), prohibits discrimination and empowers the state to make special provision for the girl child (Article 15). The *de jure* laws are not been translated in *de facto* situation and the girl child continues to suffer from the stage of being born to the stage of attaining womanhood.

Universal Declaration of Human Rights (UDHR)

This declaration was adopted and proclaimed on 10 December 1948 by United Nations. Article 1 of the UDHR says 'All human beings are born free and equal in dignity and rights'. Article 3 proclaims the right to life, liberty and security of a person. However the fact is that this right is being denied to the girl child in India and the schizophrenic attitude of the people is not allowing her to even be born.

Convention on the Elimination of All Kinds of Discrimination Against Women (CEDAW)

This was adopted in 1979 by the UN General Assembly and later on ratified by 193 countries, is often described as an international bill of rights for women. The Convention defines discrimination against women as '... any distinction, exclusion or restriction made on the basis of sex which has the effect or purpose of impairing or nullifying the recognition, enjoyment or exercise by women, irrespective of their marital status, on a basis of equality of men and women, of human rights and fundamental freedoms in the political, economic, social, cultural, civil or any other field'. India was a signatory of CEDAW in 1980 and ratified it on 9 July 1993.

Convention on the Rights of the Child (CRC)

The Convention adopted in 1989 sets out the rights in 54 articles and two Optional Protocols. It spells out the basic human rights that children everywhere have: the right to survival; to develop to the fullest; to protection from harmful influences, abuse and exploitation; and to participate fully in family, cultural and social life. The four core principles of the Convention are non-discrimination; devotion to the best interests of the child; the right to life, survival and development; and respect for the views of the child. The Government of India ratified the Convention on the Rights of the Child on 12 November 1992. By ratifying the Convention on the Rights of the Child, the government is obligated 'to review National and State legislation and bring it in line with provisions of the Convention'.

Present Status of Declining Sex Ratio

The sex differential in mortality at the national level is the result of discriminatory treatment received by girls and women. The social practices and cultural ethos that undervalue women are stronger in some regions than in others. In an almost contiguous belt extending from north-west of India to parts of Rajasthan, Gujarat and Maharashtra, the undervaluation of women is evident in the sex ratio of their population. In fact, an increase in the deficit of young girls noted in these decennial censuses of 1981, 1991, 2001, 2011 is indicative of a strong possibility that the traditional methods of neglect of female children are increasingly being replaced by not allowing female children to be born (Table 1). It must have been welcome news for the government as the newly-released census showed a significant slowing of the population growth rate for the first time in nine decades. But, that has not changed anything for the girl child who continues to be at risk.

Table 1

Child Sex Ratio: The Rural–Urban Divide

Census	*Total*	*Rural*	*Urban*
1981	962	963	931
1991	945	948	935
2001	927	934	903
2011	914	919	902

Source: Census reports.

Despite several policies to protect the girl child, their number below six years of age has fallen sharply. Poor nutrition and healthcare, rising female foeticide and overall neglect are being pegged as the major reasons for this sharp decline. But, attitude, experts say, continues to be the biggest factor. For past three decades the ratio of girl child per thousand male child has witnessed a sharp decline in Indian villages in the last decade, according to the latest census data. Much of the literature on Indian sex ratios has focused on a North–South dichotomy. This literature has argued that the northern and western regions of the country not only have more rigid norms of female seclusion – particularly related to participation in economic activities outside the home – but also have marriage customs, such as large dowry payments that make female children economic burdens on families. In contrast, women in the South and the East enjoy greater autonomy and higher social status within the family. These cultural differences manifest themselves in the form of lower sex ratios at birth in the northern and western states than in the southern and eastern states. The data is broadly consistent with these predicted patterns, but the picture is more nuanced. For instance, the phenomenon of low juvenile sex ratios has become more pervasive over time, and has spread to states in the South and the East. States which had more balanced sex ratios – Odisha, Gujarat, Maharashtra and even Tamil Nadu – than the northern states have, more recently, seen large declines in their juvenile sex ratios (Deolalikar, 2009).

In this backdrop, this study has been undertaken to support the broad perspective and vague understanding on the consequences of declining sex ratio on the social fabric. The findings and observations could be further used as a sensitization tool, generating mass awareness to make people realize the status of women vis-à-vis men and the repercussion of declining sex ratio in socio-economic paradigm.

Methodology

In our study the research methodology adopted is the qualitative research in which personal interviews with key stakeholders and respondents were conducted with the help of semi-structured questionnaire. Along with this, focus group discussion and community meetings in identified villages across different districts selected were also carried out to obtain more information in greater depth from the interviewers. The sources of data are primary which have been collected through field visits, recording of interviews, interaction with different non-governmental organizations (NGOs) and secondary data in the form of literature available to collate the findings.

To capture the regional variations on the consequences of declining sex ratio as a fall out of female foeticide, the empirical study has been carried out in some of the villages in six districts of Uttar Pradesh (UP) where the child sex ratio (CSR) is on the declining trend (Table 2). The surveyed districts are Jhansi in Bundelkhand, Moradabad and Bagpat in Western UP, Lucknow and Hardoi in Central UP, and Mau in Eastern UP. These districts have been selected after interacting with NGOs working on this particular issue in different villages of these districts to assess the intra-regional cause-effect relationship of female foeticide.

The State of Uttar Pradesh: Now Becoming Like Grave for Girls

The state of Uttar Pradesh is still a backward state. There are four economic regions in the state, viz., Western, Central, Eastern and Bundelkhand, and vast inter-regional disparities can be witnessed in terms of development and growth amongst these regions. If we consider the historical background of these regions then the reasons for killing girls have been different in various regions. For example, the western UP is basically agrarian in nature with feudal mindset. Moreover, this part of the state is comparatively more prosperous. Hence, there is both availability and affordability of technology in this region. Further, the land ownership makes the preference for the son stronger. If we think of Bundelkhand then it has a long history of honour killings and bowing head is something considered to be below dignity. Hence, daughters are less preferred as the father of the daughter has to bow his head down in front of the groom's parents. In the eastern and central part of UP dowry, illiteracy and backwardness together results in more inclination towards the sons. It can be inferred that the cultural roots and schizophrenic attitude of the people in the state has led to drastic decline in female-male ratio. Going extensively through the available literature, we all have been talking about why and how of female foeticide but the effects of this act are yet to be considered on a more serious note.

Table 2

Decline in Child Sex Ratio in UP (0–6 years)

Districts	*1991*	*2001*	*2011*
Jhansi	921	886	866
Moradabad	914	912	916
Bagpat	888	850	841
Hardoi	923	914	899
Lucknow	948	915	915
Mau	949	946	926
Total	945	916	902

Source: Census of India, various years.

The problem of female foeticide is a complex problem when viewed in context of social, economic and regional dynamics. The survey work was conducted in rural communities across different regions of the state and respondents selected were representative of total population in order to produce a miniature inter-regional analysis. This article will focus on direct and indirect repercussions of deficit of girls in the community and how the cultural, social and economic factors interplay in determining the status of today's woman.

Findings and Analysis

The issue of female foeticide raises the emotive and touchy concern for million of girls in India who fail to appear on the social scene not figuratively but in real demographic terms. The findings generated from the survey conducted across the chosen villages in the districts reflect a sorry state of affairs as far as the status of women is concerned.

Bridal Diaspora: Brought/Bought Women

Marriage remains universal and socially compulsory norm in India forcing the parents to marry their sons or daughters to whomever, wherever and at whatever cost. This seems to be the underlying rationale of a phenomenon which is called 'Bengali bridal diaspora' by

Ravinder Kaur (2010) whose observation and research shows that Bengali brides are to be found in almost all parts of the country, especially in northern region stretching from Kashmir down to Haryana, Punjab, towards the west in Gujarat and Rajasthan and across to UP in the north. We would like to call it only 'bridal diaspora' as during our field visit to different villages in the states, we found that the brides are coming not only from Bengal but also from other adjoining states like Bihar, Odisha and Chhattisgarh. These brides are migrating from far flung rural destinations away from their homelands to culturally strange new destinations. UP has a fairly large number of brides from across the border from Bangladesh as documented by Blanchet (2005) and also witnessed by us during the survey. This cross-cultural marriage which is actually the case of brought or bought women is termed as 'paro practice'. In the states where sex selection is most rampant, there are entire villages where men cannot find women to marry. So they are 'buying' women from other states. And, in some instances, where the family can afford to buy just one woman, she is expected to 'serve' all the men in the family. Meanwhile, according to recent reports, in villages in UP and Haryana, women are being sold as 'wives' for as little as ₹ 3,000. Impoverished women from Bihar, West Bengal, Odisha and Jharkhand are finding themselves in households where they do not speak the same language as their 'husbands' who have paid for them. An increasing number of studies and reports are now revealing that this is happening not just in Punjab and Haryana, the states with the worst sex ratios, but also in some districts of UP. It is possible that such incidents could be occurring in other states as well but have not yet been reported (Sharma, 2007). More studies devoted to the impact of past sex ratio distortions in north-west India have already shown that men unable to marry locally have resorted to the importation of brides from distant regions, lower economic backgrounds or lower caste groups. While this solution is compatible with hypergamy, strict caste rules may have to be stretched in order to allow marriage with distant communities. Moreover, dowry demands are likely to be reduced in order to facilitate such arrangements. These marriages may also be difficult to organize, thereby creating new networks (of villages, of match makers) or, at times, criminal organizations (women traffickers). Such practices are, of course, bound to intensify in the future, with unmarried men compelled to broaden their search radius even wider in order to reach women from other regions, low-status groups (UNFPA, 2007). The impact of female foeticide and declining sex ratio has resulted in desperate need of brides from other state. These cross-cultural marriages have been propelled due to female spousal shortages in the state as a whole. We also came across various such cases during our field visit to different villages in the districts of Lucknow, Jhansi, Mau and Hardoi where girls aged between 15–20 years were bought from Odisha, West Bengal, Chhattisgarh and Bihar (two from Bangladesh) in the name of marriage. The reason cited by the villagers for this cross state marriage was lack of availability of girls in their own or nearby villages.

The common feature in these cases has been poverty at their native place which has been a pushing factor for the girl's parents to marry their daughters to grooms from other state. Another interesting observation is that in all the cases interviewed the girls have more than three sisters which becomes a second reason for their parents to marry them to such grooms. The long distance marriage occurs due to its 'dowryless' nature as the expenditure is taken care by the needy groom. The males are so needy that despite of their having no means of earning, they arrange for funds so as to marry the girls from distant places. The need for women, for productive and reproductive purposes, is being addressed through unconventional marriages that are uniting rural, illiterate Indians across boundaries of region, language, religion, and even caste.

'Marriages are increasingly coming to note in which men from UP, Haryana, Punjab and Rajasthan are marrying women from West Bengal, Assam, Bihar, Andhra Pradesh and Tamil Nadu' (Kaur, 2004). An important implication which has surfaced from this analysis is that the social inclusion of these brought/bought girls is not always smooth. Furthermore the effect of declining sex ratio is that the girls are pushed into marriage market at very tender age indicating the failure of government efforts towards raising age of marriage of girls and also affecting their reproductive age.

Emergence of Dalals

It is in place to mention that the role of dalal or mediator is important in arranging marriages. Dalal/dalali refers to a male/female broker, agent or go between. The word often depicts a negative connotation. This mediator plays an important role in inter-state migration of persons in the form of marriages. Blanchet (2005) also reports about these kinds of mediators who indulge in trafficking women in the name of marriage. Kaur (2004) talks about the brokers and money spent in travel and the celebration of the marriage by the groom side. In the focus group discussion people from all communities categorically indicated that girls are not wanted in the village and this practice of non-preference of girls has increased further since last one decade.

There are two obvious reasons for this bridal diaspora or paro practice. Bengal, Odisha and Bihar remain the poorer states of India indicating failure of development and planning process. Going through the cases interviewed, at times women from poorer background are reduced to marry men who are not prosperous and have other disadvantages like they were much older, had been married earlier, were widower with many children or suffered from some physical disability. In the bride receiving societies the perception formed was not that such men could not find local brides because they did not have sufficient land or were jobless but given the shortage of local brides in the state, such men were unable to compete in local marriage market for brides, hence, were forced to look outside the state. Hence now in the market it is the survival of the fittest for the grooms.

It can also be interpreted that the *swayambar pratha* is re-emerging as the grooms are at the receiving end, and brides have the choice to whom they want to marry. When these boys are rejected in local market they move out to look for their partners in the foreign market. The sex selective abortion practice has disturbed the demand supply dynamics of brides. Families sell their daughters for some money to get some respite to their poverty thus ignoring the suitability factor of the perspective groom. Hence it is always the poor girl or women who are bearing the brunt of changing dynamics of marriage and are in no way being benefited of the so called shortage or the declining sex ratio. This practice is breaking the law of demand which states that if demand for anything is less then the price is high. In the marriage market although demand is high for the girls yet the price is not high instead they are often been married to old, unemployed and physically challenged males. It can be noted that males from the deficit state of UP are buying brides from other surplus states like Bihar, West Bengal, Odisha, etc., and if this trend of sex-selective abortion continues then many more healthy males shall also go for Paro Practice in years to come. UP's *chhatpat* weddings are the latest addition to the larger national marriage market that functions along a complex and intricate network of brides, grooms and agents. States such as Punjab and Haryana have taken to sourcing brides from states as far away as West Bengal, Assam, Bihar and Tripura, apart from neighbouring Himachal Pradesh (Sethi, 2007). Inter-state marriages is a common phenomenon in urban areas but in rural areas this kind of marriage alliance was earlier neither preferred nor welcomed and even today given a choice people would prefer to marry in their own community.

Mental Agony of Brought/Bought Women

The negative impact of marriage distance on women's status and autonomy (Dyson and Moore, 1983) is likely to be further heightened under cross-region marriage migration. Here, the marriage distance (defined as the distance between the bride's natal and conjugal home) can stretch to hundreds of miles taking a woman completely away from her familial, regional, linguistic and cultural contexts, compounding greater spatial distance with greater social distance (Kaur, 2004). As per our observations, the following factors put the brought/bought women in an uncomfortable state of mind:

(i) Women coming from other states are unable to relate with people around them. At times they are even boycotted from making their appearance in social functions like marriage or *sangeet* ceremony in village due to the language problem, communication barriers and cultural differences. Due to rigid attitude of rural people they face problem in cultural mixing.

(ii) They are not allowed to visit their native place due to paucity of funds at times or due to the fear factor that they might not come back to their respective husbands. Their right to expression is also violated as they fail to express themselves at their in-laws place due to communication problem.

(iii) Many a time these women are abused by the males of the village when they are socially not accepted in the community.

(iv) In few cases it is the children who also suffer in terms of their cognitive development because they speak in their mother tongue and finds themselves unable to mix up with other local children of their age.

Role of Frontline Workers

The frontline workers like Accredited Social Health Activist (ASHA) also have an important role to play at times in encouraging the practice of female foeticide. During our field survey in western UP it was found that one of the ASHA in Bania Kheda block in Moradabad told that she was instrumental in helping one of the couple of her village to abort the female foetus when she took the pregnant mother for ultrasound. The couple spent ₹ 5,000 and ASHA was paid ₹ 500 for this act. When we asked why did she do that she replied that the remuneration given by the government for handling each case is too less to support her family. In another case reported from village Mukari in Bagpat a brought woman from Bihar was a mother of eight girls. To our surprise when we asked her how she gave birth to so many girls, she said that out of four times when ultrasound was done the doctor misled her, every time by telling that she was carrying a boy foetus and hence she gave birth to eight girls eventually. In this case also ASHA helped to take her to ultrasound centre.

It needs to be mentioned here that at times it is not always the greed of fetching more mullas for ASHAs but their sympathetic attitude and concern for their fellow women which results in extending a hand of helpfulness by facilitating ultrasound facility to pregnant women. Here it becomes imperative to sensitize all frontline workers that how the declining sex ratio is going to affect the community in general and women in particular who are going to face various forms of violence against them.

Re-emergence of Forced Polyandry

According to social scientists, polyandry is derived from Greek word 'Polyandria' made up of 'poly' meaning many and 'andry' meaning men referring to the condition of a woman having many men. Polyandry is a form of union in which a woman has more than one husband at a time or in which brothers share a wife in common. One of the most important and probable cause of polyandry lies in demography. The disparity in sex ratio may be one of reasons for the prevalence of forced polyandry. 'The origin of polyandry must be referred to that want of balance. It is suggested that where polyandry existed, there is a surplus of male children but deficiency of females arises in all parts of the country as a biological phenomenon' (Lal, 2007). According to some researchers, the unequal distribution of family property among the brothers has indirectly encouraged the continuation of polyandry. On the other hand poverty and paucity of women may be the combined causes of forced polyandry. However, the implications are very tragic, grave, painful, and disastrous to contemplate. In western part of UP the sex ratio has become more adverse which has paved way to the issue of polyandry. In terms of marriage patterns, a shortage of potential brides may force men to delay their marriages. Marrying older is the first adjustment to adversely imbalanced sex ratios. But, the effect of delayed marriages for one generation of men will then be felt on the younger generation, as they become adults. As in a queue, unmarried men will accumulate as new cohorts of bachelors reach marriageable age. This growing pool of unmarried men will create a bottleneck that is unlikely to be solved solely by delaying marriages. Single men reaching 25 in 2025 and entering the marriage market will not only exceed the number of young women of corresponding age, but will also have to compete with a larger than expected number of older men who are still single. As a result, many of these men will not be able to marry. This means that not only will a significant share of men above 30 still be single, but also that many will never be able to marry at all. Of course, this assumes that marriage patterns do not undergo highly improbable changes, such as earlier female marriages, generalized polyandry (wherein a woman takes multiple husbands), same-sex arrangements or extremely high levels of divorce and re-marriage among women (UNFPA, 2007).

We also came across some cases of forced polyandry – *Desi Draupadi Pratha* or *Bahupati Vivah* – during the course of interviews in the villages of Bagpat and Moradabad districts in western UP where this practice is more prevalent and some of the narrations by the victims were really shocking. One girl was married to one boy legally but was later on forced into multiple relationships with her husband's brothers. In local proverbs this practice can be summarized as *'Aja beti le le phere, yo marega to aur bahutere'* (Come daughter get married, if this husband dies there are many more).

It needs to be discussed very strongly here that the impact of skewed sex ratio is making the position of women in the society far poor and derogatory. In all the cases of forced polyandry the dignity and self-respect of the woman is at stake. Although the cultural background of western part of the state may be considered to be a reason of this kind of practice meaning thereby that given the agrarian nature and land ownership issue, it has been a hidden practice that one brother marries and the wife is shared by other siblings yet, in our surveyed cases the issue of land ownership has not existed as the girls have been married to not so rich families. Therefore, non-availability of girls is leading to re-emergence of forced fraternal polyandry.

Unmarried Overaged Males: Female Drought?

The qualitative data collected by focus group discussions and personal interviews in rural villages of western UP gave insight into this third problem which is also the resultant of daughter drought. The patriarchal structure and values are ingrained for centuries and the practice of getting rid of daughters is known to exist in these areas such that certain social groups started feeling the deficit of brides for their sons. If a boy is unable to marry till the age of 22–24 years then he becomes over aged to get marry in rural areas. The problem is that the boys and their parents have failed to find brides in their own caste and communities. According to some, a few men are forced to remain bachelors. It can be interpreted that the use of modern medical technology has been at its worst as the daughters are being eliminated by choice with the help of sex selective abortions. If girls keep disappearing at this rate then boys will be in difficulty. Whom will the boys marry? Few prominent cases of forced bachelors came into light when we went to villages in Bagpat. It needs to be mentioned here that in the cases interviewed the mothers were ready to go for brought woman but the sons were reluctant to marry outside the caste.

Here, caste dynamics has played a dominant role in selection of brides. On the other hand the parents of girls want their daughters to get married to boys who are in service and settled in cities. So they are creating a monopolistic market where they are the choosers and not takers unlike the normal situations where it is the groom side which decides which girl to marry their boys. This trend reversal is an auto catalyst reaction of female foeticide. This is creating an imbalance situation between the brides and the grooms. Either the girl is not there, if she is there she is being shared by many males or else she is brought from other states. If the girls are not allowed to be born from where will the males get their brides?

Having analysed the socio-cultural dynamics of the Indian society, UP in particular, we observed that idolizing the son and ignoring the daughter has created multiple problems and is degenerating the social fabric of the state and the country as a whole. The insensitivity to this issue has reached its zenith and the parents are not hesitating to throw away their new born girl children in jungles, dustbins, riverside railway tracks or in any open space where the baby dies of hostile weather or becomes a pray for stray dogs. They may be many more abandoned children which are not even alive as they fall pray to dogs, animals and fishes as fresh flesh implying that there may be many more cases which do not come in notice even.

Conclusion and Suggestions

After having discussed in length about the consequences of skewed sex ratio and strong son preference it needs to be pondered more seriously that how can we transform the mindset of people in a positive way. It is indeed a perplexed situation that how the policies and programmes initiated by the government to control this menace are going to work not only in rural communities but also in urban population. To conclude, it can only be suggested that sensitization is the most important thing which needs to be done else it may take generations and centuries to take people out of the son complex situation. People should be made aware of this genocide and they must join hands to save our daughters from their journey from womb to tomb otherwise we shall land into 'no girl zone' one day. In a nutshell, a few more suggestions could be:

(i) Medical audits are of primary importance. They need to be strictly enforced so as to check the misuse of ultrasound machines, hence strict implementation of the Pre-conception and Pre-natal Diagnostic Technique (PCPNDT) Act by the government.

(ii) Special incentives and grants should be given to organizations so as to facilitate them to take up research and field action projects around the issue.

(iii) Campaigns at the grassroots level should be designed to sensitize people and generate mass awareness on the issue of female foeticide and its consequences.

(iv) The processes through which religious communities are intervening on the issue is also an area which needs to be studied and documented for further replication and learning. The religious dimension to the problem needs special attention.

(v) Positive images of the women should be encouraged and support of media should be incorporated.

(vi) Counselling facilities should be made available for the couple in family way to make them aware of the importance of girl child.

(vii) Frontline workers like Auxiliary Nurse Midwife (ANM) and ASHA appointed in the villages should also play a social policing role by discouraging the practice of sex selective abortions. They should be sensitized on the consequences of the declining sex ratio so that they do not become party in providing such services on the demand of the family. Their skill should be raised to say NO to it and not to succumb under pressure out of sympathy.

(viii) The population policy of the country needs to be re-looked. By and large the general population has misinterpreted the two child norm. This slogan needs to be redefined.

(ix) Schemes that give incentives to families where there is a daughter needs to be publicized and promoted at all-India level.

(x) Societal forums need to engage more to discuss and dialogue these socio-cultural repercussions and bring them to public domain. Youth should be actively engaged in such discourse.

(This is an improved version of the article published in the *Indian Economic Journal,* Vol. 59(2), July–September 2011).

References

A Sociological Report on Female Foeticide. 2003. Inter-State Workshop organized by Plan India and Vatsalya, Lucknow by Nav Bharat Jagriti Kendra, Jharkhand.

A Study of People's Perception on Female Foeticide in Uttar Pradesh. 2000. Conducted by Vatsalya, Lucknow and supported by Oxfam India Trust, Lucknow.

Blanchet, Therese. 2005. 'Bangladeshi Girls Sold as Wives in North India', *The Indian Journal of Gender Studies,* Vol. 12, Nos 2–3.

Census of India. Various Issues, Ministry of Home Affairs, Government of India.

Croll, Elizabeth. 2001. *Endangered Daughters: Discrimination and Development in Asia*, Routledge, London, 22 February.

Dyson, T. and M. Moore. 1983. 'On Kinship Structure: Female Autonomy and Demographic Behaviour in India', *Population and Development Review*, Vol. 9, No. 1.

Kabeer, Naila. 2000. 'Inter-Generational Contracts, Demographic Transitions and the Quantity-Quality Trade-off: Parents, Children and Investing in the Future', *Journal of International Development*, Vol. 12, No. 4.

Kaur, Ravinder. 2004. 'Across Region Marriages: Poverty, Female Migration and Sex Ratios', *Economic and Political Weekly*, Vol. 39, No. 25, 19–25 June .

——. 2010. 'Bengali Bridal Diaspora: Marriage as a Livelihood Strategy', *Economic and Political Weekly*, Vol. 45, No. 5, 30 January .

Kothari, C.P. 2008. *Research Methodology: Methods and Techniques*, New Age International Publishers, New Delhi.

Lal, Madan Mohan. 2007. 'Polyandry a Social System in India: Now State of Disappearance', *http://www.articlebase.com* (accessed on 15 May 2011).

Patel, Tulsi (ed.) 2007. *Sex-Selective Abortion in India*, Sage Publications, New Delhi.

Prasad, Shweta. 2001. Report on 'Female Foeticide: A Study of Varanasi', Centre for Women's Studies and Development, BHU, Varanasi.

Report on 'A Girl's Right to Live: Female Foeticide and Girl Infanticide'. 2007. Working Group on the Girl Child, NGO Committee on the Status of Women, Geneva.

Report on 'Reflections on the Campaign against Sex Selection and Exploring Ways Forward'. 2007. Conducted by Josantony Joseph and CYDA commissioned by UNFPA, India.

Report on 'Status of Implementation of PC-PNDT Act in Uttar Pradesh'. 2009. Conducted by Vatsalya, Lucknow, supported by Plan India.

Sethi, Aman. 2007. 'India: Gender Ratio Affects Marriage Norms in Uttar Pradesh State', *http://www.thesouthasian.org/archives/2007/gender_ratio_affects_marriage.html* (accessed on 5 January 2010). Supported by UNICEF, UP.

Sharma, Kalpana. 2007. 'World without Women', *The Hindu*, 18 November.

Shrinivasan, Rukmini and Himanshi Dhawan. 2011. 'Sense of Census: Save the Girl Child', *Times of India*, Lucknow, 1 April.

UNFPA. 2007. Report on 'Characteristics of Sex Imbalances in India and Future Scenarios', Hyderabad, India.

Visaria, Pravin. 1971. 'The Sex Ratio of the Population in India', Monograph No. 10, Census of India 1961, New Delhi.

Walia, Arjinder. 2005. 'Female Foeticide in Punjab: Exploring the Socio-Economic and Cultural Dimensions', *IDEA: A Journal of Social Sciences*, Vol. 10, No. 1, August 9.

11

Image and Reality

Portrayal of Tribal Women in Media

Gomati Bodra

Media texts are perceived to be one of the prime cultural sites through which it is possible to study the position of women in society. This is an arena within which our society presents itself publicly, defines our identity, establishes the parameters of consensus and relegates what is perceived as unconventional to the margins. In today's contemporary societies, the term 'culture' is used to describe the symbolic expressions of various characteristics – the ways in which they come to be represented in language, printed texts, sound, visual images, etc. These cultural forms are primarily mass produced and disseminated to wide undifferentiated audiences and are best described as 'mass culture'. Most of these are produced, marketed and distributed by global corporation that have been described as the 'culture industries' (Aderno, 1991) and produce most of what we would call mass media cultural forms that are produced and consumed on a mass undifferentiated scale. Douglas Kellner (1995), for instance, argues that we live in a media culture to the extent that the only culture deemed to exist is that produced and disseminated by the mass media. A media culture has emerged in which images, sounds and spectacles help produce the fabric of everyday life, dominating leisure time, shaping political views and social behaviours and providing the materials out of which people forged their very identities (Kellner, 1995).

The popular discourses have the tendency to view tribal women as homogenous group having similar life experiences. The subordination of tribal women operates at various and complex levels specially which lies in the various male-centric perceptions and definitions of most discourses which are decidedly mainstream. Traditional notions related to women's roles, social position, responsibilities, privileges, economic, political and sexual rights are determined and judged from the dominant cultural perspectives that clash with the ideals of tribal traditions. Linked to this very basic form of subordination, is the injustice inherent in the motives and mindset which go into the construction of the image of tribal women in media. Representation is a political issue. Without the power to define their interests and to participate in the decisions that affects them, the tribal women in media are subjected to the definitions and decisions of others, which serve the interests of the mainstream society. Dominant patterns of representation are constructed on the basis of socially and structurally dominant values which are in turn produced and reproduced through the same set of dominant representation (Moore, 1988).

Gender, Hegemony and Media

In media studies, hegemony refers to the ways in which the media encourage people to consent to status quo power structures drawing upon Marxism. Gramsci (writings of 1920 and 1930) conceptualized the theory of hegemony, which posits that oppressive regimes are able to stay in power through a combination of coercion and consent – with an emphasis on consent – and people must be taught to consent to everyday life behaviours and practices that keep the powerful people in power. According to Dave Harris (2007), the concept 'hegemony' takes on more specific implications from its use to explain forms of domination (e.g., by classes, ethnic groups or gender) within a nation-state. Mass media can be seen as having an important role in justifying the rule of dominant groups by supporting their claims to superiority and in trying to persuade the dominated to consent to this justification. People who specialize in formulating and disseminating ideas (such as journalists, priests, public relations companies, politicians, advisors and academics) are constantly engaged in interpreting current events and debates so as to fit dominant conceptions and categories (not always conspiratorially).

According to journalist P. Sainath, one of the fundamental features of the media is the growing discontent between the mass media and mass reality. There is a structural shutout of the poor in media and there is also a corporate hijack of media agendas. Finally, media is the most exclusive and most elitist. These are the reasons that determine the media coverage and representation of women in addition to the patriarchal social structure. Media cannot be considered as autonomous from other structures of the society. Media plays an important role in any country shaping public opinions, views, disseminating information, imparting public policies, providing entertainment. Media is not neutral and above structures that produce discrimination and biases in the society. The prevailing power structures determine equally the nature of media coverage and values. Undeniably, therefore, caste, class and patriarchy are operative to understand what media does and why, what it upholds, represents, highlights and what it chooses not to represent. There is an evident predominance of upper castes, middle and upper class, English educated urban men and women. No presence of dalits and tribals in the media is a reason for the negligible understanding or empathy for the issues related to them (Panikkar, 2009).

This article seeks to analyse the representation of tribal women in print media and popular cinema with the help of small slice of the print media. Few English newspapers persuaded are Times of India, Hindustan Times, The Hindu, Deccan Herald, Indian Express, and Asian Age that have been followed almost continuously since 1999. The focus had only been on the tribal women of central and south India and not of north-east. This paper specifically examines the portrayal of tribal women in an integrated overview of globalization, media representation and gender. This study on the representation of tribal women will try to locate the various frameworks of gender discrimination based on both content analysis and semiotics of print media as well as the review of popular cinema '*Chak de India*'. What is intended to be focused on is not the representation of difference and otherness within mass culture, but on the main vehicle of this representation – the tribal women. For this study the feminist perspective for analysing representation has been pursued. Drawing from both the dominant academic discourses of Anthropology and Modern Indian Literature, it has been reflected how the popular perceptions are being constructed, strengthen within the power structure of class, ethnicity and patriarchy, which further gets reinforced by the media hegemony, power and representation.

Print Media, Globalization and Tribal Women

The important social processes within which any meaningful reading of print media and representation of tribal women can be attempted today is the process of globalization and economic liberalization initiated in India. Newspaper history in India is inextricably tangled with political history. In the struggle for freedom, journalist in the twentieth century performed a dual role as professionals and nationalist. Until a few years ago, these were to do with the 'fourth estate' notion and watchdog standing. The news media were expected to have larger and long range concerns about society not just market compulsion or competitive concerns. The print media underwent dramatic transformation with the onset of liberalization. The overall transformation lies in the fact that today it is the sponsors who lay down the rules. There is a dramatic growth on advertisement sale and market strategies. After the liberalization of the economy, the growth of industry and arise in literacy, the post-emergency boom rekindled the world's largest middle class, in news politics and consumerism while capitalist sustain national news paper, the big houses, Dalmias, Jains, Goenkas, etc., monopolized and corrupted free journalism. On the other, the family and caste controlled regional small newspapers. The top 10 newspapers controlled roughly 50 per cent of daily circulation in all languages. This paradigm shifts involves bigger issues to do with consumerism which is a global phenomenon that dictates the media priorities today. Accompanying this are frequent write ups and articles on lifestyles of the rich and famous, interviews with models and fashion icons and cover stories on consumption patterns of new generations (Chaudhuri, 2000; Rao and Vasanti, 2005).

Portrayal of Tribal Women: Always 'The Other'

Media projection of tribal women have tendency to view tribal women as homogeneous lot having similar life experience. At the same time it also highlights exclusion and marginality in portrayal of tribal women. A content analysis of the print media clearly shows that a particular image of tribal women is being constituted which is very much influenced by the popular and complex discourses in social sciences. The first discourse positions tribes at the centre stage of anthropology. Objectification of tribes as the other, the exotic, pervades the concern. Another discourse raised the issue of gender and development, thereby viewing women as either active participant in conservation of their culture or helpless victim of the forces of globalization, cultural change and modernization (Mehrotra, 2004). Media reveals fundamental principles of upper caste perceptions and patriarchal thinking. Tribal women are projected as the other, the exception, the incomplete, the damaged and the marginal. Analysis of the contents demonstrated that they are depicted as the other of Indian mainstreams society living in forest. They certainly do not behave as was expected of an Indian woman of wider society. They were often projected as overtly indulging in free and premarital sex; they drink and also sell alcohol, dress in minimal clothes, etc. Mainly restricting the presentation of women to the physical function of sex and reproduction, women personality traits are depicted as being fundamentally different in nature from those of mainstream women. *Deccan Herald* (15 May 2005) under the headline '*Efforts to create a wonderful world*' wrote about different customs prevailing in different tribal communities. Bondo girls older by many years, marry a young boy who takes care of her when she is old. Eligible teenagers in Dhruva tribe of Chhattisgarh choose their own life partners. The girls wear a bone comb in their hair. The boys choose a girl, chases her takes the comb out of her hair and runs into deep forest. Her mission is to retrieve the comb and return to the village. That can be after a day or two, when the couple has had time to explore all the sexual rituals. Returning with the comb, she decides if she wants to marry him or not. If yes the dowry is decided by the family which could be in the form of a goat, chicken, banana and mahua. *Asian Age* (21 March 2006) writes about cultural change: '.... Earlier tribal women don't wear blouses and just cover their breast with their saari, but now the younger lot has started wearing trendy bras. It was those tribal women who got jobs in the outside world. Tribal girls are also initiating their friend in city school and hostels'.

Earlier definition of Indian tribes relied almost entirely on the theories evolved by anthropologist, colonial administrators, missionaries, social reformers and nationalists and historians. Throughout the long debate, only the tribal remained silent, because they wear beyond the pale of western learning and could not contribute to anthropological research. Hence, the primitive tribal identity came to be defined by the civilized world in terms of its own self-perceived identity. The western civilized gazed divided the world neatly into two parts – the primitive and the civilized. This binary gaze constructed the primitive other in terms of it own civilized self. In the process, primitive societies came to be defined in pejorative terms, such as wild, savage, backward, perverse and even criminal. A similar dichotomy was found in an Indian anthropology and modern Indian writings (Hansdak, 2007; Mehrotra, 2004; Pathy, 2000; Yadav, 2002) and which is also reflected in media.

The general remarks presents in these newspaper articles misrepresents the tribal people in general and women in particular, who are often depicted by cultural stereotypes. The focus is like always 'the other'. A title in *Times of India* (2 July 2007) states, *'Looking for a bride? Cook for the in-laws first'* reads 'after engagement a boy in nomadic Madari community are sent to stay at their in-laws house where they cook, clean, earn all to prove that they are worthy of winning the daughter's hand in marriage.

The most common role of women portrayed in media newspapers is as victims. The preference of the media for dealing with women as victims is a double-edged sword. On one hand the media creates public awareness about tribal women, thus advancing social debates and remedies. On the one hand the media's tendency is to eroticize, trivialize and sensationalize depicts the phenomena as the private battles of passive, unfortunate women rather than a structural inherent, social problem arising from power relations and inequality. One way or the other the media continues to perpetuate the impression of female as weak, passive and in need of male protection.

Even if the problems of tribal women are mentioned, the otherness is tried to be maintained, for example, in primitive tribe of Chakotia Bhunjia of Odisha, the women are not allowed to wear blouses, petti-coats and chappals and families ostracized girls as they take as high school certificate examination. The problem of abandoned unwed tribal women in Kerala, who are being lured and exploited by non-tribal men for anything spectacular even a pair of colourful bangles and the kui women from Kandamal district of Odisha who were also being married and deserted by non-tribal men. The article reads that, in fact, this phenomenon becomes so prevalent that Pulbani was called Premnagar or the city of love (*Deccan Herald,* 18 November 2000; 22 April 2005; 7 June 2007; *Times of India,* 18 March 2007).

The news article mentions the sexual abuse of tribal women by non-tribal men, they still reinforce the stereotype that adivasi women enjoy more freedom than the women of mainstream society as they are free from the pernicious practice of child marriage, dowry or prohibition of widow remarriage. Such perceptions view that tribal women are better placed than their non-tribal counterparts. Another indication of gender equality was sexual freedom which tribal women enjoy. Autonomy in terms of choosing the spouse and easy access to divorce, remarriage, etc., are perceived as great markers of their liberation or higher status. But all these are an upper caste perception (Mehrotra, 2004).[1]

The plight of the ordinary tribal women is also being pointed out. Health problems like miscarriage, still births, etc., among tribal women in Jadugora the site of India's uranium mines in Jharkhand and life of adivasi women head loaders who are the sufferers due to development induced displacement as land and forests being taken away by mega projects are mentioned. The plight of those tribal women is also being highlighted who are branded as witches and subjected to brutal torture and also killed in Jharkhand and Odisha. Another problem which the media points out is that minor tribal girls are trafficked in the name of marriage and then pushed into prostitution. But write ups are in a very different manner ... as stricken by poverty, the girls are eager to escape to a better life in Mumbai or Delhi. This somehow reflects a different almost negative attitude towards the freedom of movement which a tribal woman enjoys. This becomes much clearer with another issue of tribal domestic workers in Delhi. If one article writes about abuse and ill treatment of young maids who are lured into this job then another news piece on the same issue comes with a headline '*Delhi maids get upwardly mobile*' and '*Made to order maids makes a difference to Delhi themselves*' and it also refers them as maid in Manhattan (a 2002 Hollywood romantic comedy) The article reads '... when Maggi came to Delhi, she was terrified of traffic signals. After eight years – mostly with upper crust families – she's on to a blue chip all expense paid and no taxes career. She speaks English, bakes bread and take messages from American teacher of her employer's child .... They are being quoted saying, "I wouldn't get married and blow it up all". It further reads that maids from far away villages are arriving here to scale up their profession, like never before. Artless, rural girls are transforming themselves into smart and urbane professionals' (*Times of India*, 6 March 2003).

This again misrepresent the tribal domestic worker those who migrate from Jharkhand, Odisha and Chattisgarh and are concentrated in the lowest level of unorganized sector and these live-in-maids are constantly at the mercy of their employers (Alam, 1988; Wedge, 1995). Again this reinforces the stereotype since the physical mobility and earning of tribal women is depicted as empowered women who are free to make choices in life especially regarding migration, marriage and livelihood.

Interestingly, on one hand, she is being projected as a victim, but at the same time she is also considered to be brave especially when a tribal woman resists against injustice or participate in the resistance movement. But one thing is common. She is always branded as the 'other' and her activities are automatically related to the identity of that community. For example one headline in *Indian Express* (19 April 2001) read, 'Orissa tribal women admitted of murdering robber-rapist (it referred to a woman of Lodha tribe, which is a denotified tribe)'. Same is the case with women of Baawariya tribe in Delhi and National Capital Region regarding whom the media reports are that they were illegally kept in the lock-up. Women of Madhya Pradesh, Chhattisgarh and Jharkhand participating in the resistance movement or protecting forest were depicted differently as brave tribal women. Though bravery is considered to be a masculine trait, but it is associated with tribal women due to the popular perception that they are close to wilderness, forest, etc. The article further read that the '... the docile looking women armed with lathis and traditional weapons (bows and arrows), sickle, etc., roam around the forests and they confront mafia with courage – the women snatch away saws and axes, seize the vehicles'. Such depiction is to create emotional rhetoric and invasive picture which is very different and also oppose to the image of Indian Hindu and Muslim women. Who by contrast, are considered to be more sensible, homely and happily confined to domesticity. This framing of women by media was defined by Tuchman (1981) as symbolic annihilation achieved through the process of condemnation, trivialization and absence of women from media.

Globalization, Cultural Representation and Gender

Globalization has a direct bearing on the manner in tribal women are being represented within the English print media. The central consequence is that the primacy of lifestyle and its inevitability for individual agent. Simultaneously, there is a focus on selling and a construction of the ideology of consumption, individualism, free choice and good life. This new ideology celebrates the burgeoning growth of the market and main target is Indian middle class. Significantly a section as lifestyle is an integrated feature of all these national dailies (a newspaper supplement). Tribal women and their specific work many a time get featured under the column of art and culture. This particular aspect is related to traditional tribal clothes, embroidery work and jewellery which are basically a women's work and are considered to be traditional, ethnic and stylish, sellable with tremendous market value. It specially appeals to the urban upper middle class. An article in *Deccan Herald* (18 May 2004) about the art work of women in Lambani tribe in Andhra Pradesh read as '... their garment which represent high workmanship graphically depicts the different forms of art practices by Lambani tribes has always been close contact with nature. The colourful attire with all embellishments and crafty jewellery worn by their womenfolk has always fascinated the so called civilized lot. Other than their ivory bangles, jewellery is important to them as their traditional attire, silver toe rings, neck chains, specially made thumb ring, silver embellishment for the thread work used on their hair, broom takes sticks for the years, beats for the hair. A Lambani woman when she is in her traditional attire, beside colourful costumes revealing their back, they are considered extremely beautiful'. Such descriptions are also being about tribal women of Rajasthan, Gujarat and Madhya Pradesh. The cluster of binary concept used to 'make sense' of the world such as public–private, nature–culture, body–mind, reason–emotion have formed dualities in which women take the characteristics of the subordinated dependent partner which is made to appear opposite. This characterizing of women as body, emotion and nature has been used to place women's art making in connection with the home, the family and also with community. Such cultural representation states notions of gender difference, one of the key way in which gender is represented culturally is through the segregation of certain kinds of art making to women which are seen both feminine and inferior (King, 1992).

At the same time, the impact of globalization and consumer culture making in roads in tribal society is also being mentioned in a positive manner, completely ignoring negative impact. *Asian Age* (6 November and 21 March 2006) in an article titled *'Haute couture gets a vizag tribal make over'* mentioned that the tribal women of Andhra Pradesh are stitching clothes for famous brand such as Arrow, Combay, Duckhead, Enwear Nautice and D&T.[2] Another headline focused on the consumer culture *'MNC trigger cosmetic craze among tribal'.* Again the focus is marketing strategies and promoting consumer culture where even the tribal people are being looked as a potential target group.

Naked and Natural

The meaning of a representation is created by where it appears and what we bring to it (by its context and convention). The viewer and the reader are involved in a similar process. The tendency of our mind is like an art gallery and in everyday life is to classify and register our experience in terms of the known. We can see nothing; all our new seeing is formed by what we have seen before (Allen, 1992). It is very true to the use of still photographs by English print media related to most of articles about either tribes or tribal women. It clearly shows the conventional and generic understanding of the representation of tribal women.

A typical representation of exotic, conversely and her feminity is represented by half naked, dark skinned and wild. Most pictures show a tribal women of central India carrying bamboo baskets, pots or firewood, wrapping a piece of cloth, standing in the middle of the forest or selling rice beer in weekly Haat or dancing together. *The Hindu* (22 December 2006), in one of its articles titled *'Ray of hope: Rising awareness among tribal women',* wrote about the problems of health and lives. It also mentioned the life in the fortified camps of salwa judum. It read '... women are too scared, the nurse and the Anganwadi worker have stopped coming to the camps. There is no drinking water and everyday a couple of children die. No lady doctors are coming there so women are facing health problems. On one side there is police and on the other the Naxalites. People are caught between. People in camps are cut off from their livelihood .... But now few of them are being trained to become health volunteers called Mitanins, the Chhattisgadi term for friend. Mitanins are trying to take care of children and women's health especially pregnant women and also to provide nutritious meal.' Along with this article, a picture of two tribal women of Baster carrying bamboo basket on their head, wearing one piece of cloth in the middle of the forest was published. The question here is why not a photo of 'Mittian' and what if she is not a tribal women. Similar photographs were also published in *Deccan Herald* and *Hindustan Times*, along with the articles on the tribal forest bill. From this point of view, the combination of wilderness with feminity is strange, perhaps overall the images mean that for the conventional male gaze, Feminity is somewhat strange even abnormal especially when images comes from an unfamiliar culture. Roland Barth's (1972) work on images suggested that meaning are produced through the codes at work in representation and while that might appear to be natural, obvious, moment but they are in fact produced, they are constructed through identifiable process of signification at work in all representation. Meaning production takes place with social and historical context.

It seems clear that today's media draws heavily from traditional anthropological account and modern Indian writings. In most of the early ethnographic monographs, tribes are invariably represented as half clad, with only grass fibres and at times naked. Women have always figured in monographs on tribal societies. But early monographs depict them in exotic attires and poses and objectify them as things of beauty, sexuality and curiosity. This is seen in vivid pictorial forms in anthropological and other work. The basic assumption behind such account was that these groups were primitive, savage and backward. Some ethnographers like Elwin and Furer Haimendorf even celebrated such virtues among tribes. Elwin went to an extent of providing detailed narratives of the place of sex in tribal life, the sexual life of children, ideas of erotic attractiveness, wooing romance and frequency of intercourse among Baigas of central India. But such views dominated colonial ethnography and have undergone a change and does not present in today's anthropological writings (Xaxa, 2004).[3]

Even in the modern Indian writings which is apparently serious and sensitive work have the stereotype of seductive but shy, brave but submissive, hardworking but sleek 'wild women' appears and reappears in the work of many famous Indian writers (Hansdak, 2007; Yadav, 2002). Arun Joshi, winner of Sahitya Academy award for literature describes a tribal girl Bilasia in his famous novel *The Strange Case of Billy Biswas* only in terms of her anatomy and her magical, secret powers of seduction and in contrast to the social celebral, philosophical, conjugal, even spiritual dimensions awarded to the male protagonist (an urban middle class and US returned anthropologist named Billy Biswas who teaches in Delhi University). He also eroticicized the tribal women by speaking of uninhibited sexuality. Bilasia, who not only drinks and dances with abandon, but also chooses him (Billy) as her lover is consciously contrasted with Billy's civilized wife Maya. Another Oriya novelist cum senior administrator in the civil service, Gopinath Mohanthy in his famous novel *Paraja* eroticized tribal women by dwelling on her nakedness which emphasize sexuality that is innocent and unrestrained. There is an incident where Jilli and her sister Bili bathe naked at a pool under the surreptitious gaze of the forest guard. In *Paraja* Mohanty described the tribal dormitory as an idealized site for spontaneous love to flourish. Here young men address elaborate love songs to the women they love, to the accompaniment of the drum. The courtship ends with meeting often in the privacy of the forest. Sometimes, there are festivals where the young people dance through the night. This is also a secret world where all the courtship rituals are conducted at night and only young people participate. Moreover, the unending chorus of dancing and lovemaking seem to continue even while the lives of the people disintegrate (Hansdak, 2007).

Former secretary of the Sahitya Akademy and famous author Prabhakar Machwe's short story *Soma* which is about an orphaned tribal girl also depicts the gay abandon with horned dances and drinking parties. Here the author tries to draw a parallel between the tribal youth dormitory (Ghotul) and American dating culture, of course in a discussion between the male protagonist and the Christian priest. A Ghotul is being described where young men and women sleep together and pick up their life partner by trial and error method. The tribal woman is being referred as 'wild bird' living in the company of nature without any dress or apparel ... except a necklace of stones and a very small long cloth to hide her waist and below. This miniskirt also girded only when she had to visit the weekly bazaars. But, the Gond girl is also being referred as 'young smart nurse' when she is picked up by the missionary and trained as a nurse. But this transformation is short lived and on a festival day, '... when the drums were sounding hauntingly inviting, almost like under hypnotic charm ... she dropped her uniform and ran to the forest as if civilization was chasing her like an unseen abstract ghost'. The story ends with, '... the only thing she left behind was the dress she wore, the cape, the frock and even the underwear. She went back in the Eve's dress, in which she was born'.

Even Gita Mehta's novel '*A River Sutra*' is being criticized as she mentions the tribal only as decorative elements in a manner similar to their appearance in commercial Hindi films. There are suggestive references to 'sturdy tribal women' 'their sturdy bodies', etc., they are given to 'provocative laughter' and 'insinuative teasing'. As against their 'fierce' menfolk, they have 'slender' brown arms and full breast. These women, the narrator feels are knowingly voluptuous. The description of the tribal prototype Rima is couched in sensuous details ... Nitin Bose's story (male protagonist) is about 'the power of women who had enchanted him .... Her body encircled mine like a flowering creeper grips a tree ... the slender shoulders pulled forward by the weight of her breast ... the perspiration shinning on the narrow waist above the mango curve of her hips. In reality Rima, Nitin himself came to know latter is a coolie's wife whose limbs are "squat and ugly" and who is only one of the "bovine tea pickers", but the fact remains that "always she surprised my senses" "seduced ... with tribal songs"' (Pathak, 2003).

Most of the Indian novelists, while writing about tribal societies, assume the position of the outsider and are influenced by mainstream discourses on tribes and often reproduced the familiar stereotypes. There is the tendency to ignore the context and particularly the codes and ethics which governed the tribal life even in youth dormitory. According to Spivak, 'Context is seen as to anti-essentialism as to contextualize is to expose the history of what might otherwise seen outside history, natural and thus universal'. The obsession with nudity continues further in some of the well meaning, non-fictional documents like the well known Hindi writer Shanni's undoubted concern for the Maria Gonds in *An Island of Sal* notwithstanding, his description of Kosi has the making of an erotic poster, glossy and highly salable, '... She was then naked from head to navel, from ankles three fourth of her thighs. Her brown skin gleamed in the transparent clear air as she glided past on the forest path, arms raised to support the pitcher, higher convex breast ...' (Yadav, 2002).

Many a time this nudity of tribal women is tended to inspire the visual art which appeals to an urbanized aesthetic sense especially the male gaze. Sunil Janah, a young photo journalist from Assam, earned international acclaim first for his photographs of the 1943 Bengal famine and then of the Indian tribes. It is noted that Janah's photographs predominantly featured young tribal women. Explaining this reference, he said that, 'She represented youth, charm and vitality which are not quite destroyed in such people and which appear as irrepressibly as the hunger, I had gone to portray. For Janah, his frequent depiction of the innocent nudity of young tribal women contained an element of voyeurism (Hansdak, 2007).

Even in acclaimed flims like *'Aranyer Din Ratri'* and *'Agantuk'* by Satyajit Ray and *Mrigaya* by Mrinal Sen, the image of tribal women under the benign gaze of non-tribal value system, definitions and priorities is reduced to the stereotype of an innocent, earthy, sensuous, indispensable item in the bigger, more important scheme of things.

Representation of tribal women defined by and confined to the body and senses deprive them of their totality. They take the focus away from occasional flasks of the real possible present. Most of the newspaper articles on tribes and tribal women are supplemented with photos of half clad tribal women captioned as 'beautiful' 'attractive', etc., some are quite vague and unceremonious, 'mirth and merry making in tribal land', just like the ethnographic depiction, the literature. The visual art, for the English print media the female body remains a text indistinguishable from the subject that is woman. An act of discrimination involves the degradation of the subject and also its presentation as something exotic. The process of romanticization and exploitation is related one in that together they demean and commodify. Here, the so-called civilized gaze which is urban, non-tribal, upper caste is conveniently blended with male gaze (even though this media gaze is more impersonal and controlled) at the primitive other, and if the focus is women that it apparently becomes strange, exciting and exotic. According to Kumkum Sangari, in such representation, the tribals especially the woman is dark, inscrutable a kind of repository of unrepressed, orgiastic, magical sexuality, therapeutic powers and the unconsciousness and such a solution for the urban malaise (Hansdak, 2007).

But it is not that all writers and artists have eroticized the female tribal body. Famous Bengali writer Mahasweta Devi in most of her novels and stories uses the beauty of the primitive body to evoke a disturbing and horrifying image as well as a bitter critique of the dominated cultural perception. In her short stories '*Draupadi*' and '*Witch Hunt*' nakedness is used as a reminder of the exploitation a tribal woman suffers. In this discussion of media representation and images of tribal women, Mahasweta Devi's story '*Behind the Bodice*' requires a special mention. In this story the photographer who sells the photographs of the beautiful, nude Gangor, has no inkling of the consequences they would lead to. He is just one of the 'innocent' non-tribal who sell pictures of the nude and semi-nude tribal women to be printed on calendars, posters, etc. Her story is about the consequences of such 'harmless' exercises. Far from being entertainment or art, such images when repeated in the media deny women their dignity as humans and 'places them at risk'. Pornographic material, erotic art and newspaper might not fall under the same category, but they can lead to similar effects in everyday life of the underprivileged. They humiliate, embrass, commodify and demoralize women at every newspaper stall (Yadav, 2002).

In practice images are always seen in context they always have a specific use value in particular time and place of their consumption. This together with their formal characteristic, conditions and limits the meaning available from them at any one moment. Moments do not reside in the image then; they are circulated between representation, spectator and social formation.

Power and Representation

Popular culture is often identified as instrument for the imposition of hegemonic ideas; in Althussar's term one of the important ideological state apparatuses which ensure social conformity without use of naked force. In the popular Hindi cinema which is commercially oriented, popular art form, the tribals generally are not featured prominently. But even in some rear instance, the blatant bias is clearly visible, a Bollywood film in 1960s *'Shalimar'*, the tribals were presented as caricatures at the best, they were half clad men and women sporting feathers and beads, are seen either slaving or dancing for the benefit of their white western bosses (Yadav, 2002). In this section, I discussed the issues of power and representation within the operation of mass media, in representing tribal women. How it has been presented and explored in the cinematic narrative of 2007 popular Bollywood movie *'Chak de India'*. This movie was a landmark in so many different ways. It was based on sports, which is not a very successful genre in Bollywood. Directed by Shimit Amin it was not based on stereotypical romances with song-dance sequences or sentimental family drama.

This film has to be applauded as for the first time the tribal women were given some space as compared to other mainstream media like television or Bollywood cinema. At the same time their representation in the movie was not exoticized in their ethnic grab, as it was in anthropology and modern Indian writings but they were being portrayed as member of Indian women's national hockey team, playing for their country in the international arena. It shows the struggle of the two tribal girls who are unfamiliar to the dominantly spoken Hindi language and also to the civilized society. How they are the helpless when bullied by their team mates.

Indirectly *'Chak de India'* brings fore the actual problems of speechless tribal women of central India, who are being deprived of basic amenities like education, healthcare and employment, etc. The low grade education provided by the government schools does not equip students with proper linguistic ability, which is the least requirement to get a descent job. Irrespective of being very hard working the tribal women are still in the periphery of Indian society in general and tribal society in particular.

But my main focus over here is popular cinema's deployment of discriminatory stereotypes of women. This 'stereotyped-centred' approach is useful because it unpacks oppressive patterns of prejudice to show that such reduction are not just errors of perception but forms of social control. It reduces a complex variety of representation into a pre-established categories (Gosh, 2005). The portrayal was a complete contrast to the actual tribal field hockey players of Jharkhand, who have made it to the national team and have represented India in the international circuits. Even though they belong to small towns like Sundergarh and Simdega, most of them have done their schooling in Ranchi. Most of them are educated up to 10+2 level and few up to graduation. Most of them are employed with Indian Railways. Before making it to the national team, they have played for various states like Bihar, Odisha, Mumbai, Punjab, etc., and also organizations like Railways in various domestic circuits including Federation Cup and Senior National Tournaments. This gives them enough exposure to the mainstream world, as for being selected for the National team, these girls have to compete on the basis of their physical and mental strength.

The point which I am trying to argue is that education, white collar employment, exposure to the mainstream culture, competence and equal opportunity does bring a change in the personality and makes them quite assertive in their everyday life. As the popular picture of tribal women in cities is of construction labourer or of domestic worker (who come to the city for the first time and are severely exploited) which is more acceptable to the mainstream society and such projection help in maintaining the status quo and caste-class based social inequality. And popular cinema just like print media portrayal and also the modern Indian literature didn't give enough space to the changing tribal women and the tribal is invariably reduced to a silent subject (Hansdak, 2007).

Media images are ethnocentric in their construction of tribal women, they are implicated in the same landscape of stereotype which is organized around the needs, desires and demands of the mainstream society especially men, the exotic, savage on the one hand and the helpless victim on the other. Ethnocentricism has not only been limited to the media images. Historically, anthropology has emerged out and been sustained by a dominant western cultural bias. Anthropology has been and still critically involved in coming to terms with its own colonial past and with the power relationship which characterizes the encounter between those who study and those who are being studied (Asad, 1973; Moore, 1988). Women with different ethnic background and social class work within different representational framework. A difference of culture also implies a difference in generic understanding and conventions.

Conclusion

India is a multi-cultural country in which caste, religion, language, region, and ethnic background form important parameters for an individual identity. Gender identities are complicated by intersecting identities of class, caste, region, religion, language, ethnicity, age and sexual preference, signalling the inadequacy of gender only identity politics. Gender is obviously a critical ground of social positioning and influence on the scopic regime. It is based on the idea that individual's subjective capacity to interpret visual imagery is significantly moduled by his or her social position among other factors. Michel Foucault who explored the constitutive relationship of power and knowledge in a variety of discursive practices, Foucault's theory of controlling 'gaze' exercised through modern instruments of 'surveillance' has been particularly influential in interpreting artifacts of visual culture. All women neither feel nor read images the same way. Women's responses are as diverse as are women. What may be empowering for one person may be critiqued or ignored by another. Similarly, one women's negative image may be another's empowerment. Making sense of representation and cultural praxis hinges on a recognizing of identities as multiple, unstable, historically situated and products of ongoing differentiation (Gosh, 2005; Uberoi, 2006). A woman is not something fixed for all time, but is subject to transformation, contestation and change. While it is as important to be aware of continuity as well as change, this does not mean that it is an abstract women identity or condition which transcends history. Put bluntly, what it meant to be a woman in 1920 is different to what it meant to be a woman in 1990 or 2000. At the same time, while analysing representation it is also important to interrogate cultural issues especially certain aspects of culture. Such as national or regional history, ethnic identity, religious affiliation and sexual identity enter into the making and consumption of media messages and social relations associated with this process, though one finds evidence of creeping change in the images of the tribal women in media, but still an unrealistic picture of the world presented by the media leaves women at the margins of the social, economic, cultural and political processes. There is a need to recognize them as specific individual rooted in historically and culturally specific contexts, as well as active participants in socio-economic and political life of India.

Ethnic minorities like tribes are underrepresented as media persons and the role of active audience is missing in the case of tribal women that are one of the reasons for such constructed, negative and unequal representation of tribal women, which are often depicted by cultural stereotypes. It may reflect historically longstanding patterns of ethnic inequality. The non-prejudicial representation in media does not mean hiding cultural differences behind contrived sameness. In fact the cultural differences enrich the overall Indian culture, but representation of tribal as the unequal other however seems to call forth images that reflect and feed ethnic stereotypes harboured by many Indians. It is true that tribes practically live on the fringes of the so-called civilized sections of society that generally define the norms for national culture. The failure of media demonstrated to larger issues involving the nation-state's failure to accommodate all dimensions of its social structure in its self-representation.

The exclusion and marginality of tribal women from the public sphere especially the forum of political, cultural and economic power is achieved through processes of self-negation of self-identity, abrogation of rights and repressions. The media did not invent women's inequality and victimization and they cannot be held solely responsible for the existence of discrimination. Yet the images they present can reinforce by glorifying the situation and presenting it as the normal or expected state of affairs. Constant distorted depiction may even mislead or blind people and it also tempts to believe that ethnic minorities like tribes are non-existent and unimportant part of Indian society. Exposing the ideological ties between socio-economic and political reality and media images representing it is but one step toward cracking the walls of hegemony.

Notes

1. Taking the meaning of images as self-evident and extracting them from both the context of the text in which they appear and a wider cultural context in which they are produced and consumed is highly problematic. It is necessary to consider how the meaning of the text will be constructed differently according to the discourses (knowledge, prejudices, resistance, etc.), brought to bear on the test by the reader. For example, the media images that the white, middle class, professional Betty Friedan interpreted as damaging to the women in 1950s were the very same images of femininity which some working class women may have found liberating. For details, see Joanne Hollows (2000). *Feminism, Femininity and Popular Culture*, Manchester University Press, New York.
2. Quite similar to this is the Vogue photo shoot, where the rural Indians are used as props to sell haute couture. Neither can they afford them nor can they fit into the aesthetic qualities expected by media, managed by middle-class professionals and catering to middle-class audiences. But these media images are at times appropriated for the fetishism of

commodities referred to as ethnic or for an elite conception of a diverse nation. For details, see Kishore Budha (2008). 'Subaltern Media', *Critical Stew*, 10 December, *http://criticalstew.org*. accessed on 10 December 2012.

3. According to V. Xaxa, tribes have been primarily studied either with reference to the values of the European Enlightenment, viz., freedom, equality and fraternity or in relation to values prevalent in the dominant Indian society in which freedom is often scorned and hierarchy is much valued. Hardly any attempt has been made to study them in terms of values prevalent in tribal society.

References

Aderno, T. 1991. *The Cultural Industry* (originally published in 1944), Routledge, London.

Alam, J. 1988. 'Urban Migration Among Tribal Women: Obvious Reasons Hidden Impact', *LILA-Asia Pacific Women's Studies Journal*, Vol. 7.

Allen, Richard. 1992. 'Analysing Representation', in Frances Bonner, Zizbeth Goodman, Richard Allen, Linda Janes and Catherine King (eds), *Imagining Women: Cultural Representation and Gender*, Polity Press, Cambridge and London.

Asad, Talal (ed.). 1973. *Anthropology and the Colonial Encounter*, Ithaca Press, London.

Baehr, Halen and Ann Gray. 1996. *Turning It On: A Reader in Women and Media*, Arnold Publishers, London.

Barth, Roland. 1972. *Mythologies*, translated by Annette Lavers (first published in 1957), Les Lettres Nouvelles, France.

Blackwell Encyclopedia of Sociology. 2007. Blackwell Publishing, Malden, *http://www.blackwellreference.com*. accessed on 12 December 2012.

Chaudhuri, Maitrayee. 2000. 'Feminism in Print Media', *Indian Journal of Gender Studies*, Vol. 7, No. 2, p. 2.

Dave, Harris. 2007. 'Hegemony and Media', in George Ritzer (ed.), *Blackwell Encyclopedia of Sociology*, Blackwell Publishing, Malden, available at www.blackwellreference.com, accessed on 12 December 2012.

Gosh, Shohini. 2005. 'The Troubled Existence of Sex and Sexuality', in Mala Khullar (ed.), *Writing the Women's Movement: A Reader*, Zubaan Publications, New Delhi.

Harris, Dave. 2007. 'Hegemony and the Media', in *Blackwell Encyclopedia of Sociology*, Blackwell Publishing, Malden.

Hansdak, Ivy. 2007. 'The Nation and the Indian Tribes: A Diachronic View', in Meenakshi Mukherjee, Harish Trivedi and Vijay Kumar (eds), *Nation in Imagination*, Orient Longman, Hyderabad.

Kellner, D. 1995. *Media Culture*, Routledge, London.

King, Catherine. 1992. 'Making Things Mean: Cultural Representation in Objects', in Frances Bonner, Zizbeth Goodman, Richard Allen, Linda Janes and Catherine King (eds), *Imagining Women: Cultural Representation and Gender*, Polity Press, Cambridge and London.

Machwe, Prabhakar. 2008. 'Soma', in Suresh Kohli (ed.), *Modern Indian Short Stories*, Imprint One, New Delhi.

Mehrotra, Nilika. 2004. 'Situating Tribal Women', *The Eastern Anthropologist*, Vol. 57, No. 1, p. 1.

Marries, Paul and Sue Thornham (eds), 1997. *Media Study: A Reader*, Edinburgh University Press, Edinburgh.

Moore, Henrietta. 1988. *Feminism and Anthropology*, Polity Press, Oxford, UK.

Panikkar, Sumati. 2009. 'Women and Media: An Unequal Relationship', *Women's Link*, April–June, Vol. 15, No. 2.

Pathak, R.S. 2003. *Marginalised Voices: Indian English Literature*, Creative Books, New Delhi.

Pathy, J. 2000. 'Tribe, Region and Nation in the Context of Indian State', in S.L. Sharma and T.K. Oommen (eds), *Nation and National Identity in South Asia*, Longman, New Delhi.

Rao, N. Bhaskara and P.N. Vasanti. 2005. 'Media Scene as India Globalizes', *http://www.cmsindia.org*. accessed on 12 December 2012.

Ross, Karen and Carolyn M. Byerly (eds), 2004. *Women and Media: International Perspectives*, Blackwell Publishing, Malden.

Tuchman, G. 1981. 'The Symbolic Annihilation of Women by the Media', in S. Cohen and J. Young (eds), *The Manufacture of News*, revised edition, Constable, London.

Uberoi, P. 2006. *Gender, Family and Popular Culture in India*, OUP, New Delhi.

Wedge, A. 1995. 'The Tribal Domestic Worker at Crossroads: A Search for Alternatives', a Report on Status of Domestic Working Women in India, New Delhi.

Xaxa, V. 2004. 'Women and Gender in the Study of Tribes in India', *Indian Journal of Gender Studies*, Vol. 11, No. 3, September–December.

Yadav, Kumkum. 2002. 'You and I Belong to Two Different Worlds: Feminism, Tradition and Modernity in Relation to the Representation of Tribal Women in Modern Indian Writing', in Chandrakala Padia (ed.), *Feminism, Tradition and Modernity*, IIAS, Shimla.

12

Changing Face of Women Entrepreneurship in the Globalized Indian Economy

Mir M. Amin and Farooque Ajaz Shah

In the present era of globalization, any economy's strength is known by its quality of 'human and knowledge capital'. There are evidences to believe that countries, which have proportionately higher percentage of entrepreneurs in their population, have developed much faster as compared to countries, which have lesser percentage of them in the society. India with her vast human resources can progress and prosper more, if and only if, the women population is put into productive use. Entrepreneurship is one of the main tool through which women can become economically independent, gain empowerment, social recognition, status, and equity. Evidence suggests that entrepreneurship in general contributes in various ways to economic development and job creation. From a public policy perspective, promoting the entrepreneurial dynamic of a country should be an integral element of any government attempt to boost overall economic growth and prosperity.

It is very difficult to draw a clear-cut distinction between entrepreneur and entrepreneurship. Broadly, an entrepreneur is defined as an innovator with potentialities of doing things in a new way while entrepreneurship represents the dynamic process concerned with various actions with a view to bring about breakthrough product/service innovations. Thus, entrepreneurship reflects the process which involves taking the initiative, preparing a blueprint, then implementing, building enterprise, maintaining and achieving goal rather than conceiving ideas but not able to pursue the process of commercialization of new ideas or the existing new knowledge.

In India, entrepreneurship among women is comparatively a recent phenomenon. Women entrepreneurs may be defined as a woman or a group of women who initiate, organize and operate a business enterprise. The Government of India has defined a women's entrepreneurship venture as an enterprise owned and controlled by women, having a minimum financial interest of 51 per cent of the capital and giving at least 51 per cent of employment generated in the enterprise to women.

A woman entrepreneur is an individual with an eye for opportunities, an uncanny vision, a commercial acumen, a capability for tremendous perseverance and above all, a willingness to take risks with the unknown because of the adventurous spirit she possesses. She, like a male entrepreneur, has to perform many functions like exploring the prospects of starting a new enterprise, undertake risks, introduce new innovations and technologies, administer, coordinate and control business and provide effective leadership in all facets of business.

Review of Some Selected Literature

Economic empowerment business ventures usually focus on income-generating activities, which allow women to acquire their income independently. Income-generating activities encompass a wide range of areas, such as small business promotion, cooperatives, job creation schemes, sewing circles and credit and savings groups (Albee, 1994). Women entrepreneurship creates job for the entrepreneur as well as income. Woman entrepreneur is an individual who takes up a challenging role in which she constantly interacts and adjusts herself with social, resource and support spheres in a society (Pareek, 1992).

Women entrepreneurship is expanding around the world. Studies have shown that women-owned businesses comprise between one-quarter and one-third of businesses in the formal economy and are likely to play an even greater role in informal sectors (Peacock, 2003). From the 1990s, with increased levels of education, more women have opted for entrepreneurial careers in plastics, electronics and leather related industries. However, overall women entrepreneurs gravitate towards ventures with low investment and lesser technological barriers (Lakshmi, 1998; Lalitha Rani, 1996; Sharma and Dhameja, 2002).

According to economists, entrepreneurship and its creation (organization) are a result of inappropriate value-price composition in the market place. This view, of course, assumes reasonable efficiency in the economic environment. From the technological perspective, entrepreneurship is technology-driven and innovation enabled. It is a means by which superior products and services can be identified and delivered in a competitive or consumer sensitive market. A third view suggests that entrepreneurship is a business process by which creative individuals seek and identify market opportunities and organize a set of activities to respond positively to such opportunities. Often entrepreneurship is seen as an extended version of an individual's leadership, passion, personality and conviction. In the developed world, this is a standard form of wealth creation and distribution. In the developing countries, this is a positive response to inefficient organization of products and services. In an emerging economy like India, the relevance of entrepreneurship is not only pronounced but also critical.

A really path-breaking contribution to the analysis of entrepreneurship from a broad historical perspective was offered by Joseph Schumpeter in his book *The Theory of Economic Development* (1934). Starting from a circular flow of goods and money of a given size in a static context, he argues that without growth or economic progress there is no scope for entrepreneurship. At best, it generates additional jobs and (financial or non-financial) incomes for other people. Schumpeter (1961) defined entrepreneur as an agent for change – an innovator.

The third Millennium Development Goal (MDG), i.e., promoting gender equality and the empowerment of women, has given prominence to recent efforts to address 'gendered poverty'. Gendered poverty is the recognition that women and men face poverty for different reasons and both experience and respond to it differently. Research on gendered poverty has found that impoverished rural and urban women face many of the same constraints. They both suffer from low socio-economic status, lack of property rights, environmental degradation and limited health and educational resources. Many studies have recognized the importance of economic empowerment in improving the status of impoverished women. Women entrepreneurship is thus a powerful means to increase her economic status in the society.

In the process of entrepreneurship, women have to face various problems associated with entrepreneurship and these problems get doubled because of her dual role as a wage earner and a homemaker. According to Reddi (1991), women entrepreneurs in Goa feel frustrated at times because they need to spare their time and energy, both towards their business as well as domestic affairs. Women in India constitute a larger proportion of total unemployed population and hence it is imperative to find out the entrepreneurial constraints faced by them.

A strong small business sector and entrepreneurship are generally linked to a strong economy (Beck, Demirguc-Kunt and Levine, 2005). Across developed and developing countries, entrepreneurship has become a critical part of economic development strategies. Entrepreneurship achieves important functions related to efficiency, competition, product innovation, pricing and industry survival by acting to disequilibrate (Schumpeter, 1934) to equilibrate (Kirzner, 1997) or to do both (Hall, 2007) in the market.

Since the seminal work by Hisrich and Brush (1984) in which they profiled distinguishing characteristics of female entrepreneurs, the past 25 years have seen a steady increase in the number of studies on women entrepreneurs. Key issues addressed have included educational and work background, psychological characteristics, motivation, perceptions of career efficacy, training and skill development, comparative earnings levels, management practices, external networking, desire to succeed, and obstacles encountered (Birley, 1989; Brush, 1992; Dumas, 2001; Green et al., 1996; Robinson, 2001; Stevenson, 1986). At the same time, only limited attention has been devoted to understanding the growth aspirations of women entrepreneurs in different sectors of the Indian economy.

It has also been observed that women start ventures which grow at a slower rate than those owned by men (Cliff, 1998; Hisrich and Brush, 1984) notes that, compared to males, female entrepreneurs tend to set lower business size thresholds beyond which they prefer not to expand and to be more concerned with risks attached to fast growth. These conclusions are backed by more recent statistical evidence. Female entrepreneurs tend to be older and have children in more instances than their male counterparts when starting a business (Sarri and Trihopoulou, 2005). Women-owned businesses tend to be smaller with less capital, have lower revenues and fewer employees and reside in lower-profit industries.

Women tend to be sole owners and have less managerial experience (Hisrich and Brush, 1984). In terms of personal characteristics, women demonstrate lower levels of self-confidence (Brush et al., 2004; Chaganti, 1986) suggest that the broader stated aspirations of women business owners actually create a detrimental perception that women are less focused and driven to succeed in their businesses than men, resulting in difficulties obtaining institutional- or venture-capital financing.

Entrepreneurship offers tremendous opportunities for women across the world by opening doors to greater self-sufficiency, self-esteem, education, and growth – not only for the women themselves, but also for their families and their employees. And women are changing the face of business ownership internationally; between one-quarter and one-third of the world's businesses are owned by women. As their numbers grow and as their businesses prosper, they will change the way the world does business.

Objectives of the Study

From the above literature survey, it came to light that till now no study has focused specifically on the changing role of women. Thus, the purpose of this article is to obtain a clearer and more comprehensive picture of women's contribution and to discuss the concrete barriers and constraints that are responsible for poor women entrepreneurship in India. Therefore, in the light of above, the present article is designed to cover the following objectives:

(i) To study introductory background, characteristics and causes of women entrepreneurship in Indian context.

(ii) To assess the participations of women in the Small and Medium Enterprises in India.

(iii) To identify and analyse the various problems faced by women in business in India.

(iv) To present some recommendations and suggestions so that women may be encouraged to take small, medium and big size entrepreneurial ventures in India and they can be empowered economically and contribute significantly to the Indian economy.

Women and Work: A Snapshot

At present nearly 48 per cent of India's population are women, i.e., nearly 50 crore. Of the total workforce of 39.7 crore, 12.4 crore are women. Out of the 10.6 crore women working in rural areas, 75 per cent of them are in agricultural sector and overall 7 per cent of the total workforce is in organized sector and 93 per cent in unorganized sector (including agriculture). A big example where women are working in unorganized sector with unskilled jobs is found in construction sector carrying bricks, sand, mortar, etc., whereas the skilled job like masonry, carpentry are carried out by men. In India, women these days play a crucial role in all walks of life and they contribute to the national economy both in terms of Gross Domestic Product (GDP) and Gross National Product (GNP). According to one of the estimate, invisible work of housewives contributes nearly one-third of India's GNP. It is regrettable to state that even after this large contribution, women's contribution continues to be unaccounted and invisible. Thus, they are usually discriminated and deprived due to one factor or the other and this may be due to lack of access to education, skills, healthcare, sanitation, etc. But unfortunately very few women entrepreneurs are in the big enterprises. They are mainly concentrated in the small-scale industry (SSI) working as owners, managers or employees of the enterprise.

In the current scenario of globalization, one can identify a large number of women preferring and participating in diverse, dynamic and non-traditional areas. Some of them participate in establishing their own business enterprises, while the small ones prefer to take different professions like banking, insurance, teaching, trainers, etc. And it is interesting to point out that changes in the nature of women's work, volatility of employment, increase in unpaid work, massive increase in women's migration for work, etc., are some of the characteristics of women's work in India. There is no doubt that during the last 10–15 years, there has been perceptive progress of women education especially higher education whereby quite a large number of educated women have acquired professional and technical degrees and skills. Thus, many of these women could be identified and encouraged to be associated with the women enterprises. Moreover, in order to improve the success rates of women entrepreneurs, they may be motivated to take up women entrepreneurship as self-employment activities. As a result of this, increasing number of women are now-a-days entering the workforce in India due to the factors like greater participation in higher education, women emancipations, increased economic need, additional measures of managing different set of problems at workplace, various women oriented training programmes, policies, government programmes and schemes, etc.

In the twenty-first century, women are taking part in every segment and sector of the economy. Thus, they are competing neck to neck with the men in professional and non-professional activities, enjoying more freedom and power than ever before. However, they are still disadvantaged when compared to men in almost all aspects of life in terms of equal access to education, healthcare, capital, and decision-making powers in the political, social and business sectors. According to the United Nations, men are credited with performing three quarters of all economic activities in developing countries whereas women actually perform 53 per cent of the work. The United Nations Human Development Report, 2005 comments that 'an estimated 16 trillion dollars in global output is currently "invisible", of which 11 trillion dollars is estimated to be produced by women'.

The real tragedy is that women are often better economic stewards of capital than men. Research has shown that women more likely to reinvest profits back into human capital than men. When women have economic power (defined as control of income and capital) they gain more equality and control over their own lives, while contributing directly to their children's development (nutrition, health and education) and thereby indirectly to their nation's income growth and development.

Factors Responsible for Women Entrepreneurship

In this part of the article, characteristics of women entrepreneurs and subsequently factors responsible for women entrepreneurship are highlighted. Woman entrepreneurs tend to be highly motivated and self-directed. They also exhibit a high internal locus of control and achievement. Researchers contend that women business owners possess certain specific characteristics that promote their creativity and generate new ideas and ways of doing things. Generally women business owners are found to have high risk-taking propensity, intense focus, high energy level, personal motivations, general business management skills, social adroitness, interpersonal skills, competence in finance, and in managing relationships.

Women are becoming entrepreneurs at a more than proportionate rate compared to men (Renzulli et al., 2000). One of the qualities that women entrepreneurs cite as key to their success is the ability to focus intensely. For example, Neff and Citrin (1999) have pointed out that Elizabeth Dole, as the former head of the Red Cross (one of the world's largest non-governmental organization), managed 1.3 million volunteers, revenues of 2.l billion dollars, and supplied relief to victims of more than 60,000 natural and man-made disasters each year. According to Dole, '*focus*' was the key for 'the management of inner resources'. Other women entrepreneurs also cited '*focus*' as a principal characteristic enhancing their successes. Women business owners' opinions are supported by a comparative study in Estonia, Russia and Scandinavia by Kauppinen-Toropainen (1993) and by interviews conducted by Neff and Citrin (1999).

Women are choosing both the traditional (toy-making, pickle-making, candle-making, etc.) as well as the non-traditional (garment shop, beauty parlour, computer training, school management, etc.) activities and are performing well. Training approach is important for helping women in non-traditional, high skill, male dominated activities and also to build-up the confidence among women to meet their requirements (Kirve and Kanitkar, 1993). Training to develop good entrepreneurial skills is useful and essential to women (Padmavati, 2002; Sathyasundaram, 2004).

In sum, we can say that women entrepreneurs share characteristics like sharp communication skills, intuitive people skills, consensus building competencies and nurturing, integrating abilities. Women need to use all these skills as they strive to make appropriate decisions for their families and for their business enterprises. The reasons for the women to enter into the field of business and pursue entrepreneurship are slightly different from those of men. These factors may be categorized as pull and push factors. Pull factors may be defined as those which naturally initiate entrepreneurial activities by women. These factors may be instrumental in bringing about a dynamic change from the regular 'housewives' to 'entrepreneurs' and thus help them to transform from being home economist to market economist. These factors may be mentioned as follows:

(i) A strong urge to prove themselves in the society,
(ii) A high need for achievement factor,
(iii) A dominant will to exploit dormant and latent entrepreneurial skills,
(iv) To become an independent individual by breaking the shackles of the age-old societal confinements,
(v) To hold a position in the society, contribute and harness the growth of the country's economy.

The push factors are those which are external in nature. There may not be an internal will and wish to become an entrepreneur but external circumstances leave no choice before them, other than to start their own business enterprise. These factors may be summed up as follows:

(i) Women resorting to move out and venturing into business due to the financial problems of the family,
(ii) Unemployment of the spouse or low wages earned by the other members of the family,
(iii) Extreme and dire requirements for money to have a basic livelihood, etc.

As a result of the above factors, the role of women worldwide is undergoing a dramatic change. Working women are no longer a rarity and are now accepted as integral part of the working force. Indian organizations, now-a-days, have experienced a steady increase in the number of women entrepreneurs and this pattern is bound to continue in the future. Women recently began to join the ranks of leaders in large numbers. For example, there are women who are working shoulder to shoulder with men in big business. They all are successful women entrepreneurs and are also now big names in the business world, for example, Ekta Kapoor, Creative Director, Balaji Telefilms; Kiran Mazumdar Shaw, CEO, Biocon Limited; Maureen Wadia, President, Gladrags Beauty Pageants; Shahnaz Hussain, CEO, Shahnaz Herbals; Parameshwar Godrej, Godrej; Indra Nuyi, PepsiCo; Chanda Kochar, ICICI Bank; Veena Patil, Kesari Travels; Vimlaben M. Pawale, Ex-President, Sri Mahila Griha Udyog Lijjat Papad (SMGULP); Anu Agha, Thermax;

Rajashree Birla, Birla Group; Bector, Cremica Industries Limited; Vandana Luthra, VLCC.

For any country, the availability of entrepreneurial skills is an important asset and an instrumental force for its economic development. General Gunderson has rightly remarked that 'not resources, not protestant ethics but entrepreneurship explains economic growth'. In India, entrepreneurship among women is significant for the following reasons:

(i) more status and respect in the society which raises self-confidence,
(ii) makes women economically self-dependent,
(iii) fullest utilization of available human resources,
(iv) accelerated pace of industrial development,
(v) availability of best and non-controversial policy related to empowerment of women, and
(vi) promotion of equality and opportunity and human dignity.

Besides, now-a-days, companies encourage having maximum women in their workforce. For example, IT giant Wipro Technologies are proud to announce that the ratio of women workers in Wipro rose to 21.22 per cent in April 2005 from 18.75 per cent in 2004. Even in Infosys, the number of IT professional women has increased from 19 per cent in 2003 to 22 per cent in 2004 and 24 per cent in 2005.

Women's Participation in Small and Medium Enterprises (SMEs)

SMEs sector is the only sector where the presence of women is extremely visible. The participation of women in this sector can be identified in terms of three different roles. Some women are the owners of enterprises, some are managers of enterprises and some are the employees. SMEs sector in India is very large in nature consisting of approximately 3.57 million units, which produces more than 8,000 products. The share of the sector in overall export of the country is 34 per cent and in direct export it is 45 per cent. The sector generates 19.96 million employment of the country.

According to Annual Report of 2011–12, the total number of women enterprises in the total SMEs sector was estimated at 2.15 lakh (13.72%). The estimated number of enterprises actually managed by women was also 13.72 per cent. In the states of Mizoram, Odisha, Karnataka, Goa, Lakshadweep, Kerala, Tamil Nadu and Puducherry, the share of women employment is significantly higher (more than 20%). Table 1 shows the position of women entrepreneurships and women enterprises spread all over the country.

Table 1
State-wise Women's Participation in SMEs Sector

Name of State/UT	*No. of Enterprises Managed by Women*	*No. of Women Enterprises*
Jammu & Kashmir	5,640	5,742
Himachal Pradesh	3,515	3,722
Punjab	30,190	29,068
Chandigarh	2,059	2,243
Uttaranchal	8,706	8,804
Haryana	10,087	9,620
Delhi	13,368	14,383
Rajasthan	29,785	36,371
Uttar Pradesh	54,491	72,667
Bihar	38,170	49,443
Sikkim	30	98
Arunachal Pradesh	131	150
Nagaland	207	179
Manipur	9,168	10,745
Mizoram	3,076	3,700
Tripura	631	863
Meghalaya	3,658	3,580
Assam	11,189	11,757
West Bengal	71,847	69,625
Jharkhand	7,271	7,865
Odisha	33,274	38,233
Chhattisgarh	11,766	10,034
Madhya Pradesh	62,351	68,823
Gujarat	55,361	53,703
Daman & Diu	167	213
Dadra & Nagar Haveli	167	213
Maharashtra	80,662	1,00,670
Andhra Pradesh	77,347	77,166
Karnataka	1,01,264	1,03,169
Goa	677	810
Lakshadweep	61	67
Kerala	137561	1,39,225
Tamil Nadu	1,30,289	1,29,808
Puducherry	1,089	1,065
Andaman & Nicobar Islands	53	110
All India (Total)	9,95,141	10,63,721

Source: Annual Report, Ministry of SSI, Government of India (2005–06).

About 13 per cent of the women enterprises were in the registered SMEs sector and the remaining 87 per cent were in the unregistered SMEs sector. With regard to the enterprises managed by women, 11.5 per cent were in the registered SMEs sector and 88.5 per cent were in the unregistered SMEs sector.

The total number of female employees in the SMEs sector in 2005–06 was estimated at 33,17,496. About 57.62 per cent of the female employees were employed in the SMEs units located in the States of Tamil Nadu, Kerala, Karnataka, West Bengal and Andhra Pradesh, with Kerala is having the highest female employment rate, 37 per cent in proportion to the total female employment in the states. The overall female employment rate to the total employment in India varies at 13.31 per cent. Table 2 shows the state-wise employment scenario in registered and unregistered SSI units.

Table 2

State-wise Employment of Females in SMEs Sector

Name of State/UT	*No. of Female Employees*			*Percentage of Female Employment in the Total Employment of the State*
	Regd. SSI Sector	*Unregd. SSI Sector*	*Total*	
Jammu & Kashmir	3,313	8,153	11,466	7.51
Himachal Pradesh	4,016	4,134	8,150	6.26
Punjab	11,757	36,013	47,770	5.26
Chandigarh	659	1,975	2,634	5.46
Uttaranchal	2,940	13,240	16,180	8.28
Haryana	15,651	14,889	30,540	5.52
Delhi	6,306	35,798	42,104	6.72
Rajasthan	15,003	46,065	61,068	7.04
Uttar Pradesh	23,506	1,80,918	2,04,424	5.11
Bihar	8,353	68,908	77,261	7.14
Sikkim	212	9	221	16.72
Arunachal Pradesh	342	104	446	12.10
Nagaland	637	2,574	3,211	5.65
Manipur	3,853	19,485	23,338	17.06
Mizoram	2,188	4,636	6,824	27.46
Tripura	4,294	3,325	7,619	13.38
Meghalaya	3,139	5,664	8,803	13.42
Assam	9,077	16,988	26,065	6.08
West Bengal	26,549	3,04,969	3,31,518	15.28

Cont'd...

...Cont'd

Jharkhand	5,105	8,907	14,012	5.08
Orissa	11,723	2,13,123	2,24,846	24.36
Chhattisgarh	10,177	52,476	62,653	11.78
Madhya Pradesh	29,612	1,11,703	1,41,315	10.51
Gujarat	41,189	79,990	1,21,179	9.57
Daman & Diu	6,106	126	6,232	14.83
Dadra & Nagar Haveli	6,106	126	6,232	14.83
Maharashtra	78,731	1,62,700	2,41,431	11.77
Andhra Pradesh	60,693	2,70,026	3,30,719	15.46
Karnataka	1,17,934	2,23,142	3,41,076	20.81
Goa	5,309	1,833	7,142	24.37
Lakshadweep	26	405	431	26.31
Kerala	1,89,640	2,24,491	4,14,131	37.15
Tamil Nadu	2,70,936	2,23,050	4,93,986	24.48
Pondicherry	5,613	2,670	8,283	23.52
Andaman & Nicobar Islands	124	294	418	5.59
All India (Total)	9,74,713	23,42,783	33,17,496	13.31

Source: Annual Report, Ministry of SSI, Government of India (2005–06).

The impact of globalization on the SMEs and the level of entrepreneurship is not straightforward and can be both negative and positive. Globalization involves the integration of world markets and offers numerous opportunities for people involved in business. Moreover, globalization involves creating new opportunities for all firms by the disappearance of trade barriers. As a result, increasing competition in international markets may have a negative impact on the survival rates of women (small) entrepreneurs in SMEs.

The major threats that women entrepreneurs face in the global markets are competition from foreign products arising from trade liberalization, technological advancements outpacing current technology now used within one's business, and insufficient skills to conduct business in the global market place. To combat these obstacles, the role of women business enterprises in every region of the India should be to prepare aggressively and carefully for future participation in the global economy by providing access to intensive training on how to shape niche markets and develop new, innovative and interactive marketing skills. In this way, these strategies may pay the way for women entrepreneurs to survive as well as grow in the fast growing forces of changing competitive Indian economy.

Main Reasons for Poor Women Entrepreneurship in India

Some of the major obstacles faced by women entrepreneurs include being accepted as a woman in business, lack of a role model, lack of professional interaction, difficulties in gaining the confidence of their clients and suppliers, lack of adequate training, and lack of related experience (Belcourt et al., 1991; Collerette and Aubry, 1990; Goffee and Scase, 1985; Hisrich, 1986; Kent, 1988; Lee-Gosselin and Grise, 1990; Timmons, 1986). Age-old gender discrimination, deprivation and fragmented education have had detrimental effects on women entrepreneurship that has produced subdued personalities with respect to independent thinking and decision-making. There are a number of factors that influence the status of women, such as income, reproductive health and environmental and socio-cultural constraints.

According to the Food and Agriculture Organization of the United Nations (Lambrou, 2005), women rarely have formal title to agricultural land and therefore are deprived of asset-based security. Income-generating activities are seen as 'entry points for channels of communication and vehicles by which women can meet their needs' (Rogers and Youssef, 1988).

To be brief some of the major reasons for the slow growth of women entrepreneurs in India are:

(i) acceptance of entrepreneurship as sheer economic necessities and not a challenge or choice of career,
(ii) lack of training, motivation and counselling services,
(iii) lack of availability of sufficient finance from right resources and right kind of skilled manpower,
(iv) lack of time due to family responsibilities,
(v) lack of assets in their names and family oppositions,
(vi) faulty socializations, public prejudices and cultural values, and
(vii) lack of abilities and confidence for convincing the people, public and business practice.

But, it must be pointed out that it is true that the situation is now changing rapidly in urban and well developed areas, especially in metro and big cities where women have come out of their homes and have opted for different businesses/professions voluntarily. The situation in villages and smaller towns will have a still long way to go in this direction. Recent political move of reservation for women even in village panchayats is certainly going to give them some confidence and in the longer perspective may promote a culture of women oriented programmes. This significant measure may slowly breed the culture of economic empowerment as well as women entrepreneurship in India.

Conclusion

To sum up, we can say that the Indian society needs to bring about an attitudinal change in regard to the role of women as an entrepreneur. The following words of Pandit Jawaharlal Lal Nehru are worth to note down that *'when women move forward, the family moves, the village moves, society moves, country moves ...'.* Thus, there is an urgent need to bring the womenfolk in the mainstream of progress so that the objective of social and economic development is achieved.

Moreover, in the present dynamic and global world, all women entrepreneurs must have the flexibility and creativity to meet the challenges they face and encash the opportunities. The above gaps in information have serious consequences for the development of women-friendly national and global economic and social policies and in transforming the forces of economic globalization to be beneficial rather than hostile to women. Policy makers often hold the assumption that women are primarily workers and not entrepreneurs, or that businesswomen mostly serve their own communities and have little use for international support programmes. The full measure of impact of economic globalization and other policies on women and the development of progressive policy measures to counter these measures will not receive the attention it deserves until this dominant knowledge base is challenged and reconstructed. Often policy makers overlook the fact that women entrepreneurs – as a result of their unique social position – need different programmes than men. In fact, policy makers consider business to be gender neutral and they experience difficulty implementing different credit and training programmes based on gender.

To conclude, we remember the word of Kollan and Parikh (2005):

> ... the next millennium offers a space beyond the present horizon where, instead of hope there is active engagement with the world, instead of dreams there are commitments, instead of aspiration there are choices, instead of ideals there are convictions and instead of searching for bestowal's and affirmation there is the acknowledge of one's own uniqueness of identity. It is in this discovery that a woman can create and build an industrial empire from the first step that she would have taken.

Recommendations and Suggestions

It is to be noted here that until and unless women are given the same opportunities that men are, entire society will be destined to perform below their true potential. Thus, concerted action to educate women, give them equal access to credit, and generally empower them, are critical components in battling major global issues such as poverty, unemployment, population growth, violence, etc. Some of the important recommendations and suggestions are mentioned below so that women may be encouraged to take small, medium and big size entrepreneurial ventures so that they may be empowered economically and contribute significantly to the Indian economy:

(i) Women entrepreneurs should be encouraged to work from their homes, so that they can manage both home tasks and entrepreneurial work. This is possible with the help of Information and Communication Technology (ICT) programmes.

(ii) Most of the women entrepreneurs do not take any Entrepreneurship Development Programmes and training. Thus, there is a need to keep aware all women entrepreneurs about Entrepreneurship Training and Development Programmes available all over the country in different Entrepreneurship Development Institutes (EDIs). In this direction, professional and social organizations need to play an important role in mobilizing the women entrepreneurs.

(iii) The government should also provide women entrepreneurs with financial, marketing and training assistance so that they can start up their business. Thus, in order to bring upliftment in the quality and work skill of the women entrepreneurs they should be given proper training and support.

(iv) Publicizing the central role of women in national economies and of 'success stories of female entrepreneurs' through mass media, to assist in changing public attitudes towards women's involvement in economic decision-making and encourage women to become entrepreneurs.

(v) In the new economic environment of globalization, liberalization and increased competition there is a great need to provide gender-sensitive training to officials and representatives in the governmental, non-governmental and private sectors to promote women's interests in relevant regional and international forums and training in marketing, export development and joint venture promotion to female entrepreneurs, and relevant women groups in India.

(vi) Entrepreneurship education must address the equivocal nature of business entry. Student selection at 10+2 or college level is the first step and then those selected students need to be motivated. After the motivation phase, they should be given special entrepreneurship skills and trainings. Moreover, this type of education must include skill-building courses in negotiation, leadership, new product development, creative thinking and exposure to technology innovation. Other areas identified as important for this education include an awareness of entrepreneur career options, sources of venture capital, idea protection, ambiguity tolerance, etc. Consequently, there is a need to actively pursue education in relevant areas to get the skills and expertise necessary to embark on the entrepreneurship role.

(vii) Availability of finance for women entrepreneurs should be easily available at cheaper rates of interest so that large number of women are encouraged to take up the entrepreneurship as their life-time career option. Besides, new financial products and policies should be explored to encourage existing financial institutions to extend credit/micro-credit freely to women in all sectors of the economy. This may be done by developing or adapting legal frameworks that eliminate the gender biases of financial institutions.

(viii) Generally, it has been found that mere financial assistance does not help the women. They need institutional support. Non-financial inputs in the form of awareness, knowledge, skill training and marketing know how, etc., should be treated as an integral part of the programme and the mechanism of providing these through convergence with line departments needs to be reviewed. Information on the latest available technology also plays a significant role in the sustenance of the entrepreneurial culture among women in the longer run.

(ix) Awareness about Women's Entrepreneurship should be popularized and then the participation of women entrepreneurs in international trade and the global economy should be increased with a specific target through developing different attractive programmes, policies and schemes (which are women centric in nature) in different sectors of the economy.

(x) Increasing inclusion of poor women and other vulnerable groups to give them a voice in economic bodies and financial structures;

(xi) Developing policy frameworks that allow women to move away from the ghetto of micro-finance to mainstream economic policy and structures.

(xii) Women entrepreneurs should be kept abreast of knowledge about new techniques, financial institutions, new schemes, training institutions and marketing linkages.

(xiii) Vocational and technical training of women in particularly non-traditional areas along with appropriate skill training, technical upgradation, and entrepreneurship under public-private partnership within a region-specific context.

(xiv) There should be a tax incentive to encourage women entrepreneurial ventures in big industries other than SMEs where there are low numbers of women workers and/or management.

References

Albee, A. 1994. 'Support to Women's Productive and Income-Generating Activities', UNICEF Evaluation and Research Working Paper Series No. 1.

Beck, T., A. Demirguc-Kunt and R. Levine. 2005. 'SMEs, Growth and Poverty: Cross-Country Evidence', *Journal of Economic Growth*, Vol. 10, No. 3, pp. 199–229.

Belcourt, M., R.J. Burket and H. Lee-Gosselin. 1991. 'The Glass Box: Women Business Owners in Canada', background paper published by the Canadian Advisory Council on the Status of Women.

Birley, Sue. 1989. 'Female Entrepreneurs: Are They Really Any Different?', *Journal of Small Business Management*, Vol. 27, No. 1, pp. 32–37.

Brush, C. 1992. 'Research on Women Business Owners: Past Trends, a New Perspective and Future Directions', *Entrepreneurship Theory and Practice*, Vol. 16, No. 4, pp. 5–30.

Brush, C., N. Carter, E. Gatewood, P. Greene and M. Hart. 2004. *Clearing the Hurdles: Women Building High Growth Businesses*, Prentice Hall, New Jersey.

Chaganti, R. 1986. 'Management in Women-Owned Enterprises', *Journal of Small Business Management*, Vol. 24, No. 4, pp. 18–29.

Chant, S. 2003. 'Female Household Headship and the Feminization of Poverty: Facts, Fiction and Forward Strategies', Gender Institute, London School of Economics and Political Science.

Chattopadhyay, Arundhati. 2005. 'Women and Entrepreneurship', *Yojana*, Vol. 49, January, pp. 27–33.

Cliff, J. 1998. 'Does One Size Fit All? Exploring Attitudes Towards Growth, Gender and Business Size', *Journal of Business Venturing*, Vol. 13, pp. 523–42.

Collerette, P. and P. Aubry. 1990. 'Socio-Economic Evolution of Women Business Owners in Quebec', *Journal of Business Ethics*, Vol. 9, April–May, pp. 417–22.

Dhameja, S.K. 2002. *Women Entrepreneurs: Opportunities, Performance and Problems*, Deep and Deep Publications, New Delhi, pp. 11–17.

Dumas, C. 2001. 'Evaluating the Outcomes of Microenterprise Training for Low Income Female: A Case Study', *Journal of Developmental Entrepreneurship*, Vol. 6, pp. 97–128.

Goffee, R. and R. Scase. 1985. *Women in Charge: The Experiences of Women Entrepreneurs*, Allen and Irwin, London.

Green, R., J. David, M. Dent and A. Tyshkovsky. 1996. 'The Russian Entrepreneur: A Study of Psychological Characteristics', *International Journal of Entrepreneurial Behaviour and Research*, Vol. 2, No. 1, pp. 49–53.

Hall, J.C. 2007. 'Entrepreneurship and Economic Progress', *Review of Austrian Economics*, Vol. 21, Nos 2–3, pp. 219–22.

Hisrich, R. and C. Brush. 1984. 'The Woman Entrepreneurs: Management Skills and Business Problems', *Journal of Small Business Management*, Vol. 22, No. 1, pp. 31–36.

——. 1987. 'Women Entrepreneurs: A Longitudinal Study', proceedings of the Seventh Annual Babson College Entrepreneurship Research Conference, Frontiers of Entrepreneurship Research, pp. 187–99.

Hisrich, R. 1986. 'The Woman Entrepreneur: Characteristics, Skills, Problems, and Prescriptions for Success', in D. Sexton and R. Smilor (eds), *The Art and Science of Entrepreneurship*, Ballinger, Cambridge.

Kaufmann, P., D. Welsh and N. Bushmarin. 1995. 'Locus of Control and Entrepreneurship in the Russian Republic', *Entrepreneurship Theory and Practice*, Vol. 20, No. 1, pp. 43–56.

Kauppinen-Toropainen, K. 1993. 'Comparative Study of Women's Work Satisfaction and Work Commitment: Research Findings from Estonia, Moscow, and Scandinavia', in V. Moghadam (ed.), *Democratic Reform and the Position of Women in Transitional Economies*, Clarendon Press, Oxford, pp. 198–412.

Kent, C. 1988. 'Business Education for Women Entrepreneurs', *Journal of Business Education*, pp. 28–33.

Kirve, H. and A. Kanitkar. 1993. 'Entrepreneurship at the Grass-roots: Developing the Income-generating Capabilities of Rural Women', *Journal of Entrepreneurship*, Vol. 2, No. 2, pp. 177–97.

Kirzner, I.M. 1997. 'Entrepreneurial Discovery and the Competitive Market Process: An Austrian Approach', *Journal of Economic Literature*, Vol. 35, No. 1, pp. 60–85.

Kollan, Bharti and J. Parikh. 2005. 'A Reflection of the Indian Women in Entrepreneurial World', Working Paper No. 2005–08–07, August, IIM, Ahmedabad, Gujarat, India.

Lakshmi, C. Swarajya (ed). 1998. *Development of Women Entrepreneurship in India: Problems and Prospects,* Discovery Publishing House, New Delhi.

Lalitha Rani, D. 1996. *Women Entrepreneurs*, APH Publishing Corporation, New Delhi.

Lambrou, Y. 2005. 'Monitoring the Millennium Development Goals from a Rural Perspective', FAO Discussion Paper.

Lee-Gosselin, H. and J. Grise. 1990. 'Are Women Owner-Managers Challenging Our Definitions of Entrepreneurship? An In-Depth Survey', *Journal of Business Ethics*, Vol. 9, Nos 4–5, April–May, pp. 423–35.

Neff, T.J. and J.M. Citrin. 1999. *Lessons from the Top*, Doubleday, New York.

Nijkamp, Peter. 2009. 'Entrepreneurship Development and the Spatial Context: Retrospect and Prospect', Research Paper No. 2009/08, United Nations University, World Initiative for Development Economics, February.

Padmavati, D. 2002. 'Training Women for Entrepreneurship', *Social Welfare*, Vol. 49, No. 2, pp. 15–18.

Pareek. 1992. *Entrepreneurial Role Stress*, Mimeographed, Indian Institute of Management, Ahmedabad.

Peacock, S. 2003. 'Women Entrepreneurs Worldwide Voice Optimism', CWBR, 3 March 1998 in Maria Minniti and Pia Arenius, *Women in Entrepreneurship*, UN Headquarters, 29 April.

Reddi, P.N. 1991. 'Problems of Women Entrepreneurs in Goa: A Pilot Study', *Khadi Gramodyog*, Vol. 37, No. 4, pp. 157–59.

Renzulli, L., H. Aldrich and J. Moody. 2000. 'Family Matters: Gender Networks and Entrepreneurial Outcomes', *Social Forces*, Vol. 79, No. 2, pp. 523–46.

Robinson, S. 2001. 'An Examination of Business Ownership by Rural and Non-Rural Men in Pennsylvania', Allied Academies International Conference, Las Vegas.

Rogers, B. and N. Youssef. 1988. 'The Importance of Women's Involvement in Economic Activities in the Improvement of Child Nutrition and Health', *Food and Nutrition Bulletin*, Vol. 10, No. 3.

Sarri, K. and A. Trihopoulou. 2005. 'Female Entrepreneurs Personal Characteristics and Motivation: A Review of the Greek Situation', *Women in Management Review*, Vol. 20, No. 1, pp. 24–36.

Sathyasundaram, I. 2004. 'Encouraging Womens Entrepreneurship', *Social Welfare*, Vol. 50, No. 12, pp. 13–15.

Schumpeter, J. 1934. *Theory of Economic Development*, Cambridge University Press, Cambridge.

——. 1961. *The Theory of Economic Development: An Enquiry into Profits, Capital, Credit, Interest and the Business Cycle*, Harvard University Press, Cambridge.

Sharma, D.D. and S.K. Dhameja. 2002. *Women and Rural Entrepreneurship*, Abhishek Publications, Chandigarh.

Stevenson, L.A. 1986. 'Against All Odds: The Entrepreneurship of Women', *Journal of Small Business Management*, October, pp. 30–44.

Stevenson, L. 1990. 'Some Methodological Problems Associated with Researching Women Entrepreneurs', *Journal of Business Ethics*, Vol. 9, Nos 4-5, pp. 439–46.

Timmons, J.A. 1986. 'Characteristics and Role Demands of Entrepreneurship', *American Journal of Small Business*, Vol. 3, No. 1, pp. 5–17.

United Nations. 1995. 'Women in a Changing Global Economy: 1994', World Survey on the Role of Women in Development, New York.

13

Sex Education in India

Expectations and Experiences of Young Women

Niharika Tripathi and T.V. Sekher

Family life education (FLE) refers to a broad programme designed to impart knowledge regarding practices, values and attitudes affecting family relationships. It aims to develop the qualities and attitudes on which successful family life depends. The real purpose of family life/sex education is the transfiguration of a boy child into manhood and of a girl child into womanhood. Many psychologists believe that sex education begins at an early age and continues throughout the life of an individual (Devi et al., 1988). Sex education includes the information about conception, contraception and sexually transmitted diseases. It is a continuous process of developing attitudes, values and understanding regarding all situations and relationships in which people play roles as male or female (D'Souza, 1979). More than biological facts sex education should also include social and moral behaviour, proper attitudes and values towards sex, love, family life, and interpersonal relations in society. Adolescent life/sex education has been one of the most controversial issues in Indian society. Due to increasing incidences of Human Immunodeficiency Virus (HIV), Acquired Immune Deficiency Syndrome (AIDS), Reproductive Tract Infections (RTIs), Sexually Transmitted Diseases (STIs) and teenage pregnancies, there is a need to impart sex education among youth. However introducing sex education at school level always received opposition from various segments of Indian society. The study on child abuse in India, conducted by the

Ministry of Women and Child Development, reports that 53 per cent of the boys and 47 per cent of the girls surveyed faced some form of sexual abuse (Government of India, 2007). The problem of overpopulation also demands family life education including family planning as a priority as many of the young people about to be married should be aware of responsibilities they would have. The National Population Policy also reiterates the need of educating adolescents about the risks of unprotected sex (ibid., 2000). In this chaper an attempt has been made to understand the expectations and experiences of young women aged 15–24 years in India regarding FLE.

Objectives of Family Life/Sex Education

Following are the main objectives of FLE/sex education:

(i) To help emotionally stable children and adolescents who feel sufficiently secure and adequate in making decisions regarding their conduct without being carried away by their emotions.

(ii) To provide sound knowledge not only of the physical aspects of sex behaviour but also its psychological and sociological aspects, so that sexual experience can be viewed as a part of the total personality of the individual.

(iii) To develop attitudes and standards of conduct which will ensure that young people and adults will determine their sexual and other behaviour by considering its long range effects on their own personal development, the good of other individuals, and welfare of society as a whole (D'Souza, 1979).

The rapidly changing western society has for a long time recognized the importance of sex education. In 1984 it was found that around 50 per cent of Canadian schools introduced family life education programme (Nolte, 1984). The scenario in India is somewhat different, as sex education is considered as a 'taboo' by many. Children as well as parents feel hesitant and embarrassed while discussing such issues. Curiosity to know about sex is inseparable and inevitable thirst of humans. Its necessity has been realized and imparted throughout the history of human societies within its variant cultural settings, though with restrictions. But in the modern society, under the strong influence of mass media, the taboo regarding sex has lost its meaning. Adolescents and youth are getting affected mainly because of various misconceptions on sex.

The first organization in India to sponsor sex education was All India Moral and Social Hygiene Association founded by Keshab Chander Sen, who led the movement for improving the status of women (Forbes, 1963). The Family Planning Association of India (FPAI) pioneered the population education in 1960s and moved on to 'family life and sex education' thereafter, keeping the need of such education.

In 2007, the scheme promoted by the National AIDS Control Organization (NACO) and the Human Resource Development (HRD) Ministry that adolescence education should be introduced in the school curriculum led to a debate in India. The opponents of sex education argued for a ban of sex education in schools on the ground that it corrupts the youth and offends 'Indian values'. They felt that it may lead to promiscuity, experimentation and irresponsible sexual behaviour. On the one hand, we have a thriving economy and modernization and on the other, an uneasy debate on sex education. The critics of sex education feel that sex education may be necessary in western countries, but not in India, which has a rich culture. It will have adverse effects on young minds. On the other hand, the proponents say that conservative ideas have little place in a modernizing country like India where attitudes towards sex are changing rapidly. The states of Gujarat, Madhya Pradesh, Maharashtra, Karnataka, Kerala, Rajasthan, Chhattisgarh and Goa declared that the course content as suggested by HRD Ministry was unacceptable and banned the programme (Motihar, 2007).

Even while the politicians have opposed the introduction of sex education in schools, studies show that Indian adolescents, youth, even men getting married do not have enough information about sex, thereby increasing the possibility of marital rape and other forms of sexual violence. TARSHI (Talking about Reproductive and Sexual Health Issues), a non-governmental organization, running a helpline on sexual information, received over 59,000 calls from men, seeking information on sexual anatomy and physiology. An analysis of this data showed that 70 per cent of the callers were Hindi speaking and below 30 years of age while 33 per cent were in the age group of 15 to 24 which indicates that young people do have the need but no source to receive information in a positive manner. The introduction on sex education in schools is opposed on the ground that it being anti-ethical to Indian culture whereas the World Health Organization (WHO) reports conversely show that promotion of sex education resulted in delayed age of entering into sexual relationship, reduced number of partners, increase use of safer sex and contraception, and other positive behaviour (Chauhan, 2007).

A survey of 35 sex education projects conducted by WHO in 1993 showed that sex education in schools did not encourage young people to have sex at earlier age; rather it delays the start of sexual activity and encourages young people to have safer sex (Dhiman, 2007). India has become the second largest hub of HIV/AIDS pandemic in the world. NFHS-3 (2005–06) survey shows that awareness regarding HIV/AIDS is 30.7 per cent among women with no education and 50.7 per cent among uneducated men. Those who had education of more than 10 years, among them the awareness level increased to 97 per cent and 98 per cent for women and men respectively. The proponents of sex education stressed the need for providing knowledge about HIV/AIDS, teenage pregnancies and information about sexual health. Both the critiques and supporters of sex education shared same ideology of 'sexual restraint' (Anandhi, 2007). In a survey of college students conducted by the All India Educational and Vocational Guidance Association, it was reported that 54 per cent of males and 42 per cent of females did not have adequate knowledge regarding matters of sex (D'Souza, 1979).

We need to accept the fact that we are living in a complicated world leading complicated lives. Preventing access to porn or movies or TV is not practical, but adding a single chapter to the school curriculum is simple and practical (Yashwanth, 2007). Mass media being highly influential has been a part of both solution and the problem in the area of sex and youth. It has been part of the solution because it has helped to bring sexual topics into discussion. Radio and television has been a medium in opening doors to the discussions of some topics which were previously considered as taboo. A survey conducted in Mumbai found that among 695 college students, 88 per cent of the boys and 58 per cent of the girls had received no sex education from their parents and the source of information were books, magazines and youth counsellors (D'Souza, 1979).

Internet is the greatest culprit which makes pornography easily accessible in recent times. Research studies have shown that vast majority of parents do not accept the responsibility for providing sex education to their sons or daughters (Devi et al., 1988). Another study states that 68 per cent of the parents believe that they should be the primary sex educators of their children followed by schools (Alexander, 1984). The stigma attached to any discussion on sex in India is due to the fact that people tend to view sex education in a narrow sense the mere explanation of anatomical and biological differences. Ideally home is the best place for sex education and the attitudes of parents are of vital importance. It is also found that when a child feels the subject as forbidden it can lead to misleading information, if parents feel shameful and embarrassed in talking about sex with their children (D'Souza, 1979).

Review of Literature

A study by Marsman and Herold (1986) states that majority of mothers believed that discouraging pre-marital intercourse should be the most important objective of sex education and those who felt that their own sex education was inadequate were in support of sex education for their children. The study also reveals that children who had sex education were less likely to engage in pre-marital intercourse than those who did not have. Another study by Alexander (1984) found that only 68 per cent of parents were the primary source in providing sex education to their children. A study by Forbes (1963) concluded that the understanding of family life varies greatly by the type of residence. Parents should provide sex education to their children in a free and informal atmosphere so that children may get rid of the idea that sex is dirty or wicked and be aware of their responsibilities as well as prepare themselves for marriage (Israel, 1967). A survey conducted in Hyderabad and Secunderabad cities found that the major sources of sex information for adolescents were books and films, followed by friends and parents (Moses and Praveena, 1983). The study strongly indicates the need for introduction of sex education in the formal curriculum. An important observation emerging from this study is that in spite of exposure towards sex education, many adolescents did not have the correct knowledge regarding reproduction. This shows that sex education in the format being imparted in certain institutions does not have the desired impact on adolescents.

Family life education for boys and girls at the adolescent stage should be constructive enough so as to contribute to healthier emotional growth and it must prepare them to enter into a responsible and a healthier adulthood (Rao, 1988). Another study carried out in Andhra Pradesh (Devi et al., 1988) concluded that adolescent boys and girls need sound and correct knowledge about sex. The knowledge of boys regarding sex is more than that of girls, may be, because boys try to satisfy their curiosity more readily than girls. Lack of proper sex education can result in emotional and social disturbances. It was also found that educated parents help their children to clarify their doubts and anxieties about sex in a more realistic way.

The findings of National Family Health Survey-3 (NFHS-3) show that majority of men and women in India favour family life education. More than two-thirds of adults approve of teaching school children about physical changes in their bodies that come with puberty, although there is somewhat less approval of children learning about puberty in the opposite sex (Table 1).

Table 1

Opinions of Men and Women on Topics to be Included in Family Life Education

Topics to be included in family life education	*Opinion of men*		*Opinion of women*	
	Girls	*Boys*	*Girls*	*Boys*
Changes in boys' bodies at puberty	68.9	81.7	53.9	67.8
Changes in girls' bodies at puberty including menstruation	77.1	63.9	76.1	41.1
Sex and sexual behaviour	62.1	62.4	46.4	42.9
Contraception	65.4	63.7	48.5	42.0
HIV/AIDS	80.5	81.6	63.4	63.1
Condom use to avoid sexually transmitted diseases	67.7	69.8	43.6	42.8

Source: IIPS and Macro International, 2007.

According to the recent Youth Study in India (2006–07) 83.7 per cent of young men and 81 per cent of young women (aged 15–24 years) felt the need to impart family life education. There is rural–urban differential in reporting of the need for family life/sex education. Majority of respondents received family life education from schools/colleges. The survey found that 24 per cent of the women had pre-marital sex for the first time before age 15. Those who received the family life education consisted of only 23 per cent unmarried women and 17 per cent unmarried men (see Table 2).

Table 2

Perceptions Regarding Family Life Education Among Unmarried Men and Women in India

Topics	*Unmarried Women*	*Unmarried Men*
Perceived family life/sex education to be important	81.0	83.7
The best person to provide family life/sex education		
Parent	30.4	5.7
Teacher	34.9	47.7
Received family life/sex education	23.0	17.4
Source of family life/sex education received		
School/College	91.8	81.6

Source: IIPS and Population Council, 2010.

Need for the Study

Sex education has been one of the most controversial issues in Indian society. Though few micro-level studies have been conducted, yet there exists gap in knowledge and implementation. Few schools and colleges are taking initiative in imparting sex education. Since there are many supporters and opponents in introducing sex education in Indian schools, it is most important to understand the perception and attitudes of youth on this controversial subject. This study is an attempt in that direction by analysing the perceptions and experiences of young unmarried women. The data from a large-scale survey conducted across India provides a unique opportunity to gauge the attitudes of younger generation. This may also help the government in formulating appropriate strategies. In this study, the terms sex education/family life education/adolescent life education were interchangeably used. For this purpose, evidence available is from nationally representative surveys like District Level Household and Facility Survey (DLHS-3: 2007–08).

Objectives

(i) To study the perception regarding family life education (FLE) and ideal age at marriage among young unmarried women.
(ii) To examine the experiences of unmarried women on family life education.
(iii) To examine the awareness on reproductive health issues among unmarried women and the impact of family life education on their awareness.

Data Source and Methodology

Data for the present analysis is from the recently released DLHS-3 conducted by the International Institute for Population Sciences (IIPS). It is the largest ever demographic and health survey carried out in India with a sample size over six lakh households covering 601 districts of the country. The perception and knowledge about family life education, family planning, RTI/STI, HIV/AIDS and reproductive health issues were collected from unmarried women of 15–24 years, 1,66,260 unmarried women were interviewed in DLHS-3 which was carried out in 2007–08 (IIPS, 2010). Along with this secondary sources like Youth Study in India (2006–07) and NFHS-3, 2005–06 all undertaken by IIPS as nodal agency have been used.

The independent variables considered in this study are age groups (15–19 and 20–24), type of locality (rural and urban), religion (Hindu,

Muslim, Christian, and others), caste (Scheduled Caste, Scheduled Tribe, Other Backward Classes, and others), education (non-literate, less than five years, 5–9 years and 10 years or above), wealth index and employment status (employed and unemployed). Employment status has been computed by using two variables – women who were employed in the last seven days and if not, whether they were employed anytime during the last 12 months. Awareness about contraceptives has been computed based on modern methods and traditional methods. Bi-variate, tri-variate and multivariate techniques have been used in the present analysis.

Results and Discussion

The background characteristics of women surveyed are presented in Table 3. 73.3 per cent of women respondents were in the age group of 15–19 and the remaining in the age group of 20–24. Good number of women (45.3%) is having education of more than 10 years. Around 68 per cent of women are Hindus. Only 27.2 per cent were employed. Nearly 37 per cent belong to the households of highest wealth category.

Table 3

Background Characteristics of Unmarried Women (Sample)

Background characteristics	*Percentage of women*	*Total number of women*
Age Group		
15–19	73.3	1,24,537
20–24	26.7	41,723
Residence		
Rural	55.0	1,21,569
Urban	45.0	44,691
Present Level of Education of Women		
Non-literate	8.4	15,568
Less than 5 years	5.2	9,859
5–9 years	41.1	72,582
10 years or above	45.3	68,252
Employment Status		
Employed	27.2	49,786
Not employed	72.8	1,16,474
Religion		
Hindu	68.6	1,15,629
Muslim	16.5	23,987
Christian	7.4	13,131

Cont'd...

...Cont'd

Others	7.5	13,513
Caste/Tribe		
Scheduled Caste	15.6	26,816
Scheduled Tribe	17.3	33,139
Other Backward Classes	35.8	57,259
Others	31.2	49,046
Wealth Index		
Lowest	8.6	18,501
Second	12.0	24,782
Middle	17.7	34,155
Fourth	25.2	42,293
Highest	36.5	46,501
India	**100.0**	**1,66,260**

Note: Employed category includes the women who were employed in the last 7 days or worked any time during the last 12 months. Students were included in the not employed category.

Source: DLHS-3 (2007–08).

Table 4

Awareness and Perception Regarding Family Life/Sex Education among Unmarried Women

Background characteristics	*Perceived family life education is Important*	*Received family life education*	*Number of women*
Age Group			
15–19	78.7	45.9	1,24,537
20–24	86.8	55.7	41,723
Residence			
Rural	77.4	43.4	1,21,569
Urban	85.1	54.8	44,691
Present level of Education of Women			
Women			
Non-literate	50.8	16.2	15,568
Less than 5 years	57.9	18.7	9,859
5–9 years	77.6	40.2	72,582
10 years or above	92.0	65.5	68,252
Employment Status			
Employed	76.7	41.4	49,786
Not employed	82.5	51.2	1,16,474

Cont'd...

...Cont'd

Religion			
Hindu	81.2	48.5	1,15,629
Muslim	78.6	43.3	23,987
Christian	81.2	57.4	13,131
Others	82.7	51.7	13,513
Caste/Tribe			
Scheduled Caste	79.3	44.9	26,816
Scheduled Tribe	73.9	44.8	33,139
Other Backward Classes	79.7	46.7	57,259
Others	86.9	54.6	49,046
Wealth Index			
Lowest	61.2	25.1	18,501
Second	70.2	32.8	24,782
Middle	75.9	40.6	34,155
Fourth	82.6	50.2	42,293
Highest	90.1	61.9	46,501
India	80.9	48.5	1,66,260

Source: DLHS-3 (2007–08).

Table 4 shows that with the increase in age, education of women and household economic status, the perception regarding importance of family life education and the number of women who received family life education also increases. At the national level, almost 81 per cent of unmarried women felt that family life education is important. However, those received family life education is only 48.5 per cent. As expected, women belonging to urban areas, having better education and from richer households are having higher chances of undergoing sex education.

DLHS-3 asked women about their opinion regarding at what age and at what level in school, the family life education should be introduced. Table 5 shows that majority of women approve that family life education should be provided in the age group 15–17 years and in standards 8 to 10. Nearly 46 per cent of women who had schooling for more than 10 years are of the opinion that family life education should be provided in standard 10 and above. Thirty-seven per cent among Christians responded that the sex education should be provided between 12–14 years. Place of residence (rural/urban) does not show much impact on the perception of women regarding the age and the standard at which the family life education should be provided.

Table 5

*Introducing Family Life/Sex Education: Opinion of Unmarried Women**

Background characteristics	*At what age*				*From which standard*			*Number of women*
	Below 12	12–14	15–17	18 or above	Below 8	8–10	Above 10	
Age Group								
15–19	7.4	33.7	37.7	16.1	22.9	55.0	13.8	96,333
20–24	7.3	31.7	36.3	21.7	22.0	54.7	17.8	35,759
Residence								
Rural	7.8	33.1	36.1	17.2	24.7	52.9	12.9	93,891
Urban	7.0	33.3	38.7	18.2	20.4	57.2	17.2	38,201
Present Level of Education of Women								
Non-literate	7.5	28.0	31.3	12.6	21.6	21.5	16.0	7,685
Less than 5 years	8.0	30.7	32.1	13.9	31.6	24.6	18.0	5,622
5–9 years	8.5	33.8	35.5	17.0	28.7	35.4	28.0	56,007
10 years or above	6.5	33.4	39.7	19.0	17.5	34.2	45.9	62,778
Employment Status								
Employed	7.6	30.8	35.2	19.4	23.3	50.6	13.9	37,411
Not employed	7.3	34.0	38.1	17.1	22.5	56.4	15.3	94,681
Religion								
Hindu	6.7	32.9	38.2	18.2	19.8	57.2	16.2	91,899
Muslim	8.8	32.8	35.3	17.0	23.1	51.5	13.6	18,658
Christian	12.8	36.9	31.2	14.5	44.6	39.9	8.3	10,514
Others	6.0	32.8	40.2	17.7	25.8	56.1	12.8	11,021
Caste/Tribe								
Scheduled Caste	6.6	31.8	38.2	18.7	21.1	55.7	15.1	20,981
Scheduled Tribe	10.5	35.6	32.4	14.8	37.0	44.1	8.5	24,030
Other Backward Classes	6.7	32.0	38.2	18.4	19.4	55.8	16.8	45,030
Others	7.0	33.2	37.3	17.7	20.1	58.6	16.0	39,559
Wealth Index								
Lowest	8.0	32.1	32.8	15.1	28.4	43.8	7.9	11,285
Second	7.5	33.0	34.9	15.5	26.5	49.2	9.7	17,368
Middle	8.0	32.2	36.2	17.5	25.5	51.5	12.9	25,989
Fourth	8.0	32.8	37.3	18.3	23.4	55.0	15.1	35,414
Highest	6.7	34.0	39.2	18.3	19.1	59.4	18.2	42,016
India	**7.4**	**33.2**	**37.3**	**17.7**	**22.7**	**54.9**	**15.0**	**1,32,092**

*Among women who perceived family life education to be important.

Source: DLHS-3 (2007–08).

Majority of the respondents felt that the main source for providing sex education should be parents. About 55 per cent respondents felt that teacher/school/college can be the source of family life education. Fifty per cent are of the view that brother/sister/sister-in-law can provide family life education. Twenty nine per cent of women perceived that friends/peers are the ideal resource persons to impart family life education.

Among those who received family life education, overwhelming majority received either from schools or colleges (Figure 1). The other sources are NGO programmes, youth clubs, government programmes, etc. Figure 2 depicts the experiences of young women who underwent family life education. Majority women are of the opinion that family life education answered/clarified many of their questions and the teacher/trainee explained it in a way that can be understood. Forty-two

Figure 1

Source of Family Life Education Received

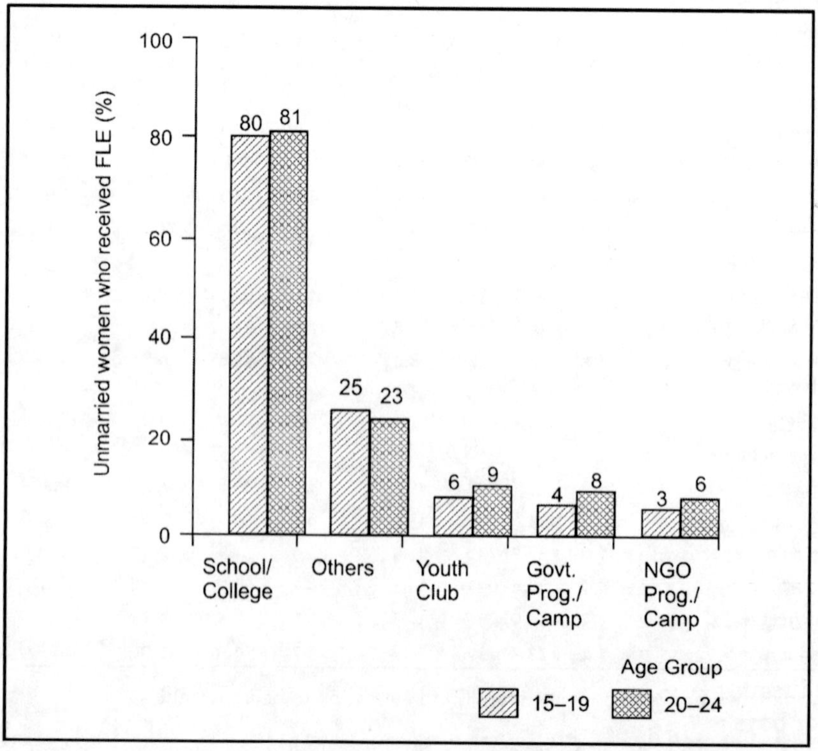

Figure 2
Experiences of Family Life Education

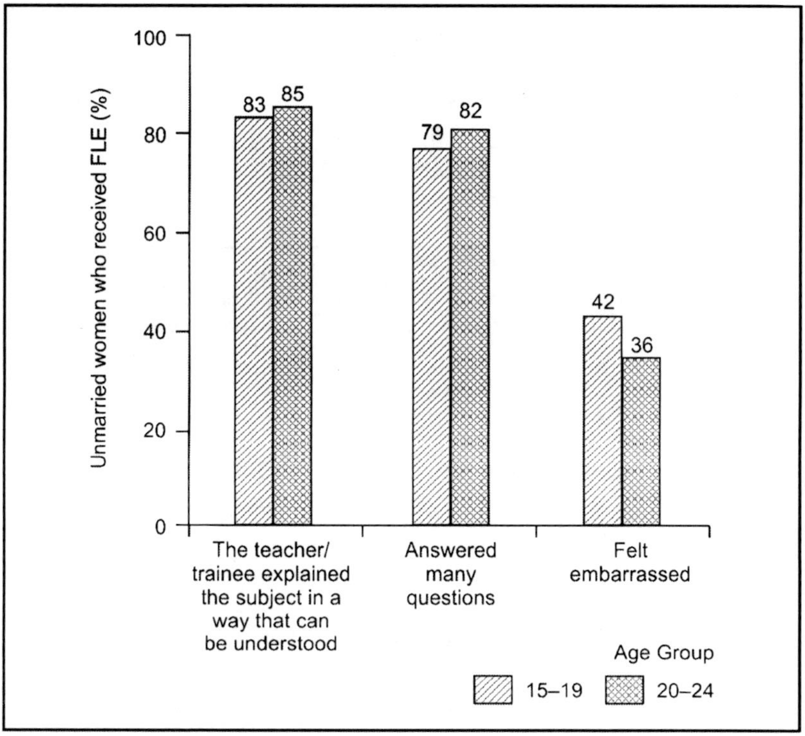

per cent of women aged 15–19 years reported that they felt embarrassed while attending family life education.

Majority of women (76%) who received family life education had the correct knowledge about the legal age at marriage for boys. Nearly 88 per cent of women who were exposed to family life education had the exact knowledge about the legally prescribed minimum age at marriage for girls in India.

It has been observed that among the women who received family life education, around 65 per cent (aged 15–24 years) say that the ideal age of marriage for boys should be more than 21 years and around 72 per cent say that the ideal age of marriage for girls should be more than 18 years (Table 6). Those who received family life education had a much liberal view regarding the ideal age at marriage for boys and girls.

Table 6

Opinion of Unmarried Women on Ideal Age at Marriage of Boys and Girls

Background characteristics	*Who received family life/sex education*						*Who did not receive family life/sex education*					
	Ideal age at marriage for boys (years)			*Ideal age at marriage for girls (years)*			*Ideal age at marriage for boys (years)*			*Ideal age at marriage for girls (years)*		
	Less than 21	*21*	*More than 21*	*Less than 18*	*18*	*More than 18*	*Less than 21*	*21*	*More than 21*	*Less than 18*	*18*	*More than 18*
Age Group												
15–19	13.9	25.9	60.2	2.2	30.5	67.3	22.3	26.4	51.3	7.6	36.0	56.4
20–24	8.2	20.5	71.3	0.9	22.5	76.6	14.3	18.6	66.8	3.7	24.7	71.6
Residence												
Rural	15.1	24.3	60.6	2.7	29.1	68.2	24.6	23.7	51.7	9.0	33.4	57.6
Urban	9.3	24.2	66.5	0.9	27.1	72.0	14.2	26.1	59.8	3.3	33.3	63.4
Present Level of Education of Women												
Non-literate	35.5	21.2	43.2	15.6	37.0	47.3	43.2	20.6	36.2	20.9	36.2	42.9
Less than 5 years	30.9	19.2	49.9	9.6	34.0	56.3	38.0	19.3	42.7	14.3	33.2	52.4
5–9 years	15.8	26.7	57.4	2.5	33.1	64.4	19.2	27.4	53.4	5.0	36.4	58.7
10 years or above	8.4	23.2	68.4	0.5	24.7	74.8	7.5	23.6	68.9	1.1	27.4	71.5
Employment Status												
Employed	15.1	22.2	62.6	3.3	27.4	69.3	27.8	23.1	49.0	10.2	33.7	56.1
Not employed	11.2	24.9	63.9	1.4	28.3	70.4	17.2	25.3	57.5	5.2	33.2	61.6
Religion												
Hindu	13.0	26.2	60.8	1.6	29	69.4	21.3	26.5	52.2	6.6	34.4	59.0
Muslim	15.2	23.4	61.4	3.7	32.5	63.8	22.5	23.3	54.1	8.6	37.3	54.2
Christian	5.9	10.5	83.6	1.0	15.2	83.8	13.5	13.3	73.2	4.8	20.4	74.8
Others	6.1	24.0	69.9	1.3	25.8	72.9	13.0	20.3	66.7	4.6	24.6	70.8
Caste/Tribe												
Scheduled Caste	14.3	25.1	60.6	1.8	29.9	68.3	23.0	25.7	51.4	6.7	34.9	58.4
Scheduled Tribe	10.2	19.3	70.5	2.4	24.3	73.4	24.2	20.3	55.4	9.8	29.3	61.0
Other Backward Classes	14.6	25.9	59.5	1.9	29.9	68.2	21.8	26.7	51.5	6.9	36.1	57.0
Others	9.7	24.5	65.8	1.5	27.2	71.3	14.7	24.2	61.1	4.4	31.6	64.0
Wealth Index												
Lowest	30.6	26.6	42.7	7.6	35.1	57.3	41.9	21.7	36.4	17.1	34.1	48.8
Second	23.6	27.2	49.2	5.1	34.2	60.7	28.8	24.9	46.3	11.0	36.4	52.6
Middle	17.4	25.1	57.5	2.8	30.8	66.4	22.0	24.7	53.4	7.0	34.2	58.8
Fourth	12.0	23.1	65.0	1.5	27.8	70.8	15.7	25.7	58.6	4.2	34.1	61.7
Highest	6.8	23.9	69.3	0.6	25.7	73.8	8.9	24.9	66.2	1.6	29.9	68.4
India	**12.1**	**24.3**	**63.6**	**1.8**	**28.1**	**70.1**	**20.5**	**24.6**	**54.9**	**6.7**	**33.4**	**59.9**

Source: DLHS-3 (2007–08).

The knowledge and awareness on reproductive health issues among unmarried women were also collected in DLHS-3. It clearly depicts that age, place of residence, education, employment, religion, caste, wealth index (economic status) are significant predictors in determining the awareness levels regarding reproductive health issues. There exist significant differentials among women of both categories (who received family life education and who did not) by their background characteristics. Urban women belonging to the households of highest wealth category and those had education of 10 years and above have more awareness than their rural counterparts. Overall, the awareness levels on various reproductive health issues indicate that women who were exposed to any form of family life education are better aware than those who did not have family life education at all. With the increasing age, education and wealth index, the awareness regarding contraception among women also increases. The awareness level is much higher among those women who had family life education.

Table 7

Results of Odds Ratio on the Perception Regarding Importance of Family Life/Sex Education

Background characteristics	*EXP(B)*
Age Group	
15–19®	
20–24	1.256***
Residence	
Rural®	
Urban	0.884***
Present Level of Education of Women	
Non-literate®	
Less than 5 years	1.346***
5–9 years	3.114***
10 years or above	8.341***
Employment Status	
Employed®	
Not employed	1.174***
Religion	
Hindu®	
Muslim	1.078***
Christian	1.259***
Others	1.069**

Cont'd...

...Cont'd

Caste/Tribe	
Scheduled Caste®	
Scheduled Tribe	0.741***
Other Backward Classes	0.939***
Others	1.150***
Wealth Index	
Lowest®	
Second	1.168***
Middle	1.274***
Fourth	1.654***
Highest	2.178***

Significance level: ***p<0.001, **p<0.05, *p<0.10

® Reference category

Table 8

Awareness and Perception Regarding Family Life/Sex Education among Unmarried Women across Major States in India

State	*Perceived family life education to be important*	*Ever received family life education*	*Number of women*
Uttar Pradesh	77.0	40.0	23,110
Uttarakhand	79.5	50.2	4,658
Rajasthan	71.1	38.1	8,416
Bihar	76.0	39.3	7,713
Jharkhand	70.8	40.8	5,063
Madhya Pradesh	74.0	35.2	9,940
Chhattisgarh	81.9	27.7	4,373
Odisha	82.4	43.6	7,257
Punjab	89.5	54.2	7,031
Haryana	89.5	44.8	5,031
West Bengal	90.4	47.0	4,325
Assam	67.9	27.8	9,286
Maharashtra	82.5	51.5	7,536
Gujarat	77.7	63.2	5,717
Kerala	91.9	71.4	2,554
Tamil Nadu	73.2	44.4	6,415
Karnataka	87.8	66.5	6,452
Andhra Pradesh	70.5	47.2	3,945
India	**80.9**	**48.5**	**1,66,260**

Source: DLHS-3 (2007–08).

Table 7 presents the results of binary logistic regression analysis on the perception of the respondents regarding the importance of family life education by various background characteristics. Respondents of age group 20–24 perceive family life education more important than the reference category of 15–19 age group. However, the respondents in urban areas are 12 per cent less likely to consider family life education to be important. This may be due to the fact that they have more options available to get knowledge about family life/sex education. So they do not consider it is as important as compared to rural women. The education, wealth index, religion and caste play a role in shaping the perceptions about family life education. Among all these, education is the most prominent determinant in moulding the positive attitude towards family life education.

In states like Kerala, Haryana, Punjab, Karnataka, and West Bengal, more than 85 per cent of women felt that family life education is important. However, those who received family life education vary considerably across the states from almost 28 per cent in Assam and Chhattisgarh to 71 per cent in Kerala (Table 8).

Table 9

Introducing Family Life Education: Opinion of Unmarried Women across Major States in India

State	*At what age*				*From which standard*		
	Below 12	*12–14*	*15–17*	*18 or above*	*Below 8*	*8–10*	*Above 10*
Uttar Pradesh	7.4	29.1	36.3	20.1	17.1	55.1	15.3
Uttarakhand	6.0	23.9	45.3	21.6	12.5	66.5	15.9
Rajasthan	7.1	35.3	40.1	13.8	26.2	59.0	9.4
Bihar	6.2	37.7	32.3	15.3	27.9	44.9	6.6
Jharkhand	8.2	35.9	32.5	12.7	24.4	53.7	6.2
Madhya Pradesh	6.1	25.5	40.8	21.1	17.9	58.0	14.2
Chhattisgarh	6.5	29.6	34.6	23.1	25.5	52.6	12.3
Odisha	9.7	42.0	32.5	11.7	32.6	50.4	11.1
Punjab	3.0	29.5	46.9	19.9	17.5	65.0	16.5
Haryana	4.7	32.5	37.4	22.2	17.2	58.8	18.3
West Bengal	6.1	38.1	35.8	14.7	33.0	48.4	8.7
Assam	7.8	40.8	30.1	13.2	31.8	46.9	10.0
Maharashtra	4.5	32.3	42.6	17.9	12.5	62.8	21.3
Gujarat	12.7	36.7	31.8	10.3	22.3	50.9	12.5
Kerala	8.7	44.0	39.1	6.8	14.8	67.4	15.8
Tamil Nadu	4.3	16.0	50.3	28.7	3.6	54.5	40.2
Karnataka	6.6	35.7	38.6	16.3	18.8	57.7	19.2
Andhra Pradesh	4.7	31.9	42.8	16.8	13.4	59.2	20.9
India	**7.4**	**33.2**	**37.3**	**17.7**	**22.7**	**54.9**	**15.0**

Source: DLHS-3 (2007–08).

Table 9 shows the opinion of unmarried women across states regarding introduction of family life education. Regarding the standard at which family life education should be introduced, most women from all states responded that it should be introduced during 8 to 10 standards. In Kerala, 67 per cent are of the view that family life education should be introduced from 8 to 10 standards in schools. Forty four per cent of Keralites also felt that the ideal age for sex education is 12 to 14 years. Interestingly, about 40 per cent of young women in Tamil Nadu felt that the sex education can be introduced after completing 10th standard of schooling.

Table 10

Perceptions of Youth Regarding Family Life Education

Perceptions	*Men*	*Women*	*Married men*	*Married women*	*Unmarried men*	*Unmarried women*
Perceived family life/sex education to be important	82.5	78.1	79.5	75.5	83.7	81.0
Perceived that family life/sex education should be provided at age (years)						
Below 12	2.8	2.6	3.3	3.2	2.7	2.1
12–14	12.1	23.6	10.7	22.6	12.6	24.7
15–17	47.5	42.6	41.7	41.5	48.7	43.7
18 or above	35.4	25.5	41.4	25.6	34.3	25.2
The best person to provide family life/sex education is						
Parent	5.9	33.8	7.4	36.7	5.7	30.4
Sibling/sister-in-law	0.4	5.6	0.4	6.5	0.4	4.8
Spouse/partner	0.2	2.4	0.3	4.2	0.2	0.3
Teacher	44.8	27.3	36.7	20.2	47.7	34.9
Friend	21.2	11.4	23.7	11.6	20.2	11.3
Healthcare provider/expert	23.2	14.5	27.1	14.7	21.9	14.2
Youth Club/Mandal/NGO Worker	0.9	0.4	0.9	0.3	1.0	0.4

Source: IIPS and Population Council, 2010.

Table 10 presents the young people's perceptions on family life/sex education, according to another survey conducted in India (2006–07). Around 83 per cent of young men and 78 per cent of young women felt that it is important to impart family life/sex education to youth. Slightly large proportion of unmarried youth (84% of men and 81% of women) as compared to married youth (79% of men and 75% of women) perceived family life/sex education to be important. Majority of young men and women approve that family life/sex education should be provided in the age group 15–17 years. Thirty five per cent of men and 25 per cent of women felt that family life/sex education should be provided at the age 18 or above. Regarding the perception of youth about the best person to impart family life/sex education, the preferences were somewhat different among men and women. Majority of young men felt that the best person to provide family life education should be teacher whereas among young women majority felt that parents are ideal persons to provide such education. As compared to married youth, majority of unmarried youth considered teacher as the best person to provide such education. Around 21 per cent of young men and 11 per cent of young women felt that the main source of providing family life/sex education should be friends.

Table 11

Experiences of Youth Who Received Family Life Education

Experiences	*Men*	*Women*	*Married Men*	*Married Women*	*Unmarried Men*	*Unmarried Women*
Source of family life/sex education received						
School/College	80.0	87.9	64.5	77.1	81.6	91.8
Government Programme/Camp	16.3	11.8	26.2	21.2	15.3	8.3
NGO Programme/Camp	6.4	5.1	13.6	8.9	6.1	3.7
Opinion about family life/sex education received						
It answered many queries	87.4	90.0	89.7	91.7	87.1	89.3
Teacher/trainer explained well	89.8	91.2	84.8	91.0	89.6	91.3
Respondent felt embarrassed	21.3	36.6	19.3	36.7	21.1	36.6

Source: IIPS and Population Council, 2010.

According to youth study in India, nearly 15 per cent of young men and 14 per cent of young women received family life/sex education (Table 11). Majority received it through schools/colleges. Among those who received formal family life/sex education majority felt that this education answered many of their queries and the teacher/trainee explained the subject well. Twenty one per cent of men and 37 per cent of women also reported that they felt embarrassed while attending family life/sex education. This, in a way suggests that we need to modify the curriculum and the method of teaching.

Policy Implications

There is no unanimity in India regarding the introduction of family life education in schools. There exists a wide gap between the proportion of women who perceive it as important and those who actually received any sex education. It was also found that women who received family life education had better knowledge and awareness on reproductive health issues than others. The study reveals that there is a need to formulate proper policy regarding family life education so as to reduce the problems faced by the youth. The present study also found that awareness and knowledge regarding family life education is more among educated, better-off sections and those living in urban areas. The growing population and increasing incidences of HIV/AIDS is a great challenge. Youth also get wrong information/messages from media and other sources. In order to prepare the youth to face these challenges, introducing sex education is an important step. The nationwide surveys clearly illustrate that overwhelming majority of young women and men are in favour of family life education. The government should initiate necessary measures to reach a consensus on this issue among various sections of the society. Imparting sex education in an appropriate manner at school level should be a national priority.

References

Alexander, Sharon J. 1984. 'Improving Sex Education Programmes for Young Adolescents: Parents' View', *Family Relations*, Vol. 33, No. 2, pp. 251–57.

Anandhi, S. 2007. 'Sex Education Conundrum', *Economic and Political Weekly*, Vol. 42, No. 33, pp. 3367–69.

Chauhan, Chetan. 2007. 'Keep off Sex Education, Teachers Told', *Hindustan Times*, 17 July 2007, *http://www.hindustantimes.com/News-Feed/india/Keep-off-sex-education-teachers-told/Article1–237205.aspx* (accessed on 8 June 2010).

Devi, G., N.V. Reddy and M. Laxmanna. 1988. 'Knowledge of Sex Education among Adolescents', *Journal of Family Welfare*, Vol. 35, No. 2, pp. 55–60.

Dhiman, Anil. 2007. *Sex Education in India*, Book Summary, *http://www.shvoong.com* (accessed on 24 April 2010).

D'Souza, Anthony A. 1979. *Sex Education and Personality Development*, Usha Publications, New Delhi.

Forbes, Grace S. 1963. 'Some Observations on Family Life Education in India', *Marriage and Family Living*, Vol. 25, No. 4, pp. 466–68.

Government of India. 2000. *National Population Policy 2000*, Ministry of Health and Family Welfare, New Delhi.

——. 2007. *Study on Child Abuse: India 2007*, Ministry of Women and Child Development, New Delhi.

International Institute for Population Sciences (IIPS). 2010. *District Level Household and Facility Survey (DLHS-3), 2007–08: India*, IIPS, Mumbai.

International Institute for Population Sciences (IIPS) and Macro International. 2007. *National Family Health Survey (NFHS-3), 2005–06: India*, IIPS, Mumbai.

International Institute for Population Sciences (IIPS) and Population Council. 2010. *Youth in India: Situation and Needs 2006–07*, IIPS, Mumbai.

Israel, Sarah. 1967. 'The Purpose, Scope and Method of Sex Education', *Journal of Family Welfare*, Vol. 13, No. 4, pp. 6–11.

Marsman, Joan C. and Edward S. Herold. 1986. 'Attitude towards Sex Education and Values in Sex Education', *Family Relations*, Vol. 35, No. 3, pp. 357–61.

Moses, S. and C. Praveena. 1983. 'Sex Education: Its Need and Attitude of Adolescents', *Journal of Family Welfare*, Vol. 30, No. 2, pp. 34–39.

Motihar, Renuka. 2007. 'Between Tradition and Modernity: Controversy in India about the Sex Education Programme in State-Run Schools', *http://www.kit.nl/net/KIT-Publicaties-output/ShowFile2.aspx?e=1421* (accessed on 2 June 2010).

Nolte, J. 1984. 'Sex Education in Canadian Classrooms', *Tellus*, Vol. 5, No. 3, pp. 13–16.

Rao, Manjula P. 1988. 'Adolescence: A Perspective and a Need for Family Life Education', *Journal of Family Welfare*, Vol. 35, No. 2, pp. 42–47.

Yashwanth, C.P. 2007. 'Need to Move with the Times', *The Hindu*, 13 May 2007, *http://www.hindu.com/op/2007/05/13/stories/200705/303521400.htm* (accessed on 11 May 2010).

14

Indian Women and Domestic Violence

Victories and Struggles in the Movement for Law and Justice

Tulika Saxena

Violence against women has been recognized internationally as serious violation of human rights. Resulting from the unequal power relations that women share with men in society at large, gender-based violence signifies the patriarchal control of men over women. Among the plethora of violence that women faces all around the world like sexual violence, honour killings, female genital mutilation, female foeticide, female trafficking, perhaps the most prevalent and invisible is domestic violence. Domestic violence is also referred to by terms like intimate partner violence or gender-based violence. Domestic violence against women is unique in the way that the perpetrator is closely related to women and mostly it happens in the privacy of home. Due to the private nature of this form of violence, its prevalence is estimated to be much more than what the available data indicates. Globally it has been estimated that one out of every three women is abused in her lifetime from a person she is well acquainted with (Heise, Ellsberg and Gottemoeller, 1999; WHO, 2002). In a developing country like India where domestic violence is a wide spread problem, it has been observed that two-thirds of married Indian women have faced domestic violence in their lives. Seventy per cent of married Indian women between the age of 15 and 50 have been physically assaulted, raped or coerced into sex by their spouses according to a report generated by the United Nations Population Fund in 2005.

Only 40 years ago, terms like 'domestic violence, gender-based violence or intimate partner violence' had yet to gain public recognition and reach the public policy agenda. It took about 20 years of feminist activism to bring about the United Nations declaration on the Elimination of Violence against Women in 1993. Since then many countries around the world have adopted policies to address violence against women, especially domestic violence. By the year 2006, 60 countries had laws on domestic violence, including India, while as much as 89 countries had some sort of legal provisions for domestic violence (UN News Centre, 2006). The Indian government officially recognized the gravity of violence against women and its adverse impact on the nation in its Country Report for the Fourth World Conference on Women in Beijing 1995, though it took about 10 years of intensive women's movement activism to come up with the legislation on domestic violence.

Despite the fact that about 60 countries have legislation in place to address the issue of domestic violence, the impact of these policies is still an under researched area. Most of this legislation is the civil laws and effective implementation is highly questionable (UNIFEM, 2009). It must be noted that the provisions of these legislations are well intended but the outcomes may not correspond accordingly as the implementation of these laws depends on the social, economical and political environment of the country. Taking the case of India, the Protection of Women from Domestic Violence Act (PWDVA, 2005) not only proposes a feminist definition of domestic violence, it also provides a single window for women with the provision of protection, shelter, medical services, interim custody of child, maintenance and compensation. But at the implementation front there are still many lacunas which need to be resolved for better outcomes for women. According to a report of Indian non-governmental organization (NGO) called Lawyers Collective Women's Right Initiative (LCWRI), 2010, the response from the 28 states and seven Union Territories of India is quite varied. As per the provisions in the Act, all states have to appoint protection officers, service providers (mostly NGOs), medical facilities, shelter homes, paralegal aid, etc. The progress till date shows huge variation among the states with respect to the mechanisms adopted and the resources invested. Considering that the environment in which the Act is being implemented is different, it can be assumed that the impact generated will also be different.

This article would provide the definitions available for domestic violence and how the domestic violence got into international agenda and in India which resulted in the passage of the landmark PWDVA 2005 and would review the present status of its implementation.

Domestic Violence

Feminist scholarship has shown that prior to the 1970, there was hardly any cognizance of the term 'domestic violence' (Hague and Wilson, 2000; Ashcraft, 2000). Dominant discourses at that time considered four walls of the home as a benevolent unit providing safety and security to all its members and generally violence inside home was a distant thought (Dobash and Dobash, 1979). Moreover, any issue happening within the purview of home was considered a private matter and the members of household were supposed to deal with it on their own.

Initially traditional dominant discourse recognized violence and abuse as deviant behaviours needing attention. Domestic violence was seen as a pathological aberration, a result of poor anger management on the part of the perpetrator. Causes were often seen as alcohol, financial issues or stress. From the 1980s there was much effort to name the issue from a feminist perspective. Feminists challenged the traditional discourse and reframed the violence as a mechanism of control and expression of patriarchy. This led to the inclusion of many more behaviours that were visibly not physically violent but were used to control the women, e.g., emotional abuse and economical abuse (Liddle, 1989).

Some authors like Johnson from Pennsylvania State University and Ferraro from Arizona State University have provided classifications of various forms of domestic violence in categories like Common Couple Violence (CCV), Intimate Terrorism (IT), Mutual Violent Control (MVC), and Violent Resistance (VR). Common couple violence is violence which happens between couples where there is no intention of control over each other. The degree of this violence can range from verbal abuse to physical abuse. Intimate terrorism is violence done with an intention of control and mostly expressed by males. Mutual violent control is violence where both couple try to control each other and violent resistance is the violence done in response to IT and is mostly expressed by females. This violence can even include homicide. Limitation of this classification is that it does not talk about the implications of degree of violence but is based on the purpose behind the violence and who the perpetrator is (Johnson and Ferraro, 2000). Moreover, this classification also recognizes the female partner along with male partner as perpetrator of violence in all the categories except IT. This reduces the gravity of gender-based violence that women face and defeats the purpose of the feminist efforts which are targeted towards having policy responses which addresses the specific needs of women who face violence.

Interestingly, there exist many views over the impact of violence. Johnson and Ferraro (2000) feel that 'an occasional slap on the face' might not have damaging impact on women as compared to habitual assaults. While during the same time, feminists were worried about even one act of cruelty and its impact. Ashcraft from Western Washington University, classified invisible behaviours which are done intentionally or unintentionally resulting in marital inequality. According to her, these behaviours are more prevalent and have damaging impact on the women.

Similarly few studies claimed that the phenomenon existed more in poor and low class sections of society (Kurz, 1998) while others described domestic violence in United Kingdom as a phenomenon which exists in every class, caste or race (Hague and Wilson, 2000). A lot was also said about the battered women syndrome and in trying to understand why women stick with abusers. Major reasons identified were around economic dependence, lack of other options of shelter, children and even conjugal bond with the perpetrator among many (ibid.). Hence, there was stress on the need for suitable shelter homes and women to be economically independent (Kurz, 1998). From 2000 onwards there was a shift from the approach of rescuing women and enabling them to escape violence. The right of the aggrieved women of domestic violence to stay in her home was recognized so that women are further not disadvantaged by the disruption caused by leaving their home (Murray, 2008).

Ashcraft highlights the problem of use of language in describing the experiences of women, which draws the attention towards the inequalities that they face and the impact of these inequalities in their lives (Ashcraft, 2000). The word 'violence' or 'abuse' was being used to cover brutal physical violence, subtle physical violence, emotional violence, domination, neglect, and deprivation of freedom and choice. This word actually reinforced the picture of physical and visible forms of violence which undermine the importance of different kinds of oppressive behaviours and inequalities which women face in their domestic relationships. These are not visible as physical abuse and are result of the desire to control the subordinate partner by dominant partner. Further labelling all active and passive behaviours as violence or abuse may result in overuse of these terms and hence render them meaningless (ibid.). Hence feminists argued that words like violence and abuse may not articulate the experience of women. These words may either provide an exaggerated account of her experience or undermine it as trivial and may result in inadequate response from welfare policies and service providers (ibid.).

Already many studies have suggested that earlier approaches to domestic violence resulted in law, policies, welfare schemes which were inadequate in supporting the violence victims (Kurz, 2000). Feminists have argued though that it might not be the failure of policies but the mismatch which results in not being able to understand the expectations of women as to what these policies are trying to provide (Suneetha and Nagraj, 2006). Again this point highlights the need of adequate language which captures the experiences of women well.

Feminists suggested that the way they understand and approach domestic violence has implications on the policy response it will generate. Bacchi (2006) points the strong links between how a problem is framed and the response that will be generated. Using 'what's the problem' approach, she claimed that when domestic violence is understood as 'social breakdown' it results in tighter social control of men and if it is understood as 'power struggle' it requires empowerment of women who needs to be free and safe from abusive men. Both ways she claims that a tendency to label a complex social issue as 'social problem' which needs to be fixed attracts responses which may not address the underlying causes (ibid.). Similarly, the popular use of the word 'victim' or 'battered' for the aggrieved women reinforces the deviant behaviour of the perpetrator and highlights the vulnerability or the powerlessness of the aggrieved. Use of language to portray such image often results in a response that victim of violence require welfare and shelter (Ashcraft, 2000).

An enhanced understanding of the domestic violence, its underlying causes and its impact on the aggrieved has led to the recent policy responses which are more holistic in understanding of the needs of women. For example the understanding of the right of a woman to stay in her own home resulted in policies which may require the perpetrator to leave the home in some countries like Australia and United States. Though it has been observed that in actual practice the belongingness and the accommodation needs of the perpetrator might be given preference by the law implementers (Murray, 2008). This theory is underdeveloped in India since the patriarchal notion of right of the male over his household is very strong. Hence, the policy only provides the aggrieved the right to stay (share) and hardly prohibits perpetrator from entering the home (LCWRI, 2009). This is yet another example of how the understanding and the social set up may have implications for the policy responses.

Policy Responses to Address Domestic Violence

An exhaustive research has been done on the government response to the issue of violence against women in 36 democratic countries (Weldon, 2002). The research concludes that a strong women's movement is a must for policy response from government. But a women's mobilization alone is not sufficient. There is a need for sympathetic allies inside the government. But these allies may be weak if women policy machinery is not present in government. An effective women's policy machinery can strengthen the policy responsiveness as they reinforce the women's movement. Though she clearly highlights that government responsiveness does not mean effectiveness. Responsiveness means quality and timeliness of the policy response while effectiveness is implementation and impact of the policy. The impact of the policy can be measured by only reaching to the end-users and changes in common attitudes towards violence against women. For this, particular policies and programmes need to be studied in greater detail (ibid.). Since most of the policies related to the domestic violence only came into effect in the last 10 years, concrete studies to show the impact of these policies are much required.

Recognition of Violence Against Women as a Human Rights Issue

During the western women's suffrage movements which peaked during 1890 to 1918, wife beating was considered as an important issue and it was hoped that it would be addressed through temperance reform was seen in 1970. The arrival of second wave of feminist movement and attention turned to the problem of pervasive form of violence against women. Domestic violence was realized as a universal problem and not just a phenomenon associated with any specific culture, community or class. Joachim (1999) describes how many international women's organizations came to realize the systemic and the widespread nature of violence that women face and were keen to bring it on to the international community agenda mainly through the United Nations. With the help of three world conferences on women, Mexico 1975, Copenhagen 1980 and Nairobi 1985 women's organizations were able to draw attention to the fact that the whole nation pays directly and indirectly for the violence that women face. In 1991, general recommendation by Convention for Elimination of Discrimination Against Women (CEDAW) which recognized gender-based violence as a form of discrimination, identified a range of measures for eradicating violence against women (Joachim, 1999). Around the same time, Roxanna Carrillo, UNIFEM human's right advisor, wrote a paper 'Violence against Women: An

Obstacle to Development' which drew attention to the fact that violence over women affects all areas of their life preventing them from contributing to a country's development and hence retards the overall development goals of the country. This paper resulted in UNIFEM taking a stance about violence against women and becoming a strong ally within the United Nations for the women's movement. Finally, in 1993, United Nations adopted the Declaration on the Elimination of Violence against Women unanimously in its General Assembly (ibid.). The result of these developments aimed at providing legal recognition of the violence against women which can be seen clearly in the study done by Weldon. The study shows that by 1994 from the 36 democratic countries, the government responses on the issue of violence over women, 32 countries had responded on one or more areas of violence.

Campaign against Domestic Violence in India

While feminist consciousness relating to violence against women was rising all over the world, during the 1970s, in India momentum was gained over the issue of violence related to dowry (Jaising, 2009; Suneetha and Nagraj, 2006). Feminist activists and many women's organization launched a campaign against dowry deaths. These seemed to peak in the early 1980s despite the fact that the Dowry Prohibition Act had existed since 1961. The efforts of the women's movement resulted in the amendments to the Indian Penal Code known as 498A and section 304B in 1983 making the cruelty against the wife cognizable and non-bailable offence. The main purpose of both the amendments was to give protection to women and justice from the cruelties related to dowry violence; hence violence which was not related to the dowry could not be invoked using these amendments.

Slowly it became clear that dowry was not the only major cause for domestic violence. The Indian movement was influenced by the American movement, where the wife battering issue was prominent, despite the evil of dowry being less of an issue (Bush, 1992). After the realization that the domestic violence faced by women is a much wider issue than dowry, attempts were made to publicize the issue and have laws, which protect women from the violence that happens in their domestic life. Bush (1992) argues that the movement against domestic violence is a hard battle due to the myth that family and polity are separate spheres. In fact, this personal/public divide is political in the sense that it helps the state and other institutions to evade accountability and responsibility. Even more, India is well known for its patriarchal social settings. The law towards domestic violence could be judged by the Delhi High Court judgement on Harvinder Kaur vs Harmender Singh case in 1984, which stated that constitutional law cannot be applied inside the family and Article 14 (Equality before Law) and Article 21 (protection of life and personal liberty) of the Indian Constitution, which have no application in the privacy of married life (Jaising, 2009).

With such a background, the women's movement challenged the assumption of the state about not interfering in the private sphere and recoined a popular feminist slogan 'the personal is political' in the Indian context (Bhasin and Khan, 1986). The dominant discourses around the use of domestic violence as a mechanism to control women and maintain unequal power relations and not only as means of obtaining dowry soon changed the way that Indian feminists approached the issue of gender-based violence. Attempts were made to publicize this issue through various innovative strategies. Women's groups conducted workshop with students, teachers and homemakers, pamphlets on domestic violence were distributed in pizza joints, 'Breakthrough', an NGO, conducted training programmes and even released music album having songs regarding the domestic violence issue. In Bengaluru, the NGO Vimochana held a three day public hearing in the city before a Truth Commission, which was comprised of a distinguished jury, lawyers and former judges. They heard of approximately 50 cases relating to violent acts against women, especially regarding dowry death and they gave their expert comments and opinions after studying the whole case. This resulted in an overall sensitization within the community, including district bureaucrats against violence inside household (Menon, 1999). Multiple stakeholders like women's organizations, health service providers and legal institutions came together to articulate domestic violence as a widespread issue rather than the compartmentalized experience of women of particular caste, class or region. They demanded a law which provides women protection from this systemic form of violence previously considered as a private matter. In the struggle for domestic violence to be recognized, the international community had a critical role to play, both in terms of putting pressure on the government and in guiding women's movement towards it. In 1993, the United Nations conference on human rights in Vienna, accepted the rights of women and girls as 'an inalienable, integral and indivisible part of universal human rights'. As already noted, the United Nations General Assembly also adopted the Declaration on the Elimination of Violence against women in the same year. In addition, the 1995 Beijing Conference gave guidance to women activists when the law about domestic violence was being talked about in concrete terms.

In 1993, the first call in India for framing legislation for domestic violence was made by the National Commission for Women (NCW). The NCW had been constituted in 1992 (Jaising, 2009). Its mandate was to 'review the Constitutional and legal safeguards for women, recommend remedial legislative measures, facilitate redressal of grievances and advise the government on all policy matters affecting women'. NCW invited LCWRI to draft a bill on domestic violence in 1993. LCWRI was able to present the first draft to NCW in 1994 but this draft bill did not see the light of day in Parliament until 2002. Between this periods though lots of efforts were done to consult with various stakeholders and to collect evidence of domestic violence.

Research studies (ICRW, 2000; Jejeebhoy, 1998; Karlekar, 1998; Rao, 1997) also presented evidence of varying degrees of prevalence of domestic violence from 35 per cent to 75 per cent in different regions of India. Most of the studies were done from the perspective of health, focusing on the impact of domestic violence on the health of women. But perhaps the first nationwide survey to collect data on domestic violence was the National Family Health Survey conducted by the Ministry of Health and Welfare. This was known as NFHS-2 and was conducted in 1998–99. This study reported that 21 per cent of ever-married women had faced domestic violence (Visaria, 2008). Being a government initiative, and from an important ministry like Health and Welfare, it was important in shaping the policy agenda.

Meanwhile, in 1998, the Lawyers' Collective, in consultation with various women's groups, proposed an alternative Bill in accordance with the United Nations Framework for Model Legislation on Domestic Violence. Under pressure from women's groups, the central government introduced a Bill on domestic violence in the Lok Sabha in 2001. The bill presented did not meet the expectations of women's groups as it was changed too much from the draft prepared earlier by the women's groups and LCWRI. The National Democratic Alliance (NDA) government tabled the bill in Parliament on 8 March 2002, International Women's Day; but it did not come up for a vote because of lack of time during the session. Meanwhile, women's groups launched a major campaign against many aspects of the proposed law. In response to this concerted opposition, a Parliamentary Standing Committee for the government's Ministry of Human Resource Development was set up to re-examine the Bill, and its report was laid before Parliament in December 2002. Except for the choice of magistrates in dealing such cases, rather than civil courts, all other demands were accepted in the Bill by this Parliamentary Committee (Jaising, 2009).

But for next two years no action was taken on this Bill and ultimately the Parliament was dissolved in 2004. The new United Progressive Alliance (UPA) government took immediate interest in the Bill and it was referred to the Ministry of Women and Child Development. In June 2005 the Bill was approved by the cabinet and in August 2005 it was passed by the Parliament. Finally it received the President's assent in September 2005 and came into life as the Protection of Women from Domestic Violence Act (PWDVA), 2005.

After that it again took one year for this Act to come into force and the rules and regulations for its implementation to be framed. Finally on 26 October 2006 it came into force in all states of India except Jammu and Kashmir.[1]

Salient Features of PWDVA, 2005

The PWDVA 2005 was the result of almost two decades of Indian women's activism. Movement is the most progressive civil law available for women in India. It is in accordance with the United Nations Framework for the model legislation on domestic violence. It defines domestic violence as all acts of gender-based violence whether physical, verbal, emotional, sexual, and economical. It also provides a woman with the right to stay at her shared matrimonial household. This Act also recognizes live-in relationships and therefore marriage need not be proved to access this law. The law also recognizes the violence that women face in their natal homes and hence the respondents under this law could also be father and brothers. Often it is hard for women to approach the police in such cases, hence to provide easier access to courts the Act introduces new support structure for women. The Protection Officer (PO) is the key person for the implementation of the law, assisting women from the very first stage of registering the case, taking the case to the court's and lastly ensuring that the court orders of relief are implemented and accepted by the respondent. This law also brings service providers into its ambit, including shelter, medical facilities and NGOs working on gender-based violence. These key institutions can assist women to register cases with POs. The police are also expected to assist women and direct her to POs for registering the case. This holistic approach is intended to provide a single window clearance for all her needs if she is victim of domestic violence. This law provides interim relief to women and can consist of:

Protection Order: Order which directs the respondent to stop the violence or threat of violence immediately.

Residence Order: Assures the peaceful occupation of the same or alternate accommodation if needed for the woman and restricts her dispossession from the shared household.

Custody Order: Temporary order till both the parties finally resolves the matter.

Monetary relief and Compensation Order: To meet the expense that occurred and compensation for the injuries or mental trauma inflicted on the aggrieved person.

Accessibility of the Act

As per the 2007 report of LCWRI women have multiple routes available to access this Act. Initially when the Act came into force many states took time in establishing the structures prescribed in the Act. Meanwhile women started accessing the Act through various routes, depending upon the availability of resources to women or the availability or non-availability of systems and structures under PWDVA. The Act is intended to provide single window clearance and can be triggered through any route that woman chooses. Ideally, a woman approaches the PO of her area; PO files the Domestic Violence Incident Report known as DIR and presents her case to magistrate which results in the protection order. But women are also free to take on alternate routes depending on their convenience. The women were reported to approach courts directly with the help of a private lawyer, without accessing POs; they also approached police who in turn directed them to POs. In a few cases, women also approached service providers and the registered service providers are also authorized to register the DIR, which is considered as the valid official document in the court by the magistrate.

Various Routes for Accessing PWDVA

Aggrieved Person→PO→Magistrate→Order

Aggrieved Person→Service Provider→Magistrate→Order

Aggrieved Person→Police→PO→Magistrate→Order

Aggrieved Person→Magistrate→Order

The Three Models of Implementation

Based on the above routes available and the pattern on which the Act was accessed by women in different states, LCWRI has suggested three models of implementation.

Private model: In this model women do not use the structures made available under this Act that is POs and service providers. Women approach the court directly through private lawyers and lodge their cases under PWDVA. Example of this model was observed in Rajasthan where in the first year of implementation there were no POs appointed.

Public model: In this model women access the Act through multiple routes but through the structures established under this Act. All the key stakeholders respond in a coordinated way, whichever route the women chooses, she is put into the loop of POs or registered service providers and DIR is lodged. In this holistic multiagency response, if women approach the police they would direct them to the POs and they assisted the women in filing the DIR. Example of this model was observed in Andhra Pradesh.

Mixed model: Women approach the PO but also hire a private lawyer and file their case with the help of both private and public resources. The example of this model is Kerala which has been documented as a case study in the 2009 report.

Progress of Implementation

Budget Allocation

LCWRI report (2007) mentions the lack of budget as major constraint in the implementation of the Act. By 2008 many states had allocated a budget for the implementation of PWDVA. But, the budget allocation pattern is very different for states, ranging from budget as high as 0.1 billion to as low as 10,000.

Protection Officers

All the states have appointed the POs but their number and level of placement varies across the states. There are states like Maharashtra which have appointed 3,892 POs, the highest among all other states while there are states like Bihar where only 16 POs have been appointed. This is nugatory, given the fact it is also a state with the second highest female population. Till now there had been no budgetary allocation in this state. The maximum number of cases 3,892, dealt by POs is in Uttar Pradesh, the state with highest population while the highest number of cases dealt by individual PO on an average is in Delhi where each PO on an average dealt with 203 cases. It is worth noting that the Delhi also has full-time POs appointed on contract basis. The second state where POs have handled 103 cases on average is Kerala, which is also a state where full-time POs exists (refer Table 1).

As per the section 8 of the Act, a full-time PO, having experience of at least three years in social sector should be appointed. Delhi, Haryana, Kerala, Tamil Nadu and West Bengal have appointed a full-time officer while all other states have vested the responsibility of PO to an existing officer, i.e., Integrated Child Development Services (ICDS) officers and Social Welfare Officers.

Table 1

POs in States and Budget Allocation

States	*Population of Women in the State*	*No. of POs*	*No. of cases dealt by POs*	*No. of cases per PO*	*Budget Allocated till 2009 (₹)*
Uttar Pradesh	14,962,548	71	3,892	55	No information
Bihar	8,048,343	16	454	28	No allocation
Maharashtra	6,558,157	3,892	400*		2,311,893
Madhya Pradesh	5,163,551	367	2,072	5.6	292,000,000
Rajasthan	5,106,492	548	Not provided	—	2,500,000
Andhra Pradesh	5,029,361	104	1,984	19	10,000,000
Gujarat	3,609,276	26	804	31	6,000,000
Karnataka	3,481,893	214	2,933	13.7	25,000,000
Kerala	1,950,023	31	3,190	103	115,000,000
Chhattisgarh	1,767,627	18	136	7.5	No information
Haryana	1,543,201	20	138	7	.01 billion
Punjab	1,481,088	148	249	1.68	.01 billion
Delhi	909,298	17	3,463	203	5,000,000
Himachal Pradesh	390,120	377	660	1.75	No allocation
Manipur	152,576	8	208	26	200,000

* 2006 to March 2008

Source: Staying Alive: Third Monitoring and Evaluation Report 2009, LCWRI and ICRW.

Service Providers and their Role in Implementation of the PWDVA

As per section 10(2) of the Act, service providers can also provide the domestic violence report which is filed in the court. Hence, the state needs to register service providers. Till now 23 states have registered service providers or are in process of registering them. Medical facilities also have a duty of examining the women and preparing medical report for PO and police station of that area.

Reporting Mechanisms

The Act does not mandate reporting at state or nodal agency,[2] nor does the Protection of Women from Domestic Violence Rules, 2006. The central government have provided a format to state and the state government based on this format is required to report to the nodal agency DWCD (Department of Women Child Development).

Review of the Implementation of PWDVA, 2005

After the rules and regulations were notified in October 2006 for PWDVA, the greatest challenge, perhaps far bigger than getting the policy on board, began. Civil laws for domestic violence often lack commitment on part of implementers as compared to a criminal law and hence may not prove to be very effective, thus the biggest limitation of the PWDVA is its civil nature (UNIFEM, 2009; Jaising, 2009; Hornbeck et al., 2009). Taking this into consideration that civil laws are prone to be not implemented very effectively, one can estimate the situation of India. The responsibility of implementing any legislation passed by central government rests on state government. This results in diverse response that a civil law may get.

Since 2007 four reports of 'Staying Alive' which monitors and evaluates the progress of PWDVA have been published by LCWRI. Perhaps, the 'Staying Alive' is the only document available in India which provides detailed account about the implementation of the Act. Since literature available on policy reforms points to the limited literature available that measures the effectiveness of the policies around the domestic violence. This is an important document for consulting constraints and the barriers in the implementation of PWDVA. A few academic papers (Hornbeck et al., 2009; Lahiri, 2009) and reports produced by NGOs (Human Rights Law Network) have also assessed on the progress of the Act. Main observation which can be derived from these reports is that there is a huge variation in the commitment and resources provided by the states.

Reporting under the PWDVA

The three 'Staying Alive' reports points out the lack of reliable data at state or national level. The Act in itself does not mandate reporting at state level to the nodal department. The format provided by central government to state government is being filled by the POs and is submitted to the nodal agency, DWCD. But the POs report might not provide the complete picture as they are able to fill the data only about the cases they themselves have handled and might not contain the cases which have gone to the court directly. The coordinated compilation of information, including that generated by police and service providers, does not exist. The data collection from courts on the cases filed under PWDVA is not easily available as there is no central depository of data. Also the bureaucratic procedures of getting permission from the relevant departments for primary data collection is time consuming and has limited the availability of data up to now.

Budget Allocation for Implementation

It is very difficult to do any meaningful analysis of the budget allocated from the data that is available till now. Allocation figures provided for states do not clarify how and where this money is to be spent. As per LCWRI (2009) there is no provision in reporting which will provide any evidence on the utilization of the budget that was allocated in the 2008. No information on how the budget was spent in 2009 report leaves ambiguity about whether the budget allocated were put to some use or they were just declarations by the state government that just remained in the planning process and never landed on concrete grounds. The information available like that of infrastructure in states also do not co-relate with the budget allocation. Thus, a very important aspect of how this budgetary allocation impacted the implementation of PWDVA, gets missed out.

Protection Officers as Key Implementers

When it comes to the appointment of POs, there is one main consideration, whether they can discharge duties part time or full time. The important point highlighted is that both types of POs have constraints and advantages in discharging their duties. While the additional charge of being a PO increases workload and puts time constraints on the officers, they enjoy certain advantages too. They are able to use various resources that are available to them and they have already built networks and presence and they are able to use that while dealing a case. On the other hand, though the contractual full-time POs are able to provide enough-time, they lack the resources and the established networks which can help them in dealing the case efficiently and effectively.

If the analysis of workload taken by full-time PO and POs having additional charge is done, it is seen that full-time POs are able to handle much more cases than the POs having additional charge. Though the aspect which remains unexplored is that independent of the number of the cases handled by the POs how much time a PO is able to provide on an average to each case. Because if handling more cases means, compromise on the time given to each case, defeating the purpose of the getting effective outcomes for the women.

Capacity Building Issues

Weldon (2002) emphasizes that government responsiveness is not complete just by introducing appropriate policy. Capacity building of implementers on the issue of violence over women and policy is the most essential requirement for the effective implementation. Given the fact that the POs are important stakeholders in the implementation of this Act, beside the appointment of POs, capacity building of these POs is an essential requirement for effective implementation of this Act. Unfortunately no systematic information is available in these reports about the number of POs trained in the states. Only some states like Delhi, Rajasthan, Andhra Pradesh, and Kerala have some information about the POs receiving training. The exact number is still not available. Of the POs interviewed by LCWRI in Delhi and Rajasthan, 80 per cent reported having received training. Andhra Pradesh and Kerala have been reported as conducting training of key stakeholders but the extent of coverage is not provided. West Bengal has conducted training for all its POs while Madhya Pradesh has been reported to have conducted 31 batches of training for all the key stakeholders.

So it can be observed that there are two issues related to the capacity building. First, the proper documentation and record maintenance of the training already conducted. Second, is the need for the training of all stakeholders which have not been covered till now.

Conclusion

Violence against women (VAW) has been recognized internationally as serious violation of human rights especially domestic violence. Globally it has been estimated that one out of every three women is abused in her lifetime from a person she is well acquainted with (Heise, Ellsberg and Gottmoeller, 1999; WHO, 2002). In India domestic violence is a widespread problem, it has been observed that two-thirds of married Indian women have faced domestic violence in their lives. Seventy per cent of married Indian women between the age of 15 and 50 have been physically assaulted, raped or coerced into sex by their spouses according to a report generated by the United Nation Population Fund in 2005.

India has taken a good measure against issue of domestic violence by passing Protection of Women from Domestic Violence Act, 2005. It makes India at par with 60 other countries which has legal provisions for domestic violence (UN News Centre, 2006). As the impact of such policies on the incidences of the domestic violence is still an area which is under researched, monitoring of PWDVA, 2005 of India is an area of interest for wider international community advocating legal measures for domestic violence.

Monitoring reports that are available on the PWDVA, 2005 shows that at the implementation front there are still many lacunae which need to be resolved to achieve better outcomes for women. Regular monitoring and evaluation of the systems and structures in India is being carried out by United Nations (UN) Trust fund at a national scale through LCWRI. This monitoring and evaluation is very important tool in providing a picture of how different states are proceeding differently regarding the implementation process. There are few good examples of the implementation, for example Andhra Pradesh and Karnataka, where resource allocation and coordination of law implementers reflect the commitment of the State to make this initiative successful. However, there are poor implementation models for example Uttar Pradesh and Bihar where no specific budgets and human resources have been allocated for the implementation of this Act. The other limitations in the implementation are related to adequate and effective capacity building of law implementers, delays in registration of service providers and weak reporting structures for this Act. Over all it can be said that though there are some good practises and landmark judgements, there is still a long way to go to observe a real impact of this law on the issue of domestic violence for Indian women.

Notes

1. Jammu and Kashmir is the only autonomous State of India under section 317 of Indian Constitution where Parliamentary laws except defence, communication and foreign policy are not applicable until passed by the State of Jammu and Kashmir.
2. Nodal agency is the department which has been made responsible for the implementation of the Act.

References

Ashcraft, C. 2000. 'Naming Knowledge: A Language for Reconstructing Domestic Violence and Systemic Gender Inequity', *Women and Language*, Vol. 23, No. 1, pp. 3–10.

Bacchi, C.L. 2006. *Women, Policy and Politics*, Sage Publications, London.

Bhasin, K. and N.S. Khan. 1986. *Some Questions on Feminism and its Relevance in South Asia*, Kali for Women, New Delhi.

Bush, D.M. 1992. 'Women's Movement and State Policy Reform Aimed at Domestic Violence against Women: A Comparison of the Consequences of the Movement Mobilization in the US and India', *Gender and Society*, Vol. 6, No. 4.

Dobash, R.E. and R. Dobash. 1979. *Violence against Wives*, Free Press, New York.

Domestic Violence in India: Exploring Strategies, Promoting Dialogue. 2001. International Centre for Research on Women, Washington, DC.

Domestic Violence in India: A Summary Report of Four Record Studies. 2000. International Centre for Research on Women, Washington, DC.

Domestic Violence in India: A Summary Report of a Multi-Site Household Survey. 2003. International Centre for Research on Women, Washington, DC.

Duvvury, Nata et al. 2002. 'Women-Initiated Community Level Responses to Domestic Violence: Summary Report of Three Studies', in *Domestic Violence in India,* International Centre for Research on Women, Washington, DC.

East and Southeast Asia Regional Workshop on Domestic Violence Legislation. 2003. Moving towards Regional Networking Strategies, Bangkok, 1–3 December.

Hague, G. and C. Wilson. 2000. 'The Silenced Pain: Domestic Violence 1945–1970', *Journal of Gender Studies*, Vol. 9, No. 2, pp. 157–70.

Heise, Lori, Mary Ellsberg and Megan Gottemoeller. 1999. 'Ending Violence against Women', *Population Reports*, Series L, Vol. XXVII, No. 4.

Hornbeck, A. et al. 2009. 'The Protection of Women from Domestic Violence Act: Solution or Mere Paper Tiger?', *Loyola University Chicago International Law Review*, Vol. 4, Issue 2, *http://www.luc.edu/law/activities/publications/ilrdocs/vol4_no2/vol4_no2/hornbeck_johnson_lagrotta_sellman.pdf* (accessed on 10 August 2010).

ICRW. 2000. 'Domestic Violence in India: A Summary Report of Four Records Studies, 2000', International Centre for Research on Women, Washington, DC.

Jaising, I. 2009. 'Bringing Rights Home: Review of the Campaign for a Law on Domestic Violence', *Economic and Political Weekly*, Vol. XLIV, No. 44, pp. 50–57.

Jejeebhoy, S. 1998. 'Wife Beating in Rural India: A Husband's Right? Evidence from Survey Data', *Economic and Political Weekly*, Vol. 33, No. 15, 11 April, pp. 855–962.

Joachim, J. 1999. 'Shaping the Human Rights Agenda: The Case of Violence against Women', in Mary K. Meyer and Elisabeth Prügl (eds), *Gender Politics in Global Governance*, Rowman and Littlefield Publishers, New York.

Johnson, M. and K. Ferraro. 2000. 'Research on Domestic Violence in the 1990s: Making Distinctions', *Journal of Marriage and Family*, Vol. 62, No. 4, pp. 948–63.

Karlekar, M. 1998. 'Domestic Violence', *Economic and Political Weekly*, Vol. 33, No. 27, pp. 1741–51.

Kurz, D. 1998. 'Women, Welfare, and Domestic Violence', *Social Justice*, Vol. 25, No. 1, pp. 105–21.

Lahiri, R. 2009. 'The Protection of Women from Domestic Violence Act: The Current Situation', Human Rights Law Network, *http://hrln.org/hrln/pdf/intern_work/PWDVA%20Article%20Rakhi%20Lahiri_formatted%20by%20Karuna_.pdf* (accessed on 30 August 2010).

——. 2007. *Staying Alive: First Monitoring and Evaluation Report 2007 on the Protection of Women from Domestic Violence Act 2005*, New Delhi.

——. 2009. *Staying Alive: Third Monitoring and Evaluation Report 2009 on the Protection of Women from Domestic Violence Act 2005*, LCWRI and ICRW, New Delhi.

——. 2010. *Staying Alive: Fourth Monitoring and Evaluation Report 2010 on the Protection of Women from Domestic Violence Act 2005*, New Delhi.

Liddle, A.M. 1989. 'Feminist Contributions to an Understanding of Violence against Women: Three Steps Forward, Two Steps Back', *Canadian Review of Sociology and Anthropology*, Vol. 26, No. 5, pp. 759–76.

Menon, P. 1999. 'Focus on Domestic Violence', *Frontline*, Vol. 16, No. 18, *http://www.hinduonnet.com/fline/fl1618/16180420.htm* (accessed on 15 March 2010).

Mitra, N. 2000. *Domestic Violence as a Public Issue: A Review of Responses*, Unit for Women Studies, Tata Institute of Social Sciences, Mumbai.

Murray, S. 2008. 'Why doesn't She Just Leave?: Belonging, Disruption and Domestic Violence', *Women's Studies International Forum*, Vol. 31, pp. 65–72, NCW, *http://ncw.nic.in/frmABTBreifHistory.aspx* (accessed on 31 March 2010).

Olesen, V.L. 2000. 'Feminisms and Qualitative Research at and into the Millennium', in N.K. Denzin and Y.S. Lincoln (eds), *Handbook of Qualitative Research*, Sage Publications, Thousand Oaks.

Pooranchandra, P. 2006. 'A Domestic Violence Coordinated Project: Going Beyond Victim Support Action Aid', paper presented at the International Conference on Strength-based Strategies, Hyderabad, *http://www.strengthbasedstrategies.com/PAPERS/14%20PoornachandraFormatted.pdf* (accessed on 13 September 2010).

Rajan, A. and N. Bhatla. 2004. *Panchayat Involvement on Violence against Women: Formative Research on Interventions in the State of Karnataka*, ICRW.

Rao, V. 1997. 'Wife-Beating in Rural South India: A Qualitative and Econometric Analysis', *Social Science Medicine*, Vol. 44, No. 8, pp. 1169–80.

Report of a South Asian Workshop on Looking Afresh at Violence against Women and Girls through an Exploration of the Political Economy of VAWG and Masculinity, 29 April–2 May 2005, Goa, India.

Suneetha, A. and V. Nagraj. 2006. 'A Difficult Match: Women's Actions and Legal Institutions in the Face of Domestic Violence', *Economic and Political Weekly*, 14 October, pp. 4355–62.

The Protection of Women from Domestic Violence Act 2005, No. 43 of 2005, Ministry of Law and Justice, New Delhi, India.

UN News Centre. 2006. More Countries have Laws Banning Domestic Violence, says UN Women's Rights Official, *http://www.un.org/apps/news/story.asp?NewsID=20703&Cr=unifem&Cr1* (accessed on 12 July 2010).

UNICEF. 2000. 'Domestic Violence against Women and Girls', *Innocenti Digest*, Vol. 6, June, Italy.

UNIFEM. 2009. 'Domestic Violence Legislation and its Implementation: An Analysis for ASEAN Countries based on International Standards and Good Practices', http://cedaw-seasia.org/docs/DomesticViolenceLegislation.pdf (accessed on 10 September 2010).

Visaria, L. 2008. 'Violence against Women in India: Is Empowerment a Protective Factor?', *Economic and Political Weekly*, 29 November, pp. 60–66.

Weldon, S.L. 2002. 'Responding to Violence against Women: Practical Lessons for Democrats, Feminists and Policymakers', in *Protest, Policy and the Problem of Violence against Women: A Cross-National Comparison*, University of Pittsburgh Press, Pittsburgh.

Women Initiated Community Level Responses to Domestic Violence. 2002. International Centre for Research on Women, Washington, DC.

World Health Organization. 2002. *World Report on Violence and Health*, World Health Organization, Geneva.

15

Baring Bodies

Resistance through Resignification

Parvin Sultana

Humiliation is a moral claim against unjust treatment meted out to an individual or a community. It is a public and political claim. The claim of humiliation and resistance can be overt like open protests or covert like certain activities which may resist in a subtle way. The discourse of resistance lays down that mode of resistance varies depending upon *the actors* who are resisting and the avenues of resistance available to them. A person in a comparatively powerful social location will resist in a very overt, open way and assert their right in a powerful way. They can also use the *legal language of rights* against humiliation and exploitation. These are the modes of people who are legally, morally, politically right. Resistance of those who may be powerful but not in a politically correct position like terrorists' groups, insurgency associations will be direct, confrontationist and violent. Such groups are also working under the compulsion of making a huge impact to drive home the seriousness of the issue that they are fighting for. One can point to the activities of Maoist groups and the ethnic homeland related movements going on in northeastern states in India. Though such groups enjoy a moral high ground on the basis that their demands are just working within the context of a nation-state they indulge in subversion. Their activities are covert as the nature of modern nation-state renders them illegal; the impact of their activities is aimed to unsettle the state.

But when the discourse talks of the weapons of those who are already in a marginalized situation, it takes a sharp turn. Such groups are robbed of the luxury of open resistance against exploitation because of their disadvantageous social location. There is a strong shift to more subtler, innovative, non confrontationist but at the same time strong acts of resistance. James C. Scott (1985) in his book *Weapons of the Weak: Everyday Forms of Peasant Resistance* talks about how subordinate classes has less often been concerned with the changing of larger structures and hence have rarely been afforded the luxury of open, organized political activity. Their activities have also not been on large scale. These relatively powerless groups (Scott focuses on peasantry) use 'weapons' like foot dragging, dissimulation, desertion, false compliance, pilfering, feigned ignorance, slander, gossip, arson, sabotage and so on. Their adversary is not the exploitative structures of the state or economic regime but rather the landlord. And their choice of mode of resistance is guided by the concern to cause difficulty to these immediate adversaries. Acts like arson, feigned ignorance, gossip, sabotage, etc., does exactly that. These *Brechtian* or *Schweikian* forms of struggle needs little or no coordination, they make use of *implicit understandings* and *informal networks*, and they often represent a form of individual self help, they typically avoid any direct symbolic confrontation with the authority. These activities are not overt. A fear of negative sanctions from above makes sure that the resistance remains untraceable to the initiator. The anonymity of the resistors increases with the authoritative and regulative pressure from above. However, this does not render the impact less influential, may be more subtle. And in fact even unknowingly the peasants succeed, although in a limited way, to assert and resist their protest against exploitation. These protests in the words of James Scott are cases of resignification of everyday normal chores into modes of resistance.

Resistance has taken varied forms. From organized class action, agitation, strikes on a massive scale to interesting variations like songs and dances of protest, to individual and rather mundane activities that Gandhiji supported like using hand spun cloth. Depending on such variances in terms of scale, methodology, many of them have been called short of movements and merely isolated incidents. Another interesting form of resistance was taken up by the homosexual activists led by Kurt Krickler in Austria. In the face of homosexuality being condemned by the Christian Church he took to exposing the clandestine homosexuality of a quarter of Austria's catholic bishops. Here outing was a *dramatic* and *performative* act and aim was to firstly rob those who condemned the act, of the moral high ground of doing the same, and secondly, to drive home the point that homosexuality was not a sinful, abnormal activity as even those who condemned it in public indulged in it in private. Thus gossip, maligning one's public image is also an important method of resistance feasible in acts of hypocrisy, especially in cases where there is a possibility of the adversary indulging in the same acts while putting up a public image of opposing it.

This article talks about the naked parade of women that took place at Kangla Fort in Manipur to oppose the rape and murder of Thangjam Manorama in July 2004 and tries to situate the incident in the larger discourse of how body has been used time and again as the site of humiliation, exploitation and resistance.

Rape as a Weapon of Humiliation

Rape in general discourse is crucial to the construction of a feminine body as numerically it has been mostly women at the receiving end of the said atrocity. Rape cannot be equated with other physical assaults. Feminists have in fact made a case for understanding rape as a sexual crime. This was in response to Foucault's advocacy of rape to be desexualized and reduced only to its violent manifestations. His comments were expressed in a Round Table Conference held in 1977 discussing his book *Discipline and Punish*. For him, rape was something a man did rather than something a woman experienced. And it revolved around penile penetration. As it revolves around male physiology it does not include a number of other ways in which a woman's body might be violated. But once the tables are turned and women are no more mere objects of rape but subjects, rape can be dehumanizing. In fact it is something a social man does to a social woman and hence is intrinsic to the creation of a social woman.

The significance of the violent act of rape also changes with the context. There have been cases of rape on mass scale against women belonging to the opposite community during partition. Urvashi Butalia in her *The Other Side of Silence* has documented the tormenting stories of women who are victims of partition-related rape. Even after independence any communal riot in India has been often accompanied by rapes of women of the opposing communities. Another way in which rape at a large scale takes place is during wars. Miranda Alison talks about wartime sexual violence. Military is the ultimate exemplar of masculinity as they are the saviours and protectors of the nation and also of the population residing within. Gangrape which has been a common occurrence during war was declared as a war crime as late as in 2008. Civil war ripped countries also provide evidence of women of vanquished side being taken as sex slaves and raped over and over.

Coming to rape as a war crime, according to Alison, it is a mode of bonding amongst male soldiers along with a reassertion of their masculinity. The trajectory of wartime rape shows how women of the vanquished enemy first considered as booty of war and hence available to the soldiers, later were often used as exemplary to send the message to the defeated. Raping women and murdering them was like sending a message to other women with an aim of terrorizing and hence taming them. While martial rape or the use of rape as a weapon is an ancient practice, it acquired recent attention owing to the era of excesses of diseases like HIV. Hence, the concern for rape on such a scale came within the health discourse and concern for public health and failed to respond to questions of dignity and human rights.

In case of a few recent events, studies consisting of interviews with soldiers who indulged in wartime sexual violence show that soldiers who were reluctant initially, took alcohol and committed the rape. It had more to do with the camaraderie. Martial rape is a weapon yielded by the soldiers of a country or a dominant political, cultural group against unarmed women of other groups. In case of ethno national conflicts in an era of the nation-state, rape is committed against specific women often belonging to ethnic minority groups. Binaries are crystallized – 'Our Women' and 'Their Women'. The violation of their women is inevitable to the protection of our women. It is a spill over of a highly militarized society where society is not insulated from such violence. Rape in such cases serves more than one purpose. It can be used for domestification of women and taming them in the civilian case, in the situation of a war it can be used to taming an ethnic community which dares to question the sovereignty of the nation-state. Rape of enemy women is the symbolic victory over their men who failed to protect their womenfolk from utmost humiliation. Such women are exemplary of humiliation for men who are socially connected to them. Rape is a cross-cultural language of male domination and the vanquished communities are rendered as effeminate.

As pointed out by Ruth Seifert female body is the symbolic 'body politic' and is often equated with nation or motherland which should not be violated. Women as reproducers are reinforcers of national boundaries which need to be upheld for issue of national pride. They are the breeders of future citizens whose purity of lineage should be maintained. This makes force impregnating of the enemy women crucial. Imperial rape is aimed at genetic imperialism by causing realignments in the loyalty of their future generations. Their citizenry is put under question. It undermines family solidarity which is closely linked with the chastity of their womenfolk which in itself is a patriarchal construct. Raped women are a cause of shame even after the war is over. Forced impregnation of the enemy women undermines family which still enjoys the legal sanction of being the unit of the state. It also destroys a group's identity which is paramount to genocide. This cultural decimation manipulates the group's identity and plays into the fact that ethnic cleansing has replaced ideas of enslavement. Hence imperial rape can be seen as a political institution. To take an apt example, this was done in Bosnia and Herzegovina during the wars of 1992–95 where enemy women were impregnated by Serbian soldiers and let go only when it was too late for abortion. Forced impregnation was a part of systematic programme of Serbian soldiers. Systematic mass rape is used as an instrument of genocidal campaigns. Hence, this is humiliating a nation by humiliating and violating a woman's body.

Body as a Site of Humiliation

Michel Foucault in his works has also placed body as a site of humiliation and hence potential resistance. He talked of another way apart from rape in which body can be dominated, subordinated and hence humiliated. This as Foucault and Bourdieu would have us believe is by the construction of a 'docile body' which can be subjected, used, transformed, and even improved. It is ruled completely by its dominant other which however has internalized as its own. The dominant other is not separate from the self. Power manifests itself in a non-intrusive and subtle way and hence domination occurs through unconscious manipulation of the body. There is a constant self disciplining of body to conform to certain dominant ideas. Bourdieu also uses concepts like *Habitus* and *Symbolic Violence*. While habitus points to habituating oneself in such a way that one perceives as one is meant to, symbolic violence points to the imposition of certain values as the legitimate ones on others. One's perception of self as well as others is manipulated. Women conducting themselves in a particular way in terms of talking and walking, or how good girls are expected to behave can be apt examples of such internalization. However it is this very power relation that gives space for resistance. For Foucault power and resistance are co-extensive. Power can never ensnare us. But he has also been critiqued for undermining the potential of transformation that resistance has.

Foucault talked of resistance only after power emerged as a central concept in his work. He is credited with giving a positive connotation to power. But does he celebrate any and every form of subversion and sanction them as resistance? For Foucault resistance cannot be understood as the antimatter of power, rather it is the odd element in power. It eludes power and hence power targets it as an adversary. Power is diffused and by its very nature it creates multiple nodes of resistance.

Resistance to a diffused power must also be diffused. As opposed to the beliefs that Foucault paralyzes resistance by portraying the adversary as an all encompassing and all powerful one, he frees resistance from limits and gives it immense potential. Such struggles of resistance find its expression at the level of the body. Most prison disciplining and revolts have been around the body which is perceived as the object of power. Even in modern prisons there is a use of tranquilizers, forced isolation, etc., which regulates the body. For Foucault the use of the language of rights is not subversive as it implies an acceptance of the principles against which the resistance is aimed. He does not however lay down how struggles should take place as that might also impose limitations. For Foucault engagement provides possibilities of change as well as self creation which is extremely essential if one has to resist against internalization. Both Foucault and Bourdieu state that the main mechanism of domination operates through the manipulation of body and resistance should address it.

Some other ways in which body becomes the site of humiliation is through the portrayal of a canonical body and the compulsion to conform to a standardized, ideal body which is normalized through media, films, etc. The canonical bodies of women are often sexually objectified. The point of reference of the construction of such bodies is the male gaze. An hour glass figure or a zero size excludes and hence humiliates. Bodies are often equated with dirt, filth, e.g., in case of a people of particular social location. The discourse of hygiene also humiliates when it essentializes the linkage of filthiness to particular groups employed in a specific kind of work. Here, the example of Dalits in India being engaged in the task of scavenging can be stated. Bodies are often marked as criminal and tattooed without the consent of the person and at times with derogatory remarks. Prisoners are often tattooed with their prison numbers. Tattoos ensure that bodies are marked for life.

Bodies as Site of Resistance

Because bodies can be humiliated they can also be resignified to humiliate the humiliator. Hence bodies can also be the site of resistance through resignification that is, subverting the meaning that is imposed on a humiliated body and investing newer meanings in the same body which renders it more powerful. This resignification can take place in a number of ways. One way of resignification of bodies is through subversion during carnivals. As understood by *Bhaktin* carnivals do not acknowledge any distinction between actors and spectators. Carnival is not merely a spectacle seen and admired by others, rather people live in it and everyone participates because its very idea embraces all. It has an equalizing effect. The unattainable equality between subjects which is so lamented by Sartre becomes the cornerstone of *Bhaktin's* carnival. Hence carnivals create a different order of human relations from those constructed by and associated with representation. A destitute can dress up like a king. There is a collapse between the self and the Other or the segregation is never complete. In fact there is continuity. *Bhaktin's* carnival body or the body of 'grotesque realism' loses its individual definition and is collectivized at a trans-individual level through the epitomization of body in terms of events and activities in which boundaries between bodies are obscured and eroded. Also, a woman's evaluation was completely transformed. As opposed to the ascetic tradition of medieval Christianity which saw the woman as an 'incarnation of the sin, the temptation of the flesh', she is portrayed as the incarnation of the 'materially bodily lower stratum' which degrades and regenerates simultaneously. Similarly, the degradations which characterizes carnivals bring joy rather than the dreadful humiliation and at the same time it has the potential of challenging the dominant social relations through resignification. Hierarchies do not hold good during carnivals.

Naked Bodies as the Site of Resistance

Another equally strong way of resignification of body is through baring it. Barbara Sutton (2007) in a paper about a paradox in western societies where while human bodies and specially female bodies are turned into sexually objectified commodities, at the same time naked bodies of resistance can lead to social outrage and violent punishment. Nakedness is filled with multiple, context bound, historically specific meanings. Nakedness can be a pleasurable experience, a mundane activity or a humiliating event depending on the situation, on who is shedding the clothes, on whether there is a spectator and in that case on the spectator's relationship to the naked person. Nakedness carries gendered connotations that are embedded in history and cultural baggage of different societies and are intertwined with the ideologies of racism, sexism, classism, colonialism, homophobia, and other types of oppression. In case of the women in colour in USA, raped bodies which were paraded as spectacle became fuel for colonialist fascination and white men's desires. Hence, it is hard to articulate a 'vision of resistance, of decolonization that provides strategies for the construction of a liberatory, black female body politics'. Black female bodies are often almost portrayed within the context of patriarchal, pornographic, racialized sexualization. In the era of capitalism nudity in western society is nothing unnatural. It turns woman into a sexualized object which can be consumed by an implicit male spectator. According to John

Berger's conceptualization, while nakedness refers simply to the body without clothes, nudity entails a level of sexual objectification. He argues 'Nakedness reveals itself. Nudity is placed on display'. While a nude body is to fulfil desires of consumption of a male gaze, a naked body asserts its agency in shedding of clothes. Coming to body as a site of resistance, Sutton goes on to say that the body (clothed and unclothed) is the tool of protest par excellence. Most political protests are enacted through body – from marches, to political theatre, to the act of chaining of a body to a tree or a building. The body is a key vehicle of protest. The body also serves as a symbol, a text that conveys political meaning. She gives an example of an incident that happened in World Social Forum in 2003 in Porto Alegre in Brazil. On the site of the forum which itself represented a platform for resisting atrocities, a young woman was hassled by the police for bathing without clothes in the open. While the women protested by taking off her clothes a number of men sympathized with her and supported her. They showed their solidarity by stripping their clothes. A particular woman who caught Sutton's attention made a statement that under our skin we all are equal. This woman with her naked action perhaps strove to reclaim a position as an active subject and reconfigure nakedness on her own terms away from objectification in order to convey a broader political message. This was a performance but was it effective? Her performance might challenge the popular imagining of women's body without clothes which is voyeuristic. But at the same time does it subvert patriarchy? Men supporting them might recreate and reinforce the dominant notions of exotic, vulnerable women who need to be rescued.

As prevailing norms in most contemporary societies prescribe the use of clothing in public spaces, naked bodies can be used in quite sensational ways to call the public's attention to a social problem. Naked protests dramatically enact protestors' willingness to put their bodies on the line to advance a political cause, such as opposition to powerful capitalist and military interests especially in a context where this kind of protest might trigger violent responses against activists. For example, women in Niger Delta used the 'curse of nakedness'. Niger Delta located between mid-western and eastern parts of Nigeria is a crude oil producing area which caters to the need of a number of Trans National Oil Corporations. The oil companies' disregard for any form of good oil field practices have led to the destruction of natural environment. While the locals have often peacefully protested, a militarized state retorted violently. Women in Niger delta pushed against the wall resorted to a variety of protests like dancing, singing, demonstration, strikes, testimonies, silence, and the extreme act of stripping oneself. In the cultural context of Nigeria naked protest enjoyed a social sanction. It is used under extreme provocation and hence has remained a powerful weapon of women's collective resistance. It is effective also because stripping by married and elderly women is a way of shaming men and some of them believe that if they see the naked bodies they will go mad or suffer great harm.

However, these protests because of their very nature are often on slippery grounds. For Sutton the message sent by the naked protesting women might be reduced to something sexual. Nudity might be imposed on their nakedness and hence robbing them of agency. In similar ways the western media sidelined the exploitation in Niger Delta and feasted on the threat of nude protests. Such protest should not be understood as an event of flaunting their nudity nor practice communal prostitution. Nude protest was not specific to black women who were sexually immodest and employed their sexuality for anything. There was a tendency of giving it a primitive touch would rob the protest of its conscious assertion by right bearing citizens.

The Manipur Incident

Hence taking cue of the slippery ground on which such protests are played out and having laid down the broad outline of how a naked body can be the site of humiliation and also a site of resignification, now I will move on to situate the specific incident of the Naked Protest in the former Royal Palace of Kangla Fort in Manipur following the brutal rape and murder of Thangjam Manorama by personnel of Assam Rifles. She was picked up on suspicion of belonging to a terrorist outfit under the Armed Forces Special Power Act (AFSPA). And her bullet ridden body was found in the wee hours of 11 July 2004 at Laipharok Maring village in Imphal east. She was believed to be a victim of custodial death. Here Manorama's body was the body politic of Manipur. And raping her would tame and dominate the state which challenged the sovereignty and supreme authority of the Indian nation-state. Manipur always claimed to be independent and blamed the Indian government of making the Manipur king sign an 'Accord of Accession' under duress. The Manipur Merger Agreement is seen to be an instrument of an illegal annexation. In the gruesome act mentioned above, Manorama was 'their woman' and hence even killing her was justified as it was done in the name of the Indian nation. The army had the backing of the state because of the impunity that it enjoyed under AFSPA. This gruesome act was followed by a number of protests but the most noteworthy was the nude protest of 12 Manipuri women who paraded to Kangla Fort where the Assam Rifles was stationed. They carried banners asking the Indian

Army to rape them and kill them too. This protest sent a strong message in fact overshadowing the other kind of demonstrations going on at the same time and compelled the government to think of a humane alternative to AFSPA. Although the act is still in place, this protest was successful in sending a crucial message across. Now I would like to take a closer look at the incident.

AFSPA which is in place in Manipur for the past four decades gives tremendous power to the Army. The prevailing attitude is that the military is protecting the common Manipuris and hence it gives them the legitimate right to control them. The people of this small state in the far east of the country comprises both of tribal non-Hindu people and Imphal valley's Meiteis who are mostly Hindus. These people were seen as a community in dire need of protection. Hence, there is one Indian soldier for every 15 Manipuris. Human rights abuse under this act has been rampant in Manipur. Anybody even a woman suspected of being a sympathizer of insurgents will be branded as 'enemy' woman. The enemy man can be humiliated and hence subjugated by raping their woman. In this case Manorama's raped, mutilated, bullet riddled body became the carrier of the message from the army to the insurgents as well as the Manipuri community at large. She was used as an example for others.

Such a heinous act of the so called protectors (Indian Army) shook the community. It was not acceptable in a community where women traditionally played a strong role. Imphal's Ima Keithel or Mother's Market shows women's dominant role in the economy of the state. The historical Nupi Lan which literally meant female warfare showed that historically in case of any injustice women would appeal to the ruler as a delegate. Two famous cases of Nupi Lan – firstly, in 1904 women stopped the extraction of materials from Kabow Valley for rebuilding the house of the British Political Agent which caught fire. The women broke in the house of British Political Agent in thousands and revoked a curfew. Secondly, in 1939, to address the issue of shortage of foodgrains, they protested for banning the export of rice outside the state. More than 15,000 women demonstrated before the Darbar Hall. They ensured that the Khwairamband Bazaar was closed by boycotting it. This impacted the economy and the government had to give in to the demands of the women. These incidents of Manipur lay down a legacy of dominant women activists.

The protest was unique. The 12 women who bared their bodies in the protest are politically active and are leading groups working against the misuse of AFSPA and are closely associated with Meira Paibi. They exercised their agency in deciding to undertake the parade. Hence they were the actors. These were middle aged women and they emphasized the fact that these were mothers. This is important because when mothers strip it signifies that they are pointing to the origin of people or where they were born from, that is the mother's womb and such protest signifies their stand by showing them saying as if 'we revoke your birth' and hence condemning the very birth of men. This also ensured that the sight was not reduced to something merely voyeuristic.

Their banners asking the Indian military to come and rape them sends a strong message by showing that something as brutal as rape has become the obvious and normal way in which they confront the Indian Army. The interface between the Indian state and the civilians is rape which is being normalized as an everyday crisis. The counterinsurgency operations have turned Manipur into a highly militarized society.

But interestingly in this incident humiliation of the Indian Army was greater because the humiliator (in this case the naked women) were not on the same footing with the Army. They were the weaker sex of a community which was to be regulated in the name of the Indian government. Hence humiliation increased manifold because of the lowly location of the humiliators. These women resignified the raped mutilated body of Manorama which was stripped of clothing by shedding their own rob.

This act of protest in fact made the government rethink about the feasibility of AFSPA and the possibility of replacing it with a more humane alternative. However, even now there is contention as to whether the jurisdiction of the state government can cover this case and the findings of Justice Upendra Singh Commission remains to be looked into and Manorama's family is still to get justice. Hence this mode of protest is much stronger than the traditional weapons of the weak because despite of not being confrontationist in a violent sense it was rather upfront. Manorama's body was attempted to be made into the vessel of shaming the community. And the bare bodies of these 12 women were successful in shaming the Indian state because these bodies became much more powerful with resignified meanings being attributed to them.

Conclusion

There is a need to situate this protest in the larger context of the society's reaction to it. Although there were students' movements which supported it but the society did not come out in a large way to back such a movement. Also, there was no encouragement to carry forward similar protests. This can be explained because the very nature of the protest places it on slippery ground. It may end up being mere celebratory rather than being motivating. Although since Manipuri society, its politics and social codes of conduct are determined through patriarchal norms, women's voices for concrete solutions have received marginal attention. And despite being giving women a better position in society, such mode of protest does not exactly enjoy a cultural sanction. Especially after *Hinduisation* which started in the early part of 1700s, there was a level of *sanskritization* and the social location of women was not insulated from this phenomenon. In substantive way the women may not be powerful if they don't have the scope of making decisions along with men and authority. Their power reduces to symbolism. However one also cannot negate the fact that women's organization have been leading the protest in Manipur. All these considerations brings to mind the question whether these 12 women are powerfully bare or barely powerful?

References

Akoijam, A. Bimol. 2001. 'How History Repeats Itself', *Economic and Political Weekly*, Vol. 36, No. 30, 28 July.

Bunzl, Matti. 1997. 'Outing as Performance/Outing as Resistance: A Queer Reading of Austrian (Homo) Sexualities', *Cultural Anthropology*, Vol. 12, No. 1, February.

Cahill, Ann J. 2000. 'Foucault, Rape and the Construction of the Feminine Body', *Hypatia*, Vol. 15, No. 1, Winter.

Card, Claudia. 1996. 'Rape as a Weapon of War', *Hypatia*, Vol. 11, Issue 7, Autumn.

Ebere, Amakwe Mary John Bosco. *The Niger Delta Oil Crisis and the Victimisation of Women: A Socio-Ethnographic Analysis, http://www.theologyinafrica.com* (accessed on 25 July 2011).

Ekanola, Adebola Babatunde. 2007. 'Terror Techniques in the Niger Delta and the Question of Justice', *Journal of Sustainable Development in Africa*, Vol. 9, No. 2.

Ekine, Sokari. 2008. 'Women's Responses to the State Violence in Niger Delta', *Feminist Africa*, Issue 10.

Guru, Gopal. 2009. 'Rejection of Rejection: Foregrounding Self Respect', in Guru (ed.), *Humiliation: Claims and Context*, Oxford University Press, New Delhi.

Ilhenacho, David Asonye. 2002. 'Our Nudity, Our Weapon! Return of Old Fashioned Women's Resistance', *Nigeria World, http://www.nigeriaworld.com* (accessed on 21 July 2002).

'Inaction on Manorama Case Flayed', editorial, Wednesday, 12 January 2011, *http://www.manipuronline.com* (accessed on 15 June 2012).

'Indian Army and the Legacy of Rape in Manipur', editorial, Monday, 22 November 2010, *http://www.manipuronline.com* (accessed on 14 June 2012).

Pickett, Brent L. 1996. 'Foucault and the Politics of Resistance', *Polity*, Vol. 28, No. 4, Summer.

Scott, James C. 1985. *Weapons of the Weak: Everyday Forms of Peasant Resistance*, Yale University Press, New Haven and London.

'Six Years Down the Line, the Spirit of Manorama Continues to Haunt AR, HC Directs AR to Reply to Petitions Filed by Bereaved Mother', editorial, 11 January 2011, *http://www.manipuronline.com* (accessed on 15 June 2012).

Sutton, Barbara. 2007. 'Naked Protest: Memories of Bodies and Resistance at the World Social Forum', *Journal of International Women's Studies*, Vol. 8, No. 3.

Thapan, Meenakshi. 1995. 'Gender, Body and Everyday Life', *Social Scientist*, Vol. 23, No. 7.

Yambem, Sanamani. 1976. 'Nupi Lan: Manipur Women's Agitation, 1939', *Economic and Political Weekly*, Vol. 11, No. 8, 21 February.

Zehol, Lucy T.V. 1998. 'Women's Movement in Manipur: Some Observations', in Mahendra Narain Karna (ed.), *Social Movement in North-East India*, Indus Publishing, New Delhi.

Index